Underground
Railroad
in New Jersey and
New York

Underground Railroad
in New Jersey and New York

WILLIAM J. SWITALA

STACKPOLE
BOOKS

Published by
STACKPOLE BOOKS
5067 Ritter Road
Mechanicsburg, PA 17055
www.stackpolebooks.com

Printed in the United States of America

10 9 8 7 6 5 4 3 2 1

FIRST EDITION

Cover design by Caroline Stover
Back cover illustration: Crossing the Delaware Bay to Cape May in an Open Boat. HISTORICAL
     SOCIETY OF DELAWARE
Maps by Kevin J. Switala

Library of Congress Cataloging-in-Publication Data
Switala, William J.
  Underground railroad in New Jersey and New York/William J. Switala; maps by Kevin J. Switala.
     p. cm.
  Includes bibliographical references and index.
  ISBN-13: 978-0-8117-3258-1 (pb)
  ISBN-10: 0-8117-3258-4 (pb)
  1. Underground railroad–New Jersey. 2. Underground railroad–New York (State) 3. Fugitive slaves–New Jersey. 4. Fugitive slaves–New York (State) 5. New Jersey–History–1775-1865. 6. New York (State)–History–1775-1865. I. Title.

E450.S985 2006
973.7'115–dc22
                                                                                    2005029804

CONTENTS

PREFACE

There was a time in the history of this country when one race enslaved almost all the members of another race. This time period was prior to the American Civil War, when African-Americans were enslaved by the whites. Even though this enslavement was organized, legalized, and quite thorough, some members among the enslaved group refused to stay yoked under this burden and sought to free themselves from it. These men, women, and children became self-emancipators and fled from their bondage to distant lands to attain their freedom. Some went south to the everglades of Florida, others went southwest to Mexican Territory, but the majority of them went north to Canada. Some among this group managed their flight to freedom without any help from outside agents. Most, however, profited from the assistance given to them by people of good conscience, both black and white, who risked fines and imprisonment to help these freedom seekers achieve their goal. The escape system that developed in the years before the Civil War that helped facilitate this quest for freedom became known as the Underground Railroad.

Most of the enslaved people living in the Southern states attempted to reach Canada in order to gain their freedom. Those living along the eastern seaboard and the Mid-Atlantic region traveled through Delaware, Pennsylvania, New Jersey, New York, and New England to achieve this goal. Although some of the freedom seekers chose to stay and blend into existing black communities in these states, most used them as a conduit to reach Canada. This book is a study of the systems of escape these individuals used as they traversed New Jersey and New York.

There are many works dealing with the subject of the Underground Railroad. Some are comprehensive in nature; others deal with only small segments or the stories of individuals who managed to successfully flee their bondage. The earliest of the more comprehensive works is William Still's *The Underground Railroad: A Record of Facts, Authentic Narratives, Letters, & c.,* published in 1872. This book is still one of the most important for researchers and students of the Underground Railroad. It contains the detailed records that Still kept while he assisted fugitive slaves passing through Philadelphia on their way north. William Still managed the offices of the Pennsylvania Anti-Slavery Society in Philadelphia, and as result of this, he helped thousands in their quest for a free life. But though his work contains references to sites in New Jersey and New York, it does not offer any real description of the system of escape paths over which the freedom seekers fled.

In 1898, Wilbur Siebert attempted to offer the most comprehensive overview of the Underground Railroad in America when he published *The Underground Railroad: From Slavery to Freedom,* the first work to give an overall picture of the routes and individuals who helped operate this escape system. The book even contains a map detailing the routes as slaves passed from the South through the other states to Canada. He based his study on information he obtained from individuals who had either escaped by this system or helped operate it. Some of the routes he depicted on his map were incomplete, however, and more recent scholarship has since greatly expanded the understanding of the operations of the Underground Railroad.

A more modern study appeared in 1987. *The Underground Railroad,* by Charles Blockson, contains brief chapters on individual states and regions through which the freedom seekers passed. A major feature of each chapter is the inclusion of several firsthand accounts of escapes. Blockson added a new dimension to the study of this system by highlighting the role that free blacks played in the entire process. Other books dealing with specific regions have appeared since Blockson's, but no comprehensive modern works cover the Underground Railroad networks in their entirety in the states of New Jersey and New York.

The purpose of this book is to expand and enhance the treatment of the Underground Railroad in New Jersey and New York in several different ways. This book offers a comprehensive view of the system's networks as they functioned in these two states as a whole. Detailed, up-to-date maps reflect the most recent scholarship on the topic, and information is provided on modern highways that have been built on these old routes, so that students of this subject can retrace them. The work also gives a more in-depth overview of the effects of geography, transportation systems, free blacks, and the role of religious organizations. Data from the federal census, taken from 1790 to 1860, provide insights into demographic features in these two states that contributed to the success of the operation of this escape system.

The bulk of the research for this work was done at the Gumberg Library at Duquesne University; at the Hillman Library at the University of Pittsburgh; and through the Internet services of historical societies in New Jersey and New York, the University of Buffalo, and the University of Rochester. In addition, I acquired copies of many works written by participants in the Underground Railroad and by writers who have produced the most recent books on area studies on this topic. Finally, I managed to visit a number of the sites mentioned in the annals of the railroad in New Jersey, New York, and Canada.

Special thanks and appreciation are due to several people who provided invaluable information, guidance, and encouragement while I researched and wrote this book. I thank my wife, Suzanne, for her help and understanding during the production of this work. I also thank my son Kevin and his wife, Katie, for the maps they drew that appear in this work, and for their help in obtaining photographs of sites in New Jersey. Finally, I give special thanks to my editor at Stackpole Books, Kyle Weaver. It was through his encouragement that I launched the effort to write this book, and the guidance and suggestions he gave me during its production have proven to be invaluable.

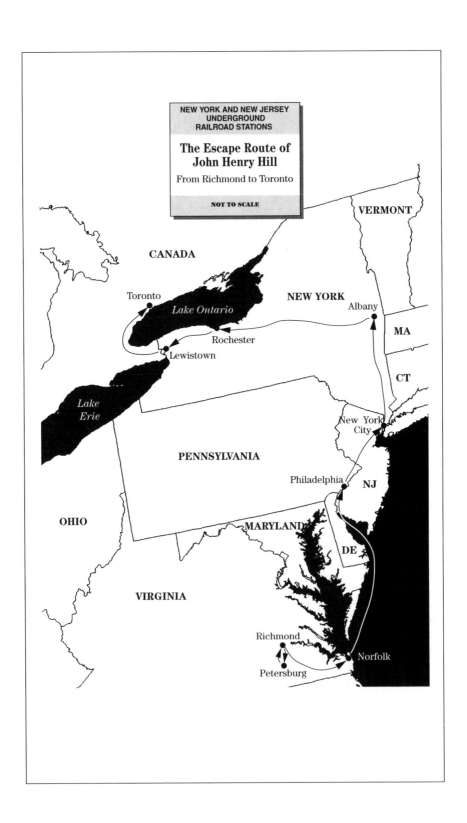

NEW YORK AND NEW JERSEY
UNDERGROUND
RAILROAD STATIONS

The Escape Route of
John Henry Hill

From Richmond to Toronto

NOT TO SCALE

The Story of
John Henry Hill

There are many stories of the successful escapes of blacks held in bondage in the South using the system known as the Underground Railroad. Most are truly heroic in nature, and many involve a degree of ingenuity that amazes the reader. The tales of Henry "Box" Brown, who mailed himself to freedom in a crate, and William and Ellen Craft, who employed remarkable disguises and daring to gain their freedom, have intrigued students of this era. Many of these sagas come to us through the careful record keeping of William Still. The main agent for the Underground Railroad in Philadelphia, Still had hundreds of fugitive slaves pass through his office. A number of these individuals later kept up a correspondence with him. It is through these letters that we have a more detailed understanding of the extent of the Underground Railroad, its successes, and its operation. One self-emancipated man named John Henry Hill wrote Still a series of thirteen letters detailing his escape, the route he took, and his resettlement in Canada. Hill also discussed many aspects of slavery as an institution and the reception he received in Canada. His story is quite interesting.

John Henry Hill was twenty-five years old when, in 1853, he managed to escape from his bondage. A muscular young man, Hill was six feet tall and had a brown complexion. Like many slaves of his era, John Henry was trained in a craft so that he could provide his services as a craftsman on his master's plantation, and so that his master could hire him out as a skilled worker, for a fee, to another plantation owner or some business concern. Many slaveowners were able to earn additional income through this practice. Hill had been trained in the art of carpentry and was quite skilled. He had a strong work ethic and was a loving father and husband. But in his heart, he had a strong desire to be free. Apparently, this deep-seated desire to gain his freedom began to manifest itself to the point where his master, John Mitchell, began to take notice of it. The Mitchell plantation, in Virginia, was not far from the border of the free state of Pennsylvania, and this caused Hill's owner to be quite apprehensive.[1]

John Henry Hill.
HISTORICAL SOCIETY OF
DELAWARE

The year before John Henry managed to escape, Mitchell had begun hiring him out as a carpenter. With his skill and hard work, Hill earned a profit of $150 for Mitchell and proved to be a good investment. Mitchell realized, however, that his slave might attempt to flee to the North at any time, so to prevent losing his investment, he decided to sell John Henry at the great slave auction that was to take place in Richmond on January 1, 1853. Mitchell gave John Henry no indication of his plans.[2]

When they arrived at the auction, Mitchell took John Henry into a building. Once inside, Mitchell and several other men attempted to handcuff him. It was at this moment that John Henry realized what was going to happen: He was about to be sold to another owner. In a flash, he decided to resist, and he attacked those trying to shackle him. Using his fists, feet, and a knife he was carrying, he surprised the four or five men trying to bind him. Stunned by the ferocity of his resistance, they fled his violent attack. Even his master, Mitchell, ran away. Taking advantage of the moment, John Henry quickly left the building, thus avoiding being sold on the auction block.[3]

John Henry Hill describes what happened to him next in an undated letter he sent to William Still:

> Nine months I was trying to get away. I was secreted for a long time in a
> kitchen of a merchant near the corner of Franklin and 7th streets, Rich-
> mond, where I was well taken care of, by a lady friend of my mother. When
> I got tired of staying in that place, I wrote myself a pass to pass myself to
> Petersburg, here I stopped with a very prominent Colored person, who was
> a friend to Freedom stayed here until two white friends told other friends if
> I was in the city to tell me to go at once, and stand not upon the order of
> going, because they had heard a plot. I wrot a pass, started for Richmond,
> Reached Manchester, got off the Cars walked into Richmond, once more
> got back into the same old Den, Stayed here from the 16th of Aug. to 12th
> Sept. On the 11th of Sept. 8 o'clock P.M. a message came to me that there
> had been a State room taken on the steamer City of Richmond for my ben-
> efit, and I assured the party that it would be occupied if God be willing.
> Before 10 o'clock the next morning, on the 12th, a beautiful Sept. day, I
> arose early, wrote a pass for Norfolk left my old Den with many a good
> bye, turned out the back way to 7th St., thence to Main, down Main
> behind 4 night watch to old Rockett's and after about 20 minutes of delay I
> succeed in Reaching the State Room.
>
> My Conductor was very much Excited, but I felt as Composed as I do
> at this moment for I had started from my Den that morning for Liberty or
> for Death providing myself with a Brace of Pistels.
>
> Yours truly J. H. Hill[4]

It is obvious from Hill's account that not only had he initiated his self-
emancipation, but he also received aid from a number of people. First, there
was the merchant in whose kitchen he had hidden. The merchant must have
known of his presence but, at great risk to himself, gave him aid. Next, the
friend of his mother, certainly another black person, tended to his needs.
Then there was the other black individual who hid him in Petersburg. This
person is referred to as being a "friend to Freedom," a coded reference to
being active in some type of system in Virginia for helping slaves gain their
freedom. Two white men now appear, and they seem to be other agents
involved in this escape system. They, in turn, are in contact with still other
agents elsewhere, and they make further arrangements for John Henry's
escape from Virginia. They procure a ticket for him aboard a steamer heading to Philadelphia. They even arrange for him to stay in a private cabin on
the steamer, at a cost of $125. The captain or another key member of the

staff on the steamer must have been involved in the plot. How else could John Henry have been permitted to stay in a private cabin aboard a Southern steamer? This part of the story illustrates a well-organized escape system for aiding fugitive slaves in their attempt to gain freedom.

When Hill reached Philadelphia, he was taken under the auspices of the Vigilance Committee and placed in the care of William Still. Still tells of Hill's concern for the wife and children he had left behind. But, as was not the case with many other fugitives who left family to gain their freedom, Hill's wife and children were already free blacks, and his father-in-law, Jack McCraey, was a free man who would certainly look after them until the entire family could be reunited.[5]

John Henry Hill writes what happened to him after he left Philadelphia, in a letter to William Still dated October 4th, 1853, sent from Toronto, Canada:

> I left your city on Saterday and I was on the way until Friday following. I got to New York the same day that I left Philadelphia, but I had to stay there untel Monday evening. I left that place at six o'clock. I got to Albany next morning in time to take the half past six o'clock train for Rochester, here I stay untel Wensday night. The reason I stay so long Mr. Gibbs given me a letter to Mr. Morris at Rochester. I left that place Wensday, but I only got five miles from that city that night. I got to Lewiston on Thursday afternoon, but too late for the boat to this city. I left Lewiston on Friday at one o'clock, got to this city at five.[6]

Hill does not explain how he got from Philadelphia to New York City, but he does say that the journey took just one day. The only way he could have traveled that distance in a day was by train or boat. Trains ran regularly and packet boats made daily trips between those two cities. Whichever he took, he seems to have had no difficulty boarding, indicating the efficiency of the Underground Railroad system linking Philadelphia with New York City.

The route that Hill followed from the city took him through Albany, Rochester, and Lewiston, until he finally reached Toronto. He writes of two Underground Railroad operatives on this journey, a Mr. Gibbs in Albany and a Mr. Morris in Rochester. A letter of introduction that he carried, written by Gibbs and addressed to Morris, acted as a safe-conduct pass between these two towns. He also openly traveled on a train from Albany to Rochester. Leaving Rochester, he seems to have continued on foot, going only five miles and traveling at night. He reached Lewiston late the next afternoon. After waiting until the following afternoon, he took a boat to Toronto, once again traveling openly.

Hill's letter to Still also gives his impression of Toronto and what he experienced on arriving in that city:

> Sir I found this to be a very handsome city. I like it better than any city I ever saw. It are not as large as the city that you live in, but it is very large place much more so than I expect to find it. I seen a gentleman that you given me letter to. I think him much of a gentleman. I got into work on Monday. The man whom I am working for is name Myers; but I expect to go to work for another man name of Tinsly, who is a master workman in this city. He says that he will give me work next week and everybody advises me to work for Mr. Tinsly as there more surety in him.[7]

Hill gives an insight into the workings of the Canadian Underground Railroad system in this excerpt from his letter. First, there were agents to whom the fugitives went. Hill bore a letter of identification from Still, as he did for Mr. Morris in Rochester. These letters were to assure the Underground Railroad agents that the bearers were truly fugitives and not impostors looking to disrupt the escape network. The Underground Railroad system in Canada provided fugitive slaves with work on their arrival, so that they could support themselves. John Henry had arrived on a Friday, and by the following Monday he had already found a job.

In addition to telling William Still about all the good things that have happened to him since his arrival in Canada, he also takes time to voice his concern for those still living in bondage back in the United States. In an undated letter to Still written between October 30 and November 12, 1853, Hill sums up his feelings on this matter:

> I wants you to let the whole United States know we are satisfied here because I have seen more Pleasure since I came here than I saw in the U.S. the 24 years that I served my master. Come Poor distress men women and come to Canada where colored men are free. Oh how sweet the word do sound to me yeas when I contemplate of these things, my very flesh creaps my heart thrub when I think of my beloved friends whom I left in that cursed hole. Oh my God what can I do for them or shall I do for them. Lord help them. Suffer them to be no longer depressed beneath the the Bruat Creation but may they be looked upon as men made of the Bone and Blood as the Anglo-Americans. May God in his mercy Give Liberty to all this world.[8]

These words contain the mix of joy and sorrow reflected in many of the narratives of escaped slaves: the exhilaration of gaining freedom, along with a sense of regret, or even in some cases a feeling of guilt, that others were left behind. For years, Southern apologists for slavery painted a picture of the black person as a brute devoid of humanity of this kind. For them, the black slave was something a little above the realm of dumb animals, but not fully human. Sentiments like those expressed in Hill's letters demolish this foolish notion and show the nobility of the black man and woman.

Hill also longs for his wife, whom he had to leave behind in Virginia. In his letter dated October 30, 1853, he gives William Still this message:

> My friend I must call upon you once more to do more kindness for me that is to write to my wife as soon as you get this, and tell her when she gets ready to come she will pack and consign her things to you. You will give her some instruction, but not to your expenses, but her own.[9]

A couple weeks later, on November 12, another letter to Still shows that Hill's longing to be reunited with his wife is growing:

> You said that you had written to my wife ten thousand thanks for what you have done and what you are willing to do. My friend whenever you hear from wife please write to me. Whenever she come to your city please give instruction how to travel. I wants her to come the faster way. I wish she was here now. I wish she could get a ticket through to this place.[10]

Hill finally realized his heart's desire in December, when his wife and children reached him in Canada. He effusively informs his friend William Still of the event in a letter written from Toronto on December 29:

> My Dear Friend:—It affords me a good deel of Pleasure to say that my wife and the Children have arrived safe to this City.[11]

The letters that John Henry Hill wrote to William Still are filled with concern for other people, most of it directed toward those in the South who had not yet gained their freedom. Hill expresses most of his feelings in a religious tone, but in a few instances he reveals a sharper side. In his second-to-last letter to Still, dated January 5, 1857, he makes a reference to the increasing number of episodes where fugitive slaves offered armed resistance to attempts by former masters and slave catchers to recapture them, voicing these words, which are almost prophetic in nature:

I hard some good Prayers put up for the suffers on last Sunday evening in the Baptist Church. Now friend still I beleve that Prayers affects great good, but I beleve that the fire and sword would affect more good in this case. Perhaps this is not your thoughts, but I must acknowledge this to be my Polacy. The world are being turned upside down, and I think we might as well take an active part in it as not. We must have something to do as other people, and I hope this moment among the Slaves are beginning. I want to see something go on while I live.[12]

These sentiments appear to be quite similar to those being expressed by many ardent abolitionists throughout the Northern states at that time. They also seem to be a premonition of the Civil War, which began just a few years after this letter.

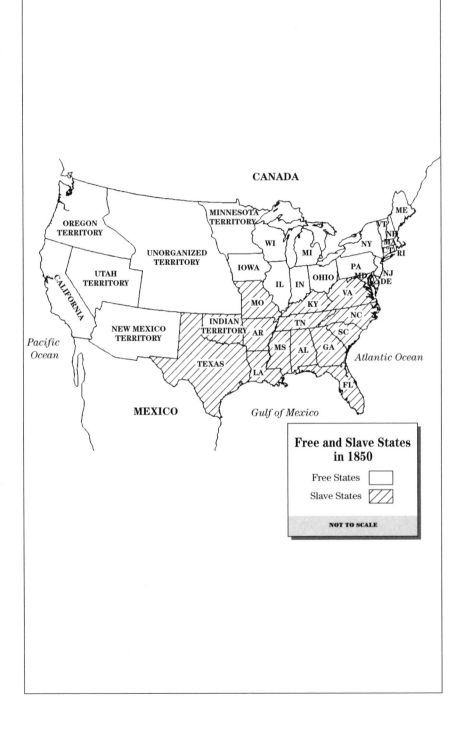

CANADA

OREGON
TERRITORY

MINNESOTA
TERRITORY

UNORGANIZED
TERRITORY

WI

MI

NY

ME

VT
NH
MA
CT RI

IOWA

PA

UTAH
TERRITORY

IL

IN

OHIO

MD
DE

NJ

CALIFORNIA

MO

VA

KY

NEW MEXICO
TERRITORY

INDIAN
TERRITORY

AR

TN

NC

SC

Pacific
Ocean

TEXAS

MS

AL

GA

Atlantic Ocean

LA

FL

MEXICO

Gulf of Mexico

**Free and Slave States
in 1850**

Free States

Slave States

NOT TO SCALE

The Setting

The setting for a discussion of the Underground Railroad in New Jersey and New York begins during the earliest years of the history of our country. Africans were forcibly brought to the shores of America shortly after the founding of the English colony of Jamestown. In 1619, twenty captured Africans were sold as slaves to the Jamestown settlers.[1] This initiated a practice that continued into the early years of the nineteenth century. During this period, slave labor became indispensable to the agricultural economy of the country. In many cases, slavery evolved into an institution rife with cruelty and inhumanity. It also spawned a countermovement of reform that ultimately led to the bloodiest conflict in our nation's history.

Slavery influenced the moral, political, and economic characteristics of every region of the country. It resulted in the emergence of individuals who were willing to risk all to aid slaves who were trying to escape their bondage and find freedom in the North. Before any discussion of who these individuals were or how slaves managed to make their way to freedom, it is necessary to consider several key factors: the demographics of these states; the legislative efforts to end slavery; the group that tried to bring an end to slavery, called the abolitionists; and the general structure of the system, known as the Underground Railroad, that helped slaves in their effort to flee their masters in the South.

DEMOGRAPHICS

The enslaved Africans who reached this country rapidly increased in numbers. The combination of regular shipments of Africans, coupled with their high rate of birth once they got here, resulted in their numbers growing steadily. One need only compare the census data from 1790 and 1860 to see this rapid growth. The census of 1790 shows that the white population of the United States was 3,953,760, and the black population was 757,208—697,681 slaves

Examining captured Africans in a Slave Market. LIBRARY OF CONGRESS

and 59,527 free individuals. The 1860 census shows an increase to 26,923,000 whites and 3,953,760 enslaved and 488,370 free blacks. This indicates that black slaves made up almost 13 percent of the population, and 3,838,765 of them lived in the South. The vast majority of the free blacks resided in the North.[2] These data show the increasing black population, but more the data also highlights the number of free blacks in the country. These free blacks played a significant role in the success of the Underground Railroad effort, in both the North and the South. Without the great number of free blacks available for aiding fugitive slaves, the escape efforts would not have been as effective as they were.

The two states examined in this study underwent important changes in population between 1790 and 1860. New Jersey had a total population of 184,139 people, according to the census of 1790. Included in this figure were 169,954 whites and 14,185 blacks, 11,423 of which were slaves. By 1850, the total population for the state reached 489,555, of which 465,509 were whites and 24,046 were blacks. The number of slaves decreased dramatically to only 236, however. All but 28 of these remaining slaves were clustered in the counties of Bergen, Middlesex, Monmouth, Morris, and Somerset, with

Monmouth having the largest number, 75. By the time of the census of 1860, there were no slaves recorded in New Jersey, and the number of blacks had risen slightly, to 25,318 out of a total population of 646,699.[3]

New York also underwent a shift in the numbers of blacks and slaves living within its borders similar to the one that occurred in New Jersey. In 1790, there were 340,241 people living in New York. Of these, 314,366 were white and 25,875 were black, of which 21,193 were slaves. The census of 1850 lists the total population of the state as 3,097,394. The number of blacks living in the state at this time had grown to 49,069, none of whom were recorded as slaves. New York City had the largest number of blacks, 13,815. Between 1850 and 1860, the black population in the state declined slightly, to 49,005, while the number of whites rose to 3,831,590.[4] (Reasons for this disparity between the number of whites and blacks are discussed later in this book.)

LEGISLATIVE EFFORTS

Efforts to eliminate or regulate the institution of slavery fell into two categories: laws passed by state or federal legislative bodies and regulations passed by organizations on this issue. Each of these helped create a climate and an opportunity in which slaves found a means for gaining their freedom.

Serious legislation was not enacted on this issue until the time of the American Revolution. Sentiments against slavery had been building in the colonies of the Northeast and some of the Mid-Atlantic areas, however. In the late 1700s and early 1800s, laws emerged in these states that either banned slavery outright or designed a process by which it would be eliminated in a gradual manner. These actions took the form of constitutional precepts, legislative statutes, or judicial rulings. The first of these steps was taken in Vermont in 1777 (at that time, Vermont was a republic and did not become a state until 1791). Following Vermont's lead were Pennsylvania, Massachusetts, Connecticut, New York, Rhode Island, and finally, in 1804, New Jersey.[5] At the national Constitutional Convention of 1787, the topic of slavery and its abolition was also raised. In August 1787, a fierce debate took place between representatives such as Gouverneur Morris, Oliver Ellsworth, and even George Mason from Virginia who argued passionately against slavery; and numerous speakers representing Southern states, especially from Georgia and South Carolina. In the end, a compromise was reached in which the importation of slaves was to be permitted until the year 1808.[6]

The month before this debate took place, a new law was passed on July 13, 1787, called the Northwest Ordinance. Article 6 of the ordinance stated, "There shall be neither slavery nor involuntary servitude in the said territory."[7] This effectively eliminated the possibility of slavery in the territory that was to become the states of Illinois, Indiana, Michigan, Ohio, and Wisconsin. The final piece of legislation in this early period of America's history affecting slavery was known as the Act to Prohibit the Importation of Slaves. In fulfilling the design of the constitutional compromise reached on slavery in 1787, Congress passed this law in 1807. It contained the proscription "that from and after the first day of January One thousand eight hundred and eight, it shall not be lawful to import or bring into the United States or the territories thereof from any foreign kingdom, place, or country, any negro, mulatto, or person of colour, as a slave, or to be held to service or labour."[8]

Not all attempts to pass laws in the states affecting or abolishing slavery were successful, however. Laws were proposed in Delaware in both 1767 and 1775 to prohibit the importation of slavery, but they were not enacted. Likewise, neither of the bills introduced in the state legislature in 1786 and 1803, urging the abolition of slavery in Delaware, was passed.[9] In 1785, the Methodist Church in Virginia petitioned the state legislature to abolish slavery on the grounds that it violated the teachings of Christianity and the tenets of the Virginia Declaration of Rights. The members of the legislature totally rejected the petition.[10]

THE ABOLITIONIST MOVEMENT

The abolitionist movement was based on the premise that slavery was an evil and those subjected to it deserved their freedom as soon as possible. Many in the North and some in the South held this sentiment. Several religious denominations even made abolitionism a basic issue in their belief system.

The earliest expression of this abolitionist view appears in the "Germantown Protest," composed in 1688 by the Quakers Garret Hendrick, Daniel D. Pastorius, and the brothers Derick and Abram op de Graeff. In it, they condemn slavery as an anti-Christian institution and include a series of arguments, based on religious principles, for the abolishment of slavery in America.[11]

A few years later, George Keith, a Quaker, printed another one in 1695 in which he also argues against the institution of slavery[12] It was followed by three other pamphlets authored by fellow Quakers. *A Brief Examination of the Practice of the Times,* written by Ralph Sanford and published in 1729 in

Pennsylvania by the press owned by Benjamin Franklin, argued strongly against the concept of slavery. In 1737, Benjamin Lay wrote an antislavery work entitled *All Slave-Keepers That Keep the Innocent in Bondage, Apostates,* arguing that slaveowners violated the basic teachings of Christianity. John Woolman published a short work called *Some Considerations on the Keeping of Negroes* in 1754.[13] This desire to abolish slavery grew within the ranks of the Quakers, and at their yearly meeting in 1754, they officially condemned the practice of slavery and urged all of their members who might own slaves to free them at once.[14] This was a critical decision, because by 1760, more than 30,000 Quakers lived in the colonies, most of them in the southeastern and southern regions of Pennsylvania and New Jersey, as well as the northern areas of Delaware and Maryland.[15]

Quakers approached the issue of abolition in various ways. Some felt that prayer was the answer. Others wanted to take a more proactive role. The great Quaker leader Elias Hicks of Long Island issued a pamphlet in 1811 entitled *Observations on the Slavery of the Africans and Their Descendents.* In it, he argued for a boycott of all goods produced through slave labor. Some were willing to aid slaves in their attempts to flee their masters[16]

Other religious groups also shared the abolitionist sentiment of the Quakers. In 1787, the General Assembly of the Presbyterian Church in America condemned the practice of slavery and began to promote abolitionism. This pronouncement was reaffirmed by the General Assembly of 1793.[17] Likewise, the Methodist Church, at its 1780 National Conference in Baltimore, stated that slavery was in contradiction to the laws of God, man, and nature.[18] Eventually the abolitionist attitude expressed by the conference led to a schism between the northern and southern branches of the Church. The northern branch remained firm in its antislavery sentiment, while the southern branch tolerated the practice.[19] The Baptist Church also had an abolitionist faction among its members. In 1789, the General Committee of Virginia Baptists passed a resolution condemning slavery. The committee also said that all legal means should be pursued to bring an end to the institution. At the same time, the Philadelphia Baptist Association endorsed abolitionism and recommended that all Baptist churches form their own abolitionist societies.[20] The members of these three denominations, along with the Quakers, were very active in the system to aid runaway slaves in the 1800s. Finally, one must not forget the role of the African Methodist Episcopal Church in the abolitionist movement. Founded in 1816 through the efforts of the Rev. Richard Allen, a black Methodist minister from Philadelphia, the A.M.E. Church universally opposed slavery and played a major role in the Underground Railroad's activities.[21]

Organized religions were not the only force fighting against slavery in America. As early as the late 1700s and the beginning of the 1800s, associations began to spring up whose purpose was to bring an end to slavery. Since their goal was to abolish the institution, they were collectively called abolitionist societies, and their members were called abolitionists. Most of these groups were located in the North. Avery Craven, in his essay "The Northern Attack on Slavery," sees the early stages of the abolitionist movement as being part of the "temperance crusade, the struggles for women's rights, prison and Sabbath reform, and the improvement of education" stirring in America. He also sees the movement as a facet of a drive to "unseat aristocrats and re-establish American democracy according to the Declaration of Independence." Craven feels that abolitionism, in its early stages, was just one of many reform movements sweeping the country, particularly the North and West. By the early 1800s, however, it became more important than all of the other movements.[22]

As slavery became the dominant issue for the reformers, it took on the mantle of being the greatest evil of the day. Craven states that the abolitionist movement had two centers of influence. The first of these appeared in the industrial areas of New England. William Lloyd Garrison, the founder and editor of an abolitionist paper there called the *Liberator*, led this faction of the movement. At first Garrison viewed slavery as a moral evil, but he later concluded that it was also a crime. He felt that the Bible and the Declaration of Independence clearly said that slavery was both immoral and a violation of basic human rights. According to Craven, Garrison viewed slavery as having "no legal status in a Christian democracy."[23]

Craven has the second center of abolitionist fervor located in upper New York and the Northwest Territories. Individuals like Benjamin Lundy and Theodore Weld spearheaded this wing of the movement. Within this faction, there were two viewpoints on how the issue of slavery should be approached. One view was grounded in the religious conviction that slavery was morally wrong, and Weld promoted this attitude in religiouslike revival meetings. Unlike Garrison, however, who also agreed that slavery was morally wrong, Weld did not urge for the immediate abolition of slavery, but opted for gradual emancipation of slaves. The other opinion on slavery, held largely in the Northwest, was grounded more in legalities than in religious fervor. The members of this group thought of slavery more in terms of a criminal act, much like Garrison's later position. They pressed the members of Congress to enact laws against the practice. By forcing Southern slaveholders to oppose this legislation, these abolitionists caused them to demonstrate how antidemocratic they really were. They also viewed their attack on the slaveholders as an antiaristocratic effort.[24]

The earliest abolitionist society in America was founded in 1775 in Philadelphia. It eventually became known as the Pennsylvania Abolition Society. In 1830, some of its key members, including James and Lucretia Mott, helped to form a new group called the Pennsylvania Anti-Slavery Society.[25] The members of this organization played a critical role in the successful operation of the Underground Railroad along Pennsylvania's border with Delaware and Maryland, and in the conducting of fugitive slaves northward through New Jersey and New York.

Two other major abolitionist societies began operating the following year, in 1831. These were the New York Committee for a National Anti-Slavery Society, organized by Arthur and Lewis Tappan, and the New England Anti-Slavery Society, headed by William Lloyd Garrison.[26] Two years later, in 1833, largely at the urging of the Motts and Robert Purvis, the black abolitionist from Philadelphia, the groups merged to form the American Anti-Slavery Society.[27] By 1837, Massachusetts had 145 antislavery societies, New York had 274, and Ohio had 213.[28]

White people were not the only ones who operated abolitionist societies. Free blacks in the North also opposed slavery and had urged its abolition for a long time. To help accomplish this goal, they formed abolitionist societies, integrated already existing major societies, published their own newspapers, and gave lectures on the topic all over the North and West. The earliest of these black abolitionist groups was formed in 1787 by Rev. Absalom Jones and Rev. Richard Allen in Philadelphia. Called the Independent Free African Society, its primary goal was to aid those who had recently gained their freedom, either through manumission or having escaped from their masters.[29]

The first of the newspapers published by the black abolitionists was the *Freedom's Journal.* It was the creation in 1827 of John B. Russwurm and Samuel Cornish. In 1828, they started another paper called *The Rights of All.* Both of these papers advocated the abolition of slavery and the granting of equal rights to all blacks in the United States. The leading abolitionists of the day regularly published articles in both papers.[30] Another black newspaper, *The Mystery*, was first published in Pittsburgh in 1847. It was the creation of the famous physician, publisher, and abolitionist Martin Delany.[31] Also joining this list of publications was the quarterly journal *The Mirror of Liberty.* It was produced by David Ruggles, a former slave, who had become a staunch advocate for the rights of blacks in the country and the elimination of slavery as an institution.[32]

Many black abolitionists also toured the United States and Europe speaking out against slavery. Powerful orators like Frederick A. Douglass, Henry Highland Garnet, and James W. C. Pennington spoke at every opportunity on the horrors of slavery.[33] Being escaped slaves, they were able to describe life as a slave with great effectiveness.

Operation
of the Railroad

The term *Underground Railroad* refers to the historic phenomenon of slaves escaping from bondage in the South by fleeing to the North before the American Civil War. It embodies a whole range of activities, from escape methods to the people who helped the runaways. The tale of the Underground Railroad has traditionally involved the stories of the slaves who set out on this perilous journey and the many terrible hardships they endured to achieve this goal. It is also the tale of the heroic individuals, both white and black, who aided them in this effort.

Some modern writers have been highly skeptical about this description of the system, however. Larry Gara, in his 1967 work, *The Liberty Line: The Legend of the Underground Railroad*, epitomizes this contemporary viewpoint. "Although the Underground Railroad was a reality," he says, "much of the material relating to it belongs in the realm of folklore rather than history."[1] He contends that the traditional literature on the subject has the fugitive slave playing a rather passive role in any escape attempt, and only through the heroic efforts of the white Underground Railroad agent did the runaway reach his or her final destination. Without this aid, few fugitives, if any, could ever reach freedom. Gara says that this view is pure melodrama and not history.[2] He is especially critical of Wilbur Siebert's 1898 work, *The Underground Railroad: From Slavery to Freedom,* as being based on faulty recollections of former agents, or the children of agents, on the railroad. He accuses Siebert of embellishing the facts, due to suspect research methods. He is also critical of the work of Robert Smedley, *History of the Underground Railroad in Chester and the Neighboring Counties of Pennsylvania*, complaining that Smedley left the reader with the impression that only white Quakers helped slaves escape.[3]

Although Gara's criticism may have some validity with respect to traditional works on the Underground Railroad, modern research has attempted to correct these shortcomings. There is a body of traditional primary source works written on this topic by individuals such as Frederick Douglass,

William Still, Rev. Calvin Fairbanks, Samuel Ringgold Ward, William and Ellen Craft, and Levi Coffin. These were people who either escaped from slavery themselves and wrote about their experiences or helped slaves escape over a period of years. In addition to these sources, government reports, letters, diary entries, and newspaper articles dating from that time period shed considerable light on the existence and organization of the Underground Railroad.

However, a caution must be given at this point. While there is sufficient evidence to support the existence of the Underground Railroad, the reader must not construe it as a unified, monolithic structure with clear lines of communication and organization. In reality, aside from some common terminology used to describe the operation of slave escape networks, these networks probably functioned on a local or county level. In many instances, these local organizations were joined loosely with one another by individuals or families. Occasionally, we see lines of communication that span broader ranges, such as William Still being in direct contact with Thomas Garrett in Wilmington, Delaware, or Cyrus Bustill in Harrisburg, Pennsylvania. There were also cases where fugitives made their journey to freedom without the assistance of any outside agents. In this context, the term "Underground Railroad" used in this work has more of a generic sense to it in order to illustrate the general concept of escape routes and systems that self-emancipating slaves used to gain their freedom.

The recent works of Charles Blockson, Tom Colarco, and Emma Marie Trusty have revealed that the Underground Railroad was not the sole property of white Quakers, as Gara has already criticized. Examples of their research on this matter will be cited throughout this work. Although they identify the Quakers as active participants in the movement, their research demonstrates the roles played by free blacks and by religious denominations such as the Presbyterians, Methodists, and Baptists. Each of these contributors will be discussed further in this book.

Because of a rekindling of interest in this topic, many local historical societies have been devoting considerable time and effort to researching the Underground Railroad in their communities, and they are making major contributions to filling in the gaps of our understanding of this enterprise. Enhancing the findings derived from new print sources is the discovery of archaeological data in some communities that give tangible evidence to the accounts in some of the escape stories and the traditions of the community on this matter. In a number of instances, these discoveries have lent credibility to many of Siebert's and Smedley's assertions. In short, modern scholarship is providing a much more accurate picture of the operation of the Underground Railroad through a critical examination of a wealth of new data.

EARLY REFERENCES TO
THE UNDERGROUND RAILROAD

The earliest documented reference to slaves receiving aid in their attempt to escape to freedom in the North comes in a letter written by George Washington to Robert Morris of Pennsylvania on April 12, 1786. In his letter, Washington mentions that a Mr. Dalby of Alexandria, Virginia, had gone to Philadelphia to take part in a lawsuit involving a slave. Quakers who lived in the area apparently assisted the slave in his effort to win freedom. Washington goes on to state that the Quakers were making a regular practice of helping runaways in the Philadelphia area.[4] In another letter, written to William Drayton on November 20, 1786, Washington complains that he had apprehended one of Drayton's runaway slaves, but when he sent the slave under guard to Baltimore to be reunited with Drayton, the slave escaped and was aided in this by some sort of escape network.[5]

Another early reference to an escape network may be seen in the work of Samuel Wright. In 1787, he laid out the town of Columbia in Lancaster County, Pennsylvania, allocating a section in the northeastern part for freed slaves. Because Columbia was not far from the Pennsylvania-Maryland border, many fugitive slaves made their way to the town, where they found refuge among the free blacks living there.[6] By 1804, there was a regular escape route from Delaware and Maryland into southeastern Pennsylvania.[7] Between 1815 and 1817, according to Wilbur Siebert, an Underground Railroad network was active between Western Virginia and the states of Ohio and Pennsylvania.[8]

ORIGIN OF THE NAME

The actual origin of the term *Underground Railroad* may never be known. Three sources give different versions of how the term began to be used. Siebert tells the tale of a slave named Tice Davids, who was fleeing his master from Kentucky in 1831. When Davids came to the Ohio River near Ripley, Ohio, he had to dive into the river and swim to the other side. His pursuers also crossed the river, but in a boat. Upon reaching the far shore, they could not find Davids. They searched everywhere but were unsuccessful. This prompted the slaveowner to state that he "must have gone on an underground road." According to Siebert, this phrase eventually evolved into Underground Railroad.[9]

A second tradition is found in Smedley's work. While discussing the importance of the town of Columbia in Lancaster County, Pennsylvania, as a major depot on the Underground Railroad escape route, Smedley writes of some slave hunters who had followed the trail of several fugitive slaves from the Pennsylvania border to Columbia.

Unable to find the runaways, they supposedly said, "There must be an underground railroad [here] somewhere."[10]

Rev. Calvin Fairbanks tells the story of three fugitive girls reaching the famous Underground Railroad agent in Indiana, Levi Coffin. When he saw that slave catchers were in hot pursuit, he hid them in his bed. The pursuers searched his house but did not locate the girls. Fairbanks records that on leaving, the slave hunters reportedly said, "That old Quaker must have an underground railroad, for once a slave gets here, he is never seen again."[11]

DESTINATIONS OF THE FUGITIVES

The chief destination for slaves fleeing from most of the states in the South was Canada, for three major reasons. First, Canada was more accessible for a greater number of slaves than were Florida and Mexico. This was especially true for those who were enslaved in Virginia, Maryland, Delaware, the Carolinas, Kentucky, and Tennessee. Once a fugitive managed to get to a free state, such as New Jersey, Pennsylvania, Ohio, Indiana, or Illinois, Canada was closer than Mexico. Second, fugitives to Canada could expect to receive help from the free blacks and whites who were part of the Underground Railroad system. And third, Canada granted freedom to slaves who crossed over its border from the United States. Slavery in the entire British empire was not officially abolished until the Imperial Act of 1833, which took effect on August 1, 1834.[12] The stage for this Act was set earlier; on May 5, 1772, Lord Chief Justice of Great Britain William Murray, earl of Mansfield, ruled that any slave reaching British soil was automatically set free.[13] The provincial government of Upper Canada passed a law in 1793 granting freedom to all children born of slave mothers when they reached the age of twenty-five.[14]

Although Canada offered a safe haven in the late 1700s for runaways, it was not until after the War of 1812 that a sizable number of fugitives found their way there. One-tenth of all the naval crews serving on the Great Lakes during the war were black. They were such an integral part of the naval operations that Capt. Oliver Hazard Perry gave them special praise for their service.[15] When these veterans returned from the war, they spoke of Canada as a land where slaves could gain their freedom. Siebert states that by 1815, a steady influx of runaway slaves was crossing into Canada.[16]

Florida was another destination for slaves seeking freedom. Before the acquisition of the Florida Territory from Spain in 1821, many slaves from

Georgia sought freedom by living among the Seminole Indians or in Spanish towns located there. The number of slaves choosing to follow this route became so large that the Georgia state legislature petitioned President George Washington in 1789 for some relief from the losses the slaveowners were experiencing as a result of the flight of their slaves. Washington, in his reply, acknowledged the financial losses and urged that this escape route be blocked to prevent Florida from becoming a destination for slaves all over the South.[17]

Other slaves fled to Mexico and the lands that were part of the Mexican Territory. The Freedmen's Inquiry Commission Report of 1864 indicates that Mexico became a goal for fugitive slaves as early as 1812.[18] The number of slaves trying to reach Mexican Territory increased in the 1820s to the point where the U.S. Congress proposed a treaty with the Mexican government in 1827 for the return of all fugitive slaves. The Mexican Senate rejected the treaty.[19] To compound the problem for slaveholders in Louisiana, Alabama, and Mississippi, the Mexican Constitution of 1829 granted freedom and equality to blacks, including the former slaves who had fled there from those states.[20]

Not all fugitive slaves went to Florida, Mexico, or Canada, however. Many stayed in the United States and blended into existing free black communities. Frequently, all a runaway needed to do was make a change of clothing, name, or hair style to elude slave catchers and former masters.

ORGANIZATION OF
THE UNDERGROUND RAILROAD

The organization of the Underground Railroad was patterned after the operation of an actual railroad. Terms such as *stations* or *depots, station agents, conductors, lines,* and *presidents* of railroads were used as a type of code to describe various activities and locations on the escape routes. According to one of the most famous operators on the Underground Railroad, Levi Coffin of Cincinnati, the depots, or safe houses, were spaced about ten to twenty miles apart. This was the distance a fugitive could travel, or be guided, in a single night.[21] When a runaway reached a depot, some signal was given, usually a rap on a window, door, or front gate. A verbal exchange took place, and the fugitive was taken inside the home. After receiving a meal, clothing, or medical attention, if necessary, the visitor was hidden in a secret room, cellar, attic, barn, or some other secret compartment until the next night. At that time, the station agent, the person who lived in the home, or someone designated as a conductor would take the runaway to the next depot. The most frequently used method of conveyance for transporting the runaway was a wagon or carriage.[22]

The Underground Railroad did not operate like a well-oiled machine, however. There was never a network that began in the South and ran, uninterrupted, directly to Canada. A better way to view this phenomenon is to consider the railroad as being a collection of smaller operations. A network could have been as large as a county, and within this geographic area, it was well run. These regional networks were then loosely connected to those in other regions, and a fugitive using these connections could eventually reach the "promised land" of Canada.

There were many runaways who never used, or received help from, the Underground Railroad in their escape attempts. Some made their way to Northern areas, and even to Canada, completely on their own.

METHODS OF ESCAPE

Slaves and their conductors used many different methods to make their way to freedom. Runaways traveled overland on foot or in some type of conveyance, on railways, or in watercraft. The most common way to travel overland, especially when escaping from Delaware, Maryland, Virginia, or Kentucky, was to simply walk to a destination from the slaveowner's plantation. The fugitives typically traveled at night. The only guide they had for heading north, where they knew freedom might be found, was to follow the North Star. They also learned that the North Star could be found by using the stars of the Big Dipper, which the slaves referred to as the "Drinking Gourd."[23]

Walking to freedom required special vigilance and creativity. The threat of being apprehended by slave catchers was always a possibility. While the fugitive was still in Southern territory, he or she could trust no one. Everyone would have been suspicious of a slave traveling alone and going north. This is why travel was done at night. During the day, the fugitive had to hide somewhere, such as in a barn or other outbuilding on a farm, in a corn shock or thicket, or under a bridge. Those lucky enough to stumble on an Underground Railroad station would have an easier time hiding during the day. Because of the difficulty of traveling constantly overland and through woods, most fugitives used roads or trails during their night travels. Always on the alert for the sound of horses approaching, the fugitive had to be ready to jump off the road into a thicket at a moment's notice. When coming to streams or rivers, the runaways waded, swam, stole boats or skiffs, made rafts, or simply clung to logs to get across.[24] If a fugitive was lucky enough to be helped by a conductor, guidance and arrangements would have made the journey less stressful.

Using a wheeled vehicle was another means of escape, usually when a runaway was in the care of an Underground Railroad network. There are stories, however, of runaways stealing wagons or horses from their masters and making good their escape in this fashion. Levi Coffin always kept a wagon at the ready to take slaves to other stations.[25] Rev. Calvin Fairbanks, a conductor who traveled south and helped lead many slaves to safety, writes that he frequently used wheeled vehicles such as wagons, buggies, or carriages. Fugitives were hidden in special false bottoms in these vehicles or under loads of hay, straw, boxes, or bags.[26] In some rarer cases, runaways disguised themselves as white people and openly drove carriages or rode in stagecoaches to the North.[27]

Railroads were another means of travel that some runaways employed. The fugitives either hid on trains and rode them to freedom, or put on disguises or used some type of subterfuge to simply ride the trains to safety. William Still tells the story of a runaway named John Thompson, who escaped from Alabama at the age of nineteen by using trains. Working on a plantation near Huntsville, Thompson had resolved to escape. He made note of those trains that passed near his plantation and were heading north. One night, he left the plantation and hid on the top of a passenger car on a train going northward. When daylight approached and the train stopped, he left the car and hid during the day. At nightfall, he climbed on top of a car of another northbound train. In this manner, he eventually made it all the way to Canada.[28] Slaves also disguised themselves as whites and rode trains to the North.

Another method of traveling northward was to use some means of water transportation. Steamboats, canoes, skiffs, and schooners were all used by fugitive slaves as means of escape. Rev. Calvin Fairbanks used the regular steamboat traffic that ran along the Mississippi and Ohio Rivers to carry slaves he was rescuing to Northern cities, especially Cincinnati and Pittsburgh. In one case, in June 1842, he guided a woman from a plantation in Montgomery County, Kentucky, by riding with her on a train to Frankfort and then getting passage for her on a steamboat going to Cincinnati. Once she got there, Levi Coffin met her and put her onto a network that eventually took her to Canada. Steamboat captains either were sympathetic to the efforts of the Underground Railroad or were bribed to carry fugitives on their boats.[29] In some instances, slaves with fair complexions disguised themselves as whites and simply booked passage on steamboats heading North.

Frederick Douglass, describing his first plan to escape from his master, tells of how he and several companions were going to paddle canoes up the Chesapeake Bay, pretending to be fishermen. When they reached a point northward, they would leave the canoes and continue on foot, following the North Star, until they reached Pennsylvania. Unfortunately, their plan was discovered, and they had to abandon the idea.[30]

Travel along the coastline in some sort of oceangoing vessel was another option some runaways employed. Portsmouth, Virginia, was the jumping-off point for a number of fugitives, who used open skiffs to sail northward.[31] Some chose to go by schooner. William Still writes about a schooner captain, whom he calls Captain F in order to hide his identity, who regularly took slaves from Virginia aboard his ship and sailed to Philadelphia with them.[32] Some fugitives would board a ship secretly and hide until the vessel reached a Northern port. Still tells the tale of three men, James Mercer, William Gilliam, and John Clayton, who got on the steamer *Pennsylvania* in Richmond before it set sail and hid in its coal bin in the boiler room. They remained there, suffering from heat, coal dust, thirst, and hunger, until the ship docked at Philadelphia Harbor on February 26, 1854. They managed to leave the ship, find the Underground Railroad office in the city, and with its help, eventually reach Canada.[33]

Perhaps the most imaginative method of escape in the annals of the Underground Railroad was reaching safety by using some type of container. Essentially, the runaway slave would hide in the container and have it shipped to some location in a free state, where it would be opened and the slave freed. William Still recounts three episodes in which slaves attained their freedom by this means. The most famous of these stories is the one of Henry Brown, a slave living in Richmond in the 1840s. In 1848, Brown resolved to escape from his bondage. Fleeing from Richmond was especially hazardous because of the number of slave catchers on the lookout. Brown concocted a plan that was both imaginative and daring. He constructed a box that was two feet, eight inches deep, two feet wide, and three feet long. He lined it with baize and put a small flask of water and some biscuits in it. On the outside of the box, he put the address of a person living in Philadelphia. He then got into the box and had a friend nail it shut. His friend took the box to the Adams' Express Office in Richmond and shipped Brown to freedom. The journey proved to be extremely agonizing, but Brown did reach Philadelphia. Still, who was an eyewitness to the event, relates that when the box was opened, Brown rose up, extended his hand, and said, "How do you do, Gentlemen?"[34] From this point on, Brown was known as Henry "Box" Brown. Still also tells the stories of two women who each fled from Baltimore to Philadelphia using containers.[35]

Punishment for trying to escape. HISTORICAL SOCIETY OF DELAWARE

A successful escape was essential for the fugitive. Being recaptured could be most painful, as slaveowners employed a whole host of punishments on runaways. One particular method is mentioned many times in the narratives written by former slaves years later. The testimony of an ex-slave named Andrew Boone from Virginia, given in the early the twentieth century, details this practice:

> Dey whipped me wid de cat-o'–nine-tails. It had nine lashes on it. Some of de slaves was whipped wid a cobbin paddle. De had forty hole in 'em and when you was buckled to a barrel dey hit your naked flesh with de paddle and everywhere dere was a hole in de paddle it drawed a blister. When de whippin' with de paddle was over, dey took de cat-o'–nine-tails and busted de blisters.
>
> By dis time de blood sometimes would be runnin' down deir heels. Den de next thing was a wash in salt water strong enough to hold up an egg. Slaves was punished dat way for runnin' away and such.[36]

Those who aided fugitives in their escape attempts were also subject to punishment. The Fugitive Slave Act of 1793 stated that assisting runaways was a federal crime. Anyone caught helping a fugitive slave was subject to a fine of $500.[37] Half a century later, the Fugitive Slave Act of 1850 made the penalties for giving aid even harsher. This law stipulated a fine of $1,000 and a jail sentence of six months for each fugitive slave helped.[38]

THE MAJOR ESCAPE ROUTES

The Underground Railroad had three major systems of escape routes to convey runaways to Canada: the western, central, and eastern routes. The western route proceeded up the Mississippi River Valley through the territories of Kansas and Missouri to Iowa and Illinois. Following this route, fugitive slaves would then be led through Michigan to Canada, frequently going through Detroit.[39] The central route originated in the heart of the South and proceeded through Kentucky, Western Virginia, and western Maryland to Ohio, Indiana, Pennsylvania, and western New York. Each of these states had Underground Railroad systems that guided fugitives to Canada. The eastern route ran from the southeastern states through Maryland, Delaware, and Virginia to Pennsylvania and New Jersey. It then went through these states to New York and New England, and thence to Canada. The reminder of this book focuses on those parts of the eastern and central routes that went through New York and New Jersey.

New Jersey—The Backdrop

New Jersey was one of the earliest areas in America settled by Europeans. In the first decade of the 1600s, the Dutch East India Company sent Henry Hudson to North America to find a water route that would allow the company's ships to traverse the continent to get to the Orient more easily than by traveling around Africa. Hudson reached New York Bay in 1609 and sailed up the Hudson River. Even though he did not find the magical route to the Far East, he did lay claim to the lands and waterways he found for the Dutch. He also sailed around what was to become New Jersey and proceeded up the Delaware River. The result of his voyage of exploration was the creation in 1624 of a Dutch empire in America known as New Netherland. It was at this time that the Dutch acquired Manhattan Island in a trade with the native population for what amounted to $24. The main area of New Netherland consisted of the lands on either side of the Hudson River, the western portion of Long Island, and the northeastern part of New Jersey. The Dutch also laid claim to the lands around the mouth of the Delaware River. The capital of this new empire was New Amsterdam.

Friction developed early between the Dutch and the colonies in New England. A war almost broke out between the two parties in the early 1600s, but because of the reluctance of Massachusetts colony, it did not materialize. The Dutch did have an armed conflict with the Swedes over the encroachment of the latter into the land around the Delaware River, which was claimed by the Dutch. The Swedes' incursion ended in 1655, when Peter Stuyvesant led a military expedition against them.[1]

The Dutch colony of New Netherland came to an end in 1664, when the king of England, Charles II, gave lands of the colony to his brother, the duke of York. The Dutch were unable to resist the superior force of the English and had to surrender their colony. The duke, in turn, gave the lands stretching from the Hudson River to the Delaware to two of his friends, Sir George Carteret and Lord John Berkeley. They named the new colony New Jersey, after the Isle of Jersey, where Carteret had once been governor.[2] The colony was split into two large areas. East New Jersey had an assembly that met at Elizabethtown. West New Jersey's assembly convened at Salem or, at times, Burlington. By 1683, East New Jersey had twenty-four proprietors, while West New Jersey had four. In 1702, the two sections were united into the Royal Province of New Jersey.[3]

Enslaved blacks made their appearance in 1639 in Pavonia, the first permanent settlement of the Dutch in the area that would become New Jersey.[4] Dutch settlers from New Amsterdam began importing black slaves from the West Indies into the northeastern portion of this area.[5] By 1680, there were about 120 enslaved blacks in the old Dutch territories of New Jersey. Of these, 60 to 70 worked on a large farm owned by a Col. Lewis Morris in Shrewsbury, Monmouth County.[6] The others worked in the ironworks located in Tinton Falls, in the same county.[7]

The number of blacks increased when New Jersey became an English colony. The new proprietors, Carteret and Berkeley, actively encouraged the importation of slaves, wanting to increase the workforce of their colony. To stimulate this enterprise, the new colony's constitution of 1664 granted settlers seventy-five acres of land for every slave they purchased before January 1, 1665; sixty acres for every one in 1666; forty-five acres in 1667; and thirty acres in 1668.[8] Even after New Jersey became a royal province, the importation of slaves continued. In 1726, the total population of the colony was 32,422, including 2,581 blacks. In 1745, there were 56,797 whites and 4,500 blacks in New Jersey. The white population continued to increase rapidly to 73,000 in 1754, but the number of blacks rose only to 5,500 in that same year. By the outbreak of the American Revolution in 1776, there were 11,000 black slaves in all of New Jersey.[9]

By 1776, most of the slaves in the colony resided in East Jersey and worked for the Dutch farmers who had settled there when the area was part of New Netherland. The slaves made up 12 percent of the total population of East Jersey. In West Jersey, the number of slaves was far fewer—only 4 percent of the population. This area was settled by Quakers, who for the most part did not make use of slave labor.[10] Most of the slaves resided in Bergen, Essex, Hunterdon, Middlesex, Monmouth, and Somerset Counties.[11]

The majority of blacks sold into bondage in New Jersey did not come directly from Africa, but from the slave populations of Jamaica, Barbados, Curacao, and Antigua. Many slaves worked in agriculture, but a large number were put to work in industries, most notably ironmaking. The major employment of slave labor in Monmouth County was in this line of industry. The iron mine and forge of Lewis Morris at Tinton Falls made heavy use of slave labor.[12]

The agricultural employment of slaves was limited because farms in the colony were not much more than 100 acres in size. The Dutch farmers typically used one or two male slaves and perhaps one female whose main tasks were related to housework. Male slaves worked as boatmen, miners, sawmill hands, carpenters, wheelwrights, bakers, cooks, stage drivers, and stablemen.[13]

After the Revolutionary War and the creation of the state of New Jersey, the black population continued to grow. As the years progressed, however, the number of free blacks far outpaced the number of slaves in the state. Table 1 displays this shift.[14]

TABLE 1.
CENSUS DATA FOR NEW JERSEY, 1790 TO 1860

Year	Total population	Slaves	Free blacks
1790	184,139	11,423 (6.2%)	2,762 (1.4%)
1800	211,149	12,422 (5.8%)	4,402 (2.0%)
1810	245,562	10,851 (4.4%)	7,843 (3.2%)
1820	273,736	7,557 (2.5%)	12,460 (4.5%)
1830	320,823	2,254 (0.7%)	18,303 (5.7%)
1840	373,306	674 (0.1%)	21,044 (5.6%)
1850	489,555	236 (.05%)	23,810 (4.8%)
1860	646,699	0	25,318 (3.9%)

These data show that the number of slaves in New Jersey was never as great as in the Southern states. After a spike in the census of 1800, the number began to gradually decline, while the number of free blacks rose. The main reason for this was the passage of a gradual abolition of slavery law in 1804. As late as the census of 1850, however, a small slave population still existed in New Jersey.

The Dutch had treated their slaves with a degree of humaneness, but this changed when the English acquired the colony. Between 1675 and 1846, the various legislatures in New Jersey passed 84 different statutes related to slaves. They governed almost every aspect of a black person's existence. In comparison, the colonial and state governments in New York enacted only 19 slave statutes between 1652 and 1841, and Pennsylvania, only 11 between 1700 and 1860.[15] Though New Jersey's statutes far exceeded those of New York and Pennsylvania, they do not come close to matching the 134 laws passed by the various governments in Virginia concerning slaves.[16]

The slave statutes of New Jersey, with some exceptions, were designed to keep the movement and daily lives of blacks in check. As early as 1675, anyone transporting an enslaved person was liable to a fine of £5. A 1682 law forbade the purchasing of goods from an enslaved person. That same year, a law was passed requiring masters to adequately feed and clothe their slaves. Two laws, in 1682 and 1685, forbade the selling of intoxicating spirits to blacks and Native Americans. The first of the runaway laws appeared in 1694, offering a reward for apprehending and returning any slave found more than five miles away from home without his or her master's permission. In 1713, a statute was passed that forbade a free black person from purchasing, inheriting, or owning land.[17] An Act for Regulating of Slaves, a major law passed in 1714, summarized many previous state laws and covered some areas that had not yet been considered. First, it reiterated the laws concerning the sale of alcohol to blacks and Native Americans, as well as the limitation as to how far a slave could be away from home without the permission of a master. Then it listed a number of crimes, such as murder, theft, and attempted rape, and the punishments that should be given to the slave for committing them. In most cases, the punishment was either death or a severe flogging. One of the provisions of the law covered the act of concealing a runaway slave. A person caught doing so had to pay a fine of 40 shillings for each time this was done. The law also reemphasized the 1713 statute that forbade free blacks from owning property. The last provision of the law stated that any master wanting to manumit a slave had to obtain a bond of £200 that was to be used to pay the freed slave an annual fee of £20 for the rest of his or her life. If the slave was freed in a will, the executor had to arrange for the bond and annual payment. If this provision was not followed, the manumission was to be considered null and void.[18] The bond and annual payments were meant to ensure that freed slaves would have a means of support.

A series of statutes passed by the legislature in 1745, 1746, and each year between 1755 and 1764 either exempted slaves from service in the military or allowed them to serve with their masters' permission. Another law, enacted in 1768, called for more severe punishment for capital offenses committed by slaves and Native Americans. The crimes of murder, conspiracy to commit murder, rape, and arson merited the death penalty. Slaves or Native Americans caught stealing something worth more than £5 could also receive the death penalty.

When New Jersey became a state, the number of laws related to slaves and free blacks continued to grow. Three laws passed in 1786 were of particular significance. The first forbade the importation of slaves brought to the United

Sates after 1776 into New Jersey, and it eliminated the bond and annual payment required to free a slave. Another made it a punishable offense to treat a slave abusively. The third prohibited freed blacks from traveling in New Jersey if they had been manumitted in another state. Those freed in New Jersey could not travel beyond the county in which they lived without carrying an official certificate stating that they had been freed.[19]

An Act Respecting Slaves, passed on March 14, 1798, was the next major law instituted by the state government. It was extremely comprehensive and contained thirty separate provisions reiterating many provisions found in earlier laws. It said that a slave was a slave for life unless manumitted by his or her master. It allowed slaves to be witnesses against other slaves in a court of law. It forbade trading with slaves without their master's permission. It strongly forbade the hiding or transporting of slaves without permission. It established a curfew for slaves and did not permit them to assemble or meet in a disorderly manner. It prohibited the importation of slaves for the purpose of sale, made it a crime to abuse one's slaves, required that slaves be taught to read, and forbade the selling of slaves to someone outside of the state without the slaves' permission if they had resided in New Jersey for one year or more. The law also had several provisions that covered the searching of vessels for contraband slaves or runaways, and it established a formal procedure by which slaves were to be manumitted by their masters.[20]

The final two state laws affecting slaves dealt with the abolition of slavery in New Jersey. An Act for the Gradual Abolition of Slavery became law on February 15, 1804. New Jersey was the last state in the North to pass such a law, which would eventually put an end to slavery within its borders. The law stated that children born of slaves in New Jersey after July 4 should remain servants of their mothers' owners until they reached the age of twenty-five for males or twenty-one for females, and at that time they should be set free. Owners of these children had to register them with the county clerk within nine months after their birth. If the owner did not want to keep the children, they could abandon that right through a formal process, and the children then became the ward of the township in which they resided. This had to be done within one year of birth, or otherwise the owners had to see to their care and maintenance until they reached the age of freedom.[21] The following is an example of one such Certificate of Abandonment:

> To the Town Clerk & overseer of the poor of this township of Piscataway
> Gentlemen this are to inform you that my Negro wench Judy was Brought
> to bed the sixteenth day of November last with a female child which she

named Sarah—I do therefore herby give you notice that I abandon all my right % title to the said female child agreeably to an Act of the Legislature in which case made & provided—Given under my hand the 6th day of June 1806.

Her

Mary Boice

Mark[22]

After the passage of this law, some slaveowners also voluntarily freed their slaves who had been born before July 4, 1804. Here is an example of one such manumission:

> Manumission of Abigal State of New Jersey, Middlesex County. These are to certify to whome it may concern, That I Ephraim Pyatt, of the township of Piscataway, State and County aforesaid, Do manumit and set free My Negrow Woman, Abigal, who is under the age of forty years and above the age of twenty one years & who appears to be of sound mind and not under any bodily incapacity of obtaining her support, and I have this day obtained a certificate for said Abigal, signed by Edward Griffin & Ephraim Runyan [sic],two of the Overseers of the Poor for the township of Piscataway, In sd [said] County and Samuel & John Randolph, two Of the Justices of the Peace for the County & State aforesaid, for her freedom. Given under my hand & seal this eighth day of August in the year of our Lord eighteen hundred and eight, 1808—
>
> Ephraim Pyatt L.S.
Witness present
Edward Griffith,
Ephraim Runyon,
John F. Randolph.[23]

An Act for the Gradual Abolition of Slavery, and Other Purposes Respecting Slaves was passed by the New Jersey General Assembly on February 24, 1820. Basically, this law restated provisions of the statutes passed in 1798 and 1804, the provisions of the original gradual abolition of slavery act, the legal procedures of manumitting a slave, the prohibition against exporting slaves out of the state, the search and seizure of ships suspected of hiding contraband slaves, and the right of slaveowners to pass through the state with their personal slaves.[24]

Why were so many laws passed in New Jersey to regulate slave behavior? The answer lies in an inordinate fear of a slave insurrection on the part of the people living there. In *History of Black Americans: From Africa to the Emergence of the Cotton Kingdom,* Philip S. Foner tells of a letter that appeared in the March 18–25, 1734, *New York Gazette* describing in detail a slave plot in New Jersey. This event caused great alarm among the citizens of the colony. Foner goes on to say that the letter appeared about the time that a number of slave uprisings were occurring in the West Indies, the place from which most of the slaves in New Jersey had originated.[25] Though these events did not have the same alarming effect on the people of New York and Pennsylvania, they did cause legislatures of New Jersey to enact measures to ensure that such uprisings would not happen in their land.

Several conditions were necessary if slaves were going to successfully escape from or through New Jersey. The first was the existence of antislavery sentiment among the state's citizens. This could take the form of abolitionist activity and the willingness of individuals, both black and white, to render assistance to fugitives trying to emancipate themselves. Another was the availability of avenues over which fugitive slaves could travel to freedom, including roads, trails, waterways, and rail lines. Still another was the establishment of an Underground Railroad network that could provide aid and guidance for runaways.

ANTISLAVERY SENTIMENT

Although New Jersey had many laws that supported the practice of slavery, there was evidence of a sentiment against this institution within the colony and state, expressed in the attempts to pass laws that would abolish slavery; the actions of abolitionist and religious organizations that were determined to do whatever was necessary to end this practice; and the role that free blacks played in assisting their brethren in attempts to escape the bondage of slavery.

The first organized attempt to legislate an end to slavery in New Jersey occurred in 1778. In that year, Samuel Allinson, a Quaker abolitionist, wrote to Gov. William Livingston, urging him to have the state legislature abolish the practice. He found a sympathetic ear in Livingston, who also opposed the institution of slavery. The governor called on the legislature to pass an abolition bill, saying that the idea of enslaving fellow human beings was unchristian and inhumane. He especially appealed to the sentiments set forth in the Declaration of Independence with respect to all people being created equal and endowed with the right to pursue happiness. The September 20, 1780, issue of the *New Jersey Gazette* contained an article by the abolitionist John Cooper, who also urged the passage of an abolition bill, citing both the Declaration of Independence and Pennsylvania's recently passed Gradual Abolition of Slavery Act.[26] The attainment of this legislative goal was not realized until 1804, when the New Jersey Gradual Abolition of Slavery Act was passed.

The first attempt on the part of New Jersey citizens to seek a federal law regulating the practice of slavery took place in 1790. Quakers from New Jersey, along with their fellow Friends from Virginia, Maryland, Delaware, New York, and western New England, petitioned the First Federal Congress to pass laws that would at least regulate the slave trade. They were joined in this effort by Benjamin Franklin and the organization of which he was president, the Pennsylvania Society for the Abolition of Slavery. The Pennsylvania petition also urged Congress to pass legislation that would discourage the trading of slaves.[27]

Another quasilegal approach to ending slavery in New Jersey was that used by the American Colonization Society. Founded between 1815 and 1817 by Rev. Robert Finley, a Presbyterian minister, the society aimed to end slavery by repatriating blacks back to Africa. Soon after its founding, a chapter formed known as the Colonization Society of New Jersey. The Princeton Theological Seminary strongly endorsed the idea of sending blacks back to their ancestral home in Africa, but African-American leaders did not accept the plan. Samuel Cornish, a black newspaper editor and abolitionist pastor of a Presbyterian church in Newark, wrote that contrary to white assertions, blacks did not yearn for a return to Africa. A convention of black leaders held in Philadelphia in 1839 soundly denounced the project.[28]

The second factor in creating a sentiment for aiding slaves in escaping from their bondage was the actions of abolitionist and religious groups in the state. John Woolman's 1754 pamphlet, "Some Considerations on the Keeping of Negroes," was one of the initial efforts to build support for the abolition of slavery. Another abolitionist pamphlet that influenced many was produced in 1783 by David Cooper, a Quaker living in Trenton, entitled "A Serious Address to the Rulers of America on the Inconsistency of Their Conduct Respecting Slavery: Forming a Contract between the Encroachment of England on American Liberty, and American Injustice in Tolerating Slavery." The pamphlet was centered around an appeal to the basic propositions of equality of humankind and basic rights as found in the Declaration of Independence. Two years after the publication of his work, Cooper appealed to the state legislature in New Jersey to pass a gradual abolition of slavery law.[29]

The Quakers led the way for the formation of the first abolition society in New Jersey when in 1792 they helped establish the New Jersey Society for Promoting the Gradual Abolition of Slavery.[30] Its president, Joseph Bloomfield, like David Cooper before him, lobbied the legislature for the passage of a gradual abolition of slavery law. After a heated debate, the bill to achieve this end failed by only one vote in 1794. Even after this setback, Bloomfield felt that the passage of such a law was drawing nearer.[31]

Religious organizations also played a pivotal role in creating a sentiment conducive to the success of slave escapes. Most active in this effort were the Presbyterian, Quaker, and African Methodist Episcopal (A.M.E.), African Methodist Episcopal Zion (A.M.E. Zion), and Methodist Episcopal (M.E.) churches. The Presbyterian Church became active in New Jersey during the 1730s. Rev. Gilbert Tennent and his brothers William Jr., John, and Charles came from the presbytery in eastern Pennsylvania where their father, William, trained ministers, and they began to minister to the members of this faith in the central New Jersey colony. In 1738, the Tennents, along with another minister, Rev. Samuel Blair, formed the New Brunswick Presbytery.[32] During the Revolutionary War period, Presbyterians in western New Jersey and in Monmouth County in eastern New Jersey became very critical of the institution of slavery. In 1787, at the General Assembly of the Presbyterian Church in America, the synods of Philadelphia and New York, which had jurisdiction over the Presbyterian churches in New Jersey, condemned the practice of slavery and approved its abolition. They did, however, opt for a moderate and gradual approach to this end.[33] By 1860, there were 211 Presbyterian churches scattered throughout the state.[34]

The Quakers came to the colony of New Jersey during its early days; arriving in the western part of the state in 1674, and by 1677, founding the town of Burlington. In 1681, when William Penn acquired the land that would become the colony of Pennsylvania, the Quakers were already well established in western New Jersey.[35] By 1860, there were sixty-one Quaker meetinghouses distributed throughout the state, twenty-six of these in Burlington County alone.[36] Antislavery sentiment emerged early among the Quakers. Pamphlets opposing the institution were written by members of the religion in Pennsylvania and New Jersey in the late 1600s and early 1700s. George Keith wrote one in 1694, and this was followed by works of Ralph Sanford (1729), Benjamin Lay (1737), and John Woolman (1754).[37] At their Yearly Meeting in 1754, the Quakers officially condemned the practice of slavery and urged all of their members who owned slaves to set them free at once.[38] The Quakers passed an even stronger measure at their Yearly Meeting in 1775, excluding any Quaker who still owned slaves from the society.[39] Quakers were instrumental in the establishment of abolitionist societies in New Jersey.

Black religious institutions such as the A.M.E. and A.M.E. Zion churches formed another group. Founded in 1816 by a black Methodist minister in Philadelphia, Rev. Richard Allen, the A.M.E. Church spread throughout the eastern United States and met the spiritual needs of African-Americans who were excluded or segregated by the established churches at that time. By 1818, New Jersey had A.M.E. congregations in Salem, Trenton, and Princeton. The number of members in each of these was small (110, 73, and 33, respectively), but the church quickly attracted both free and enslaved blacks. By 1822, the A.M.E. Church had two circuits in New Jersey. The Salem Circuit, with 293 members, consisted of churches in Port Elizabeth, Salem, Bushtown, Dutchtown (Swedesboro), Woodbury, Snowhill (Lawnside), Evesham, Tranfield, and Greenage (Greenwich). The Trenton Circuit had 227 members and included churches in Trenton, Princeton, Rockhill, Siggstown, Blandsburgh, and Brunswick.[40] Emma Marie Trusty, in her detailed study of the Underground Railroad in southern New Jersey entitled *The Underground Railroad: Ties That Bound Unveiled: A History of the Underground Railroad in Southern New Jersey from 1770 to 1861*, identifies the existence of forty-three African Methodist and A.M.E. churches in New Jersey by 1860.[41] They became key stations on the Underground Railroad routes that coursed through the state and were instrumental in helping hundreds of freedom seekers on their journey north.

Free blacks also supported attempts by slaves to emancipate themselves. Table 2 shows the distribution of free blacks throughout the state during the peak years of the Underground Railroad's operation.[42]

Some of these free blacks lived in small settlements near towns, others lived in cities, and still others resided on farms, often in isolated areas. Wherever they lived, they played a vital, and long overlooked, part in the network used by fugitives on their way to freedom.

AVENUES OF ESCAPE

A long, narrow strip of land, New Jersey contains 7,836 square miles of terrain and ranks forty-sixth in size in the United States. The state is almost a peninsula. Its western boundary is the Delaware River, to its south is the Delaware Bay, and to its east are the Atlantic Ocean and Hudson River. There is a land connection only on the northwest.

TABLE 2.
THE NUMBER OF FREE BLACKS BY COUNTY
FOR 1840, 1850, AND 1860

County	1840	1850	1860
Atlantic	234	217	194
Bergen	1,529	1,624	1,663
Burlington	1,643	2,109	2,224
Camden (created in 1844)	0	2,230	2,574
Cape May	198	247	273
Cumberland	896	1,130	1,295
Essex	1,908	2,328	1,757
Gloucester	1,631	620	707
Hudson	319	500	653
Hunterdon	778	808	796
Mercer	2,319	2,036	2,225
Middlesex	1,535	1,369	1,307
Monmouth	2,180	2,323	2,658
Morris	911	1,008	686
Ocean (created in 1850)	0	140	124
Passaic	706	615	557
Salem	1,796	2,075	2,462
Somerset	1,652	1,711	1,588
Sussex	354	340	324
Union (created in 1857)	0	0	865
Warren	455	380	386
Total	21,044	23,810	25,318

New Jersey's climate is characterized by long, warm summers and cool winters along the seacoast and snowy winters in the highlands. Ample rainfall and rich soil make the state ideal for agriculture. The land is relatively flat and includes grasslands, a mixture of evergreen and deciduous trees along the state's eastern side, and deciduous forests in its highlands. The Atlantic

Freedom seekers crossing the Delaware Bay to Cape May in an open boat. HIS-
TORICAL SOCIETY OF DELAWARE

coastal plain extends southward from a line drawn between Trenton and
Newark. To the northwest of this line is a piedmont plateau, which gives way
to a series of ridges and valleys that extend from Pennsylvania.[43]

Because New Jersey is almost surrounded by water, it has numerous
rivers that flow into the Delaware River and Bay, Atlantic Ocean, and Hudson River. These waterways provided a natural highway over which fugitive
slaves could enter the state from the south and west as they continued their
journey to freedom to the North. There are numerous tales of fugitives coming from Delaware or points farther south and crossing the Delaware River
and Bay in a wide variety of watercraft. At the other end of the state, runaways crossed the Hudson River on their way to New York State. Once they
reached New Jersey, many self-emancipators traveled up rivers and streams to
safe havens located farther inland. Commercial steamboats provided these
freedom seekers with a regular means of crossing into New Jersey or leaving
the state for New York. In the first two decades of the 1800s, steamboat ferries ran from Hoboken, New Jersey, to New York City. There was also regular service between Philadelphia and Trenton. In 1815, Aaron Ogden opened
a line between New York and Elizabethport (Port Elizabeth) in New Jersey.
This was followed in 1818 by a second steamboat service between these two

ports, operated by Thomas Gibbon. The pilot of his boat was the twenty-four-year-old Cornelius Vanderbilt.[44]

New Jersey also had a well-developed road system. A map of the state dated 1753 shows an extensive system of highways and smaller roads. Northern New Jersey, from Trenton to New York, was honeycombed with roads according to this early map. Most of them ran from west to east, coming from Pennsylvania and extending to New York. South of Trenton, the number of roads decreased dramatically, and most of those that existed at that time either ran along the eastern coastline from Cape May to Newark or extended from Cape May westward to Fairfield, Greenwich, and Salem, and then north to Trenton.[45]

This road system underwent steady improvement after the Revolutionary War. One of the early ways to upgrade roads was to make them into turnpikes that charged a toll for their use. The toll money then financed improvements to the roads. By 1829, New Jersey had about 550 miles of turnpikes, most of them in the northern and central areas of the state.

In the 1830s, road builders in New Jersey, following a national trend, began to construct a different type of road. Instead of using a macadam surface, builders used wooden planks to build roads. The road had a gravel base over which parallel wooden rails, or stringers, were placed. On top of the stringers, the builders put wooden planks that were about three inches thick and eight feet long. This type of road was considerably cheaper to build and provided a very smooth surface. By 1857, New Jersey had an extensive system of plank roads.[46]

Freedom seekers also used railroads, which began to crisscross the eastern states in the 1830s. By 1840, New Jersey had 192 miles of track, which increased to 332 by 1850 and 560 by 1860.[47] The largest railroad in New Jersey was the Camden and Amboy, which was the main line between Philadelphia and New York and had exclusive rights to all rail transportation between those two cities.[48] Other rail lines that played a role in helping runaways head north through New Jersey were the West Jersey, New Jersey Central, and Woodbury and Camden Railroads.[49]

NEW JERSEY'S
UNDERGROUND RAILROAD NETWORK

Though most accounts of the Underground Railroad give the impression that slave escapes from New Jersey were a phenomenon of the 1800s, newspaper advertisements for runaways were common during the previous century. The number of these notices grew from three in 1724 to ten in 1749, twenty in 1764, and thirty-three in 1780. Most escapees listed were males in their midtwenties or younger.[50] Following are a few examples.

From the *American Weekly Mercury* of November 15, 1722:

Runaway from William Yard of Trenton in West-Jersey, the Fifth Day of this Instant November a Negroe Man named Fransh Manuel, but commonly called Manuel, of a pretty tall stature, and speaks indifferent English. He wears a dark coloured homespun coat, an Ozenbrig Jacket, old leather breeches, Sheep-russet Stockings, new Shoes and an old Beveret hat.

He pretended formerly to be a Freeman and had passes; but he did belong to one John Raymond of Fairfield in New England and I bought him of said Raymond. And the said Negro boy has told since that he has run away, That he found a quantity of ore for his master, and that his master had given him Free. Whoever takes up said Negroe, secures him and brings him to Mr. William Bradford of New York, or to Mr. William Burge of Philadelphia or to his said Master at Trenton, shall have forty shillings reward, besides all reasonable charges, paid by me, William Yard.

From the *American Weekly Mercury* of April 6, 1727:

There is in custody of William Nichols, Esq.; High Sheriff of the County of Monmouth, a likely young Negroe man about 24 years old; he calls himself James, speaks little English and can give no account where he came from or who he belongs to. Any person who owns said Negroe paying Charges may have him.

From the *New-York Gazette* of June 24, 1734:

Runaway last Wednesday from Judith Vincent of Monmouth County in New Jersey an Indian Man named Stoffels, speaks good English, about Forty years of age, he is a House carpenter, a Cooper, a Wheelwright and is a good butcher also. There is also two others gone with him, one being half Indian and half Negro and the other a Mulatto about 30 years of age & plays upon the violin and had it with him. Whoever takes up & secures said fellow so that he may be had again shall have forty shillings as a reward and all reasonable charges paid by said Judith Vincent.

N.B. It is supposed'd they are all going together in a canow towards Connecticut or Rhode Island.[51]

The Underground Railroad network in New Jersey consisted of numerous individual escape routes that ultimately led fugitive slaves to New York and other points north. It was a network that involved many people, both black and white, who gave aid to the self-emancipators as they journeyed to freedom.

STATIONS

1. Cape May
2. Cold Spring
3. Erma
4. Port Norris
5. Port Elizabeth
6. Millville
7. Bridgeton
8. Bowentown
9. Greenwich
10. Salem
11. Malaga
12. Gravelly Run
13. Egg Harbor City
14. Port Republic
15. Atlantic City
    (Abesson Island)
16. Batsto
17. Mullica Hill
18. Swedesboro/Woolwich
19. Woodbury
20. Blackwood
21. Snow Hill/Lawnside
22. Haddonfield
23. Cherry Hill
24. Camden
25. Kresson
26. Medford
27. Evesham Mount
28. Pennsauken
29. Morrestown
30. Mt. Holly
31. Burlington
32. Bordentown
33. Trenton
34. Hamilton Twp.
35. Allentown
36. Cranbury
37. Princeton
38. New Brunswick
39. Pohatcong
40. Perth Amboy
41. Newark
42. Jersey City
43. Phillipsburg
44. Boonton
45. West Milford
46. Vernon
47. Stockholm

NEW YORK AND NEW JERSEY
UNDERGROUND
RAILROAD STATIONS

New Jersey

1790–1860

NOT TO SCALE

NEW YORK

Stroudsburg

New York
City

Easton

PENNSYLVANIA

NEW
JERSEY

Philadelphia

DELAWARE

New Jersey Routes

Wilbur Siebert, in his study of the Underground Railroad in New Jersey, describes four routes that fugitives took to cross the state, starting at four different points and progressing to New York City.[1] He even details the routes on his map of the Underground Railroad escape paths in the United States included in his book.[2] All of these routes generally merged at some point as they made their way to an area across the Hudson River from New York City. More recent research done by Trusty, Wright, and Wonkeryor has discovered additional routes besides those listed by Siebert. This study will examine these routes as they occurred in three geographic sections of New Jersey, broken down into the Southern, Central, and Northern Networks.

THE SOUTHERN NETWORK

The Southern Network of Underground Railroad routes in New Jersey crossed through counties south of a line extending from Swedesboro eastward to Barnegat on the Atlantic coast. This area included Cape May, Cumberland, Salem, Atlantic, and parts of Gloucester, Burlington, Camden, and Ocean Counties. Freedom-seeking slaves escaped from these counties, and they were also entry points for fugitives fleeing from Delaware, Maryland, Virginia, and other Southern states. The majority came from Delaware to New Jersey by crossing the Delaware or Delaware Bay. For the most part, the Southern Network channeled fugitives northward toward Camden and Mount Holly.

Three of the escape routes mentioned by Siebert began in southern New Jersey. The "Greenwich Line" began at the town of Greenwich and proceeded through Swedesboro and Evesham Mount to Mount Holly. From there the runaways went in a northwesterly direction, eventually joining the "Philadelphia Line," the main escape route in New Jersey. Another southern route began at the town of Salem and went through Woodbury and Evesham

Mount to Bordentown, north of Camden. At this point, it also connected with the "Philadelphia Line."[3] There were several other routes in southern New Jersey that Siebert does not mention. The region had an escape system far more extensive than he realized.

The Southern Network appears to have had four major geographic starting points: Cape May, Greenwich/Springtown, Salem, and the Port Republic area.

ROUTES OF CAPE MAY

The first settlers came to the Cape May peninsula in 1680s. Both Quakers and non-Quakers moved into the area, establishing homesteads and businesses such as saltmaking, whaling, and winemaking. The area grew to the point that it became Cape May County in 1692. Blacks arrived in 1688, when Daniel Coxe, one of the founders of Cape May, brought a number of slaves to the region. During the early 1700s, livestock raising, timber cutting, and farming became major industries on the peninsula. The practice of owning slaves also grew during this same time period. Families kept a limited number of slaves and often willed them to other family members. Between 1780 and 1800, there was a surge in the construction of roads, bridges, and causeways throughout the Cape May peninsula.[4] These connected the area to many other parts of southern New Jersey, providing escape paths for fugitive slaves in later years.

Jeffrey Dorwart speaks of freed slaves and runaways settling small areas in the remote woodlands of Cape May County. Two communities that played a role in Underground Railroad activity were Erma and Cold Spring. A major road ran from the town of Cape May through Cold Spring and Erma, turned west, and ran along that side of the cape, then northward to Cumberland County. Another important community of blacks developed in the 1850s in Middle Township of the county, between Goshen and Townsend's Inlet. Most of the blacks who lived in Cape May worked as farmers or domestics, although some became mariners and operated small vessels on the Delaware Bay.[5] The number of free blacks in the county rose from 198 in 1840 to 273 in 1860. These individuals would have provided a ready source of assistance for slaves trying to flee from their masters in the county and for those who had come from Delaware or other states to the south.

Siebert makes no reference to Underground Railroad activity in the Cape May region. He does not describe any routes in the area, nor does he have anyone from Atlantic or Cape May County on his list of agents and conductors in New Jersey.[6] William Still, however, includes in his work an escape story that deals with fugitives arriving at Cape May Point. He relates the tale of Thomas Sipple and his wife, Mary Ann, who, along with Henry and Elizabeth Burkett, John Purnell, and Hale Burton, left the coast of Delaware in a small skiff and crossed the Delaware Bay. Along the way, they encountered a boat full of slave catchers, whom they successfully resisted. Eventually they landed near the lighthouse at Cape May Point, where they entered the Cape May escape route and made their way to Philadelphia.[7]

The modern research of Jeffrey Dorwart and Emma Marie Trusty has filled out the details of the Cape May system and shed new light on the vital role that free blacks played in the Underground Railroad activity of the region. What emerges from their research, the references of William Still, and an examination of the geographic features of the region is that there were six escape routes that led freedom seekers from Cape May to stops north and northwest.

Cape May to Snow Hill (Lawnside)

Dorwart speaks of an Underground Railroad route that began in Cape May and proceeded all the way to the town of Snow Hill, now called Lawnside, not far from Camden. The main agent in Cape May on this route was Edward Turner. He had settled in 1850 in the small black community of Union Bethel in Lower Township, near the town of Cold Spring. Turner and his family operated a farm in the region. He is purported to have helped Harriet Tubman in her Underground Railroad activities.[8] During the summers of 1849 to 1852, Tubman worked as a cook at hotels in Cape May to help finance her Underground Railroad activities.[9] Turner used his farm as an Underground Railroad station and transported fugitives in his wagon northward. His ultimate destinations were usually the towns of Snow Hill and Haddonfield. At times he took runaways farther north.[10] Old maps of New Jersey show the route he most likely took from his home to Snow Hill and Haddonfield. Starting at Cold Spring, the main road leaving the town divided into two, one branch running northeast toward Atlantic County and the other to the northwest. Turner would have taken the northwestern one. The road ran in this direction to the town of Dennis Creek and from there to Port Elizabeth. The supposition is that from here it headed toward Camden, passing through Millville, Malaga, and Blackwood, to reach Snow Hill and Haddonfield.[11]

There are two arguments in support of the Millville route. The first is that Trusty mentions it as an alternative escape possibility for fugitives leaving Port Elizabeth when the main route was not usable.[12] The second is that West Jersey Railroad's main line ran from Millville to Camden.[13] This railroad played a role in the Underground Railroad escape routes heading out of Cumberland County. Once the fugitives reached Snow Hill or Haddonfield, they entered into the Central Network of New Jersey's Underground Railroad. There is the possibility that after reaching Port Elizabeth or Millville, Turner could have turned west and proceeded to Bridgeton, and then entered the Greenwich/Salem Underground Railroad system. That would have taken him a good deal out of his way, however, and Dorwart makes no mention of him taking this alternate route.

Cape May to Camden and Snow Hill via Gravelly Run

Trusty states that there were two main Underground Railroad routes heading out of Cape May, one of which went northwest through Gravelly Run toward Camden and Snow Hill.[14] Actually, it is necessary to go north up the eastern side of New Jersey to reach Gravelly Run from Cape May. Besides Edward Turner, other Underground Railroad agents aiding fugitives in their escape attempts from Cape May were Richard Cooper and the Trusty family.[15]

This route began in Cape May and headed north along the road that would eventually become the Garden State Parkway. At some spot near Somers Point, the fugitives probably took the road to Gravelly Point, a small town not far from Mays Landing. From here, the route proceeded northward to Egg Harbor City and then west across the state.[16] According to Trusty, this escape route passed through the communities of Mullica Hill, Kresson, and Blackwood before reaching Camden. However, an examination of the location of these towns and the roads that connected them shows that Trusty may have merged two different escape routes into one. Kresson and Blackwood are more in line with Egg Harbor City, and roads coming from that region clearly ran to those two towns in the 1850s. Mullica Hill is far to the southwest of Kresson and Blackwood, and it does not have any connecting roads with Mays Landing or Egg Harbor City on a map of New Jersey dating from 1856, although it does have roads joining it with Salem and Bridgeton, both sites on other southern New Jersey Underground Railroad routes on this map.[17] Fugitives most likely went from Egg Harbor City to Kresson and then to Blackwood before entering Camden, Snow Hill, or Pennsauken. An alternate path on this route was to leave the Mays Landing area and go to the town of Buena in the northwestern corner of Atlantic County. From there, the fugitives would proceed to Snow Hill via Malaga.[18]

Cape May to New England

The second major escape path that Trusty mentions ran from Cape May northward to New England. She gives no specific details concerning this route, but some conjectures may be made. She does detail a third route from Cape May that went to Port Republic via the old Tuckahoe Road.[19] From Port Republic, self-emancipators who wished to reach New England had two main options. The first was to hide or buy passage on a ship heading from the port to Boston or New York City. The second was to continue along the eastern seaboard of the state, passing through the Central and Northern Networks of New Jersey's Underground Railroad, until they reached New York City. From this point, they could have reached stations in the New England states. Not much evidence exists about this route, and further research is needed.

Cape May to Snow Hill via Port Republic

Another route ran along the eastern coastline before turning west toward Camden and Snow Hill. Once again, the fugitives traveled up the Tuckahoe Road, but instead of turning northwestward near Somers Point, they continued onward to Port Republic. This town was another major entry point of the Southern Network and is discussed in more detail later in this chapter.

From here, the freedom seekers turned west to Batsto or Egg Harbor City. The key agent in this area was an African-American named Joseph Trusty. The next destination was Snow Hill and the Central Network of New Jersey's Underground Railroad.[20] The map of 1856 shows good roads leading from these two sites all the way to Snow Hill and Camden.[21]

Cape May to Port Elizabeth

Yet another escape route ran from Cape May Point, through Middle Township, to Port Elizabeth. Ezekiel and Amy Cooper, the black Underground Railroad agents in this town, received the runaways there.[22] This would have been a natural path of escape, because a major road connected Cape May with Port Elizabeth as early as 1826.[23] The road eventually became NJ Route 47. The town also had a small congregation of African Methodist Episcopal church members,[24] and the church served as an Underground Railroad station. From here, the escape path went to Springtown near Greenwich. There appears to have been an alternate route that took the runaways from the port to the town of Millville.[25]

Another possible route from Port Elizabeth was by steamboat. Two steamboat lines operated between Port Elizabeth and New York City, one run by Aaron Ogden and the other by Thomas Gibbon. There are no written records of these lines being used by fugitives, but they do fit the profile of possible means of escape as described in so many stories about the Underground Railroad. It would have been easy to hide a runaway aboard one of the steamboats, bribe an officer on the boat, or simply buy a ticket for passage to New York for a fugitive in disguise.

Cape May to Port Norris

A final route from Cape May proceeded to Port Norris, about twenty-six miles away. The Underground Railroad agents Ezekiel and John Cooper took the runaways from Cape May to Port Norris.[26] This appears to be a case typical of Underground Railroad escape paths, where a backup route was used when the main one was not safe. Most likely, the next leg of the journey would have taken fugitives to the Greenwich-Springtown area and the escape route that existed there. In the event the main route was not practical, possibly because of slave catchers, an alternate route from Port Norris led the runaways to Millville.[27]

GREENWICH–SPRINGTOWN ROUTES

The second major entry point for self-emancipating slaves fleeing from Delaware, Maryland, and other Southern areas was the town of Greenwich. Located in the southwestern portion of Cumberland County, the town was near the Cohansey River, a waterway over which fugitives regularly traveled. The county had a large population of free blacks, which had increased from 786 in 1830 to 1,295 by 1860. It also had three Quaker meetinghouses that reflected a large number of proabolitionist religious group.[28] According to Payne, the A.M.E. Church also was active in the area, with a congregation that was part of the Salem Circuit centered in Greenwich.[29] A map of New Jersey dating from 1753 shows that Greenwich was well connected, with roads to Cape May to the east, Bridgeton to the north, and Salem to the northwest. By 1856, the road network was extensive and provided many possibilities for Underground Railroad routes and alternate routes from the town.[30] By the 1850s, the spur of the West Jersey Railroad ran from Bridgeton, a town just six miles to the north of Greenwich, to Camden.[31]

Greenwich appears in some of the earliest slave escape literature of the antebellum period. In telling of the escape of his family from Maryland, the black abolitionist Samuel Ringgold Ward ties Greenwich into the story. According to Ward, he was born in Maryland in 1817 to parents who were both slaves. When it was learned that his mother was to be sold to an owner in Georgia in 1819, the family decided to try to gain their freedom by fleeing. They set out for Cumberland County, New Jersey, in 1820. Ward says this site was not chosen by accident, but that the county was a major destination for runaways because of the Quaker presence there. At one point on their journey, they were overtaken by a neighbor of their former master, who ordered them to return. The man brandished a whip, but Ward's parents took it from him and gave him a sound beating. Early in 1820, they reached Greenwich safely. They found a large number of free blacks living there, as well as in a black community near the town known as Springtown. They also found numerous blacks and Quakers in nearby Bridgeton. The family settled in Waldron's Landing and remained there until August 1826, when they left for New York City because of the activity of slave catchers in the area.[32] Ward's story establishes that Greenwich, Springtown, and Bridgeton were Underground Railroad havens for fugitives, and it validates the assumption that this was so because of the assistance rendered to runaways by Quakers and free blacks in the area.

A second primary source account of the role Greenwich played in the Underground Railroad comes from William Still, who writes of his own family's escape from slavery. It is the tale of Levin and Sidney Still, who lived in bondage on the Eastern Shore of Maryland. Levin was able to purchase his freedom at some point around 1810, but his wife and four children had to remain slaves. Later, Sidney made the decision to attempt an escape with her

Charity Still twice escaped from slavery and settled in central New Jersey. She was the mother of William Still.
HISTORICAL SOCIETY OF
DELAWARE.

two young sons and two daughters. Still says that she fled to a "place near Greenwich, New Jersey." This could very well be a reference to the black community of Springtown, which was just outside Greenwich. Their stay in freedom was short-lived, however, because they were seized by slave catchers and returned to Saunders Griffin, their master in Maryland. Griffin locked Sidney in a room for several months to break her spirit. After feigning submission, she was released. A short time later, she escaped again, but this time she could take only her two daughters and had to leave her sons, Levin and Peter, behind. She went to Burlington County in New Jersey and found safety there. She changed her name to Charity Still and managed to rejoin her husband. They lived on a small farm and had other children, one of whom was William Still. Later, in 1851, William was reunited with his brother, Peter, in Philadelphia.[33]

Siebert included Greenwich as the starting point of what he called the "Greenwich Line," an Underground Railroad escape route from southern New Jersey. He cited the presence of Quaker homes and farms, as well as a swamp in which fugitives could hide, as drawing cards for runaways coming from Delaware. He says that self-emancipators crossed, or were brought across, the Delaware Bay from Dover, Delaware, at night. The boats carried signal lights: a yellow light with a blue light above it. When they saw a similar arrangement of lights on the shore, they knew that Underground Railroad agents were awaiting them. The passengers were then taken to Greenwich. From here, Siebert has the route going north twenty-five miles to Swedesboro, on the Central Network of escape routes. According to Siebert, several Underground Railroad agents helped in this effort in Cumberland County. He lists them as being Levin Bond, Ezekiel Cooper, Nathaniel Murry, J. B. Sheppard, Thomas R. Sheppard, and Alges and Julia Stanford.[34] Trusty adds the names of two black men who also were agents living in Springtown, Daniel Croker and Isaac Wright.[35] Essentially, it appears that three basic escape paths began in the Greenwich area.

Greenwich-Springtown to Swedesboro

This is the route described by Siebert. Fugitive slaves hid in the Greenwich-Springtown area, where they received aid from Underground Railroad agents. The center of this effort was the Bethel A.M.E. Church, located at 1092 Sheppards Mill Road in Springtown. It was one of the original A.M.E. churches in New Jersey, dating back to the early nineteenth century. Runaways hid either in the church or on the church's property. A swampy area near the church also made for an effective hiding place. The five black agents on Siebert's list were members of this church's congregation.[36]

Underground Railroad conductors took the runaways from Greenwich to Swedesboro, a town twenty-five miles to the northwest.[37] Siebert does not describe the route taken between Greenwich and Swedesboro, but it is safe to assume that they used the road that connected Greenwich with Salem. From Salem, they most likely took the road that ran to Sharptown, which also had an Underground Railroad station.[38] From here, they proceeded along the road to Swedesboro, in Gloucester County. Siebert lists three Underground Railroad agents in that county: William Douden, Pompey Louis, and Jubilee Sharper, the last two of whom were African-American.[39] In 1850, the county had a free black population of 620 people. It also had a Quaker presence, with three Friends meetinghouses in the county.[40] Payne identifies a congregation of the A.M.E. Church in Swedesboro that was part of the Salem Circuit, as early as 1822.[41] The black community of Small Gloucester, now called Woolwich, was just outside of Swedesboro and was the site of the Mount Zion A.M.E. Church, which was built in 1834 and was used as an Underground Railroad station. Agents Pompey Lewis and Jubilee Sharper were members of this congregation. Some of those living in this community were fugitive slaves themselves and hence more ready to aid other fugitives.[42] Taken all together, Swedesboro would have been an ideal place for an Underground Railroad operation.

The next leg of the journey ran from Swedesboro to Evesham Mount (now called Mount Laurel) and then on to Mount Holly, both of which are in Burlington County.[43] These two sites are part of the Central Network of New Jersey's Underground Railroad.

Greenwich-Springtown to Camden via Bridgeton

Another means of escaping was via the West Jersey Railroad.[44] This railroad ran from Cape May to Camden by 1869, and even earlier than that, it had a spur line from Glassboro to Bridgeton.[45] Trusty mentions Bridgeton as an alternate destination for fugitives being brought by Underground Railroad agents from Delaware up the Cohansey River, when Greenwich was not a safe stopping point. An old Indian trail also connected Greenwich with Oak Villa, a black settlement in Bridgeton. The path continued on from here to Bowentown Station, a few miles away. Agents John and Thomas Cooper received the travelers at this point. It was at this spot that some of the runaways were hidden on the West Jersey Railroad trains that stopped at the station, although this method of transporting fugitives was used on a limited basis. The "passengers" would then take the train all the way to Camden.[46]

Greenwich-Springtown to Snow Hill via Bridgeton

The West Jersey Railroad was not used to escape with any frequency. Therefore, the question remains as to what route those fugitives who reached Bridgeton, either directly from Delaware, or from Greenwich-Springtown, took to reach safety. An examination of the 1856 map of New Jersey shows that two major roads linked Bridgeton to Snow Hill and Camden. One of these proceeded northward to Mullica Hill in Gloucester County. From there, it ran through Woodbury, an Underground Railroad site in the Central Network, and joined the main highway coming from Cape May to Snow Hill and Camden. The second road left Bridgeton and, paralleling the first road, went through Centreville and Barnsboro, before reaching Woodbury.[47]

SALEM AREA ROUTE

Siebert has another escape route that began in the town of Salem in Salem County, New Jersey, and proceeded in three stages to Bordentown in Burlington County. He says that fugitives crossed the Delaware River about forty miles south of Philadelphia and made their way, either alone or with the help of Underground Railroad agents, to the town of Salem. Salem County was an excellent place for runaways. In 1850, it had a population of 2,075 free blacks, the fifth-highest number of any county in New Jersey. It also had a large number of Quakers, as evidenced by the six meetinghouses recorded in the federal census of 1850.[48] The A.M.E. Church had a strong presence in Salem County as well. Payne lists the town of Salem as the center of the A.M.E. Salem Circuit, which included churches in nine southern New Jersey towns in 1822.[49]

Siebert has two prominent personalities of Salem as agents on his list: Abigail Goodwin and Rev. Thomas C. Oliver.[50] Although Oliver was born in Salem in 1818, he did most of his work aiding runaways while he lived in Camden. Goodwin was a Quaker woman who had spent her entire seventy-three years living in and around the town of Salem. By 1838, the house in which she and her sister Elizabeth lived, at 47 Market Street in Salem, was an Underground Railroad station operated by the two women.[51] Abigail had devoted her adult life to helping the oppressed, and Still rates her as one of the most important Underground Railroad agents in the whole movement. She regularly worked to raise money that she sent to abolitionists in the Carolinas to purchase slaves for the purpose of setting them free. Her house became an Underground Railroad station for those who chose to emancipate themselves by fleeing from their bondage. Faced with the problem of providing clothing for fugitives passing through Salem, she organized a committee

*Abigail Goodwin,
a key member of the
Underground Railroad
in southern New Jersey.*
HISTORICAL SOCIETY OF
DELAWARE

of women in the town who collected wearable items and gave them to ill-clad travelers. A letter she sent to William Still summarizes her efforts and attitude regarding the work she was doing for the cause.

> Salem, February, 10 1858.
>
> Dear Friend:—Thee will find enclosed, five dollars for the fugitives, a little for so many to share it, but better than nothing; oh, that people, rich people, would remember them instead of spending so much on themselves; and those too, who are not called rich, might, if there was only a willing mind, give too of their abundance; how can they forbear to sympathize with those poor destitute ones—but so it is—there is not half the feeling for them there ought to be, indeed scarcely anybody seems to think about them. "Inasmuch as ye have <u>not</u> done it unto one of the least of these my brethren, ye have not done it unto me."
>
> Thy friend,
> A. Goodwin

The home of Abigail Goodwin in Salem. It was a major Underground Railroad station in the area. PHOTO BY KEVIN SWITALA

In another letter, she gives an excellent account of the operation of the Underground Railroad in Salem and the role she played in it.

Salem, 3 mo., 25,'55.

Dear Friend:—Thine of the 22d came to hand yesterday noon.

* * * * * * * * * * *

I do not believe that any of them are the ones thee wrote about, who wanted Dr. Lundy to come for them, and promised they would pay his expenses. They had no money, the minister said, but were pretty well off for clothes. I gave him all I had and more, but it seemed very little for four travelers—but they will meet with friends and helpers on the way. He said they expected to go away to-morrow. I am afraid it's so cold, and one of them had a sore foot, they will not get away—it's dangerous staying here. There has been a slave-hunter here lately, I was told yesterday, in search of a woman; he tracked her to our Alms-house—she had lately been confined and was not able to go—he will come back for her and his infant—and will not wait long I expect. I want much to get her away first—and if one had a C. C. Torney here no doubt it would be done; but she will be well guarded. How I wish the poor thing could be secreted in some safe place till she is able to travel Northward; but where that could be it's not easy to see. I presume the Carolina freed people have arrived by now. I hope they will meet many friends, and be well provided for. Mary Davis will be then paid—her cousins have sent her twenty-four dollars, as it was not wanted for the purchase money—it was to be kept for them when they arrive. I am glad thee did keep the ten for the fugitives.

Samuel Nixon is now here, just come—a smart young man—they will be after him soon. I advise him to hurry on to Canada; he will leave here to-morrow, but don't say that he will go straight to the city. I would send this by him if he did. I am afraid he will loiter about and be taken—do make them go on fast—he has left. I could not hear much he said—some who did don't like him at all—think him an impostor—a great brag—said he was a dentist ten years. He was asked where he came from, but would not tell till he looked at the letter that lay on the table and that he had just brought back. I don't feel much confidence in him—don't believe he is the one thee alluded to. He was asked his name—he looked at the letter to find it out. Says nobody can make a better set of teeth than he can. He said they will go on to-morrow in the stage—he took down the number and street of the Anti-slavery office—you will be on your guard against imposition—he kept the letter thee sent from Norfolk. I had then no doubt of him, and had no objection to it. I now rather regret it. I would send it to thee if I had it, but perhaps it is of no importance.

He wanted the names taken down of nine more who expected to get off soon and might come here. He told us to send them to him, but did not seem to know where he was going to. He was well dressed in fine broad-cloth coat and overcoat, and has a very active tongue in his head.

But I have said enough—don't want to prejudice thee against him, but only be on thy guard, and to not let him deceive thee, as I fear he has some of us here.

                                                    With kind regards,
                                                    A. Goodwin.[52]

This letter shows that Goodwin and her fellow agents in Salem received fugitives, clothed them, rescued some, raised money for their care, were on guard for slave catchers, and arranged for transportation to other sites. The second half of the letter discusses a special problem that agents faced. Goodwin expresses concern about the true identity of a fugitive named Samuel Nixon, based on the fact that some blacks were impostors and were actually working in concert with slave catchers, hoping to catch Underground Railroad agents off their guard. This would allow them access to other fugitives and hence enable their coconspirators to apprehend them and return them to their owners for rather large rewards.

The next stop on this route was the town of Woodbury, about twenty-five miles northeast of Salem. Siebert states that the main mode of transporting fugitives from Salem to Woodbury was by wagon.[53] A road had connected the two earlier, as is evidenced by the map of New Jersey from 1753.[54] In Goodwin's letter to Still above, dated March 25, 1855, she mentions that she is going to send a runaway, Samuel Nixon, to him on the stagecoach. This stage would have followed the Salem to Woodbury Road. This road also passed through the town of Swedesboro, a key Underground Railroad stopover. Payne located an A.M.E. church in the town, which most likely was a station

The Mount Zion A.M.E. Church in Swedesboro. The church was used as a safe haven for fugitive slaves. PHOTO BY KEVIN SWITALA

on the road to freedom for runaways.[55] A detailed accounting of the remaining stops on this route appear in the discussion of the Central Network in New Jersey.

PORT REPUBLIC AREA ROUTES

The final entry point in the Southern Network involved the town of Port Republic and its vicinity. Two escape paths had their beginnings in this area. One began at the port itself, and the other started just to its south, near Atlantic City.

Port Republic to Batsto

Fugitive slaves coming on ships and steamboats from Maryland and Virginia disembarked onto the banks of the Mullica River near Port Republic. Slaves who lived in the area also used the Mullica as a means of escaping. Both of these groups made their way up the river to Batsto, the same town that was included on a route that started in Cape May and went through Port Republic and on to Batsto. Members of the Boiling and Trusty families aided the fugitives in their quest for freedom here. From Batsto, runaways went on to Snow Hill.[56]

Atlantic City to Camden

Some runaways made their way to freedom by taking boats from Maryland, Delaware, the Carolinas, and Virginia to Abescon Island near Atlantic City. Trusty says that free blacks who worked on the Camden & Atlantic City Railroad, completed in 1854, hid the fugitives in cars and sent them on to Camden, where they entered New Jersey's Central Network.[57]

CENTRAL NETWORK

The Central Network lay in the region of New Jersey bounded by a line extending from Swedesboro to Barnegat in the south and a line from Bordentown to the Atlantic shoreline in the north. Within this section of the state are most of Burlington, Camden, and Ocean Counties, as well as part of Gloucester County. Most of the Underground Railroad activity here was confined to Burlington, Camden, and a small portion of Gloucester County, however. Period maps depict an area interlaced with well-developed roads and railroad lines.

The demographics of the Central Network indicate a strong base of support for an Underground Railroad system. In 1850, there were 4,959 free blacks living in the counties of Burlington, Camden, and Gloucester. This was one of the larger concentrations of free blacks in the state. Quakers also had a strong presence here, with thirty-one meetinghouses in these counties in 1850, twenty-five of which were in Burlington County.[58] Payne has A.M.E. churches located in Woodbury, Snow Hill, and Evesham Mount in 1822.[59] Thus the region had the qualities necessary for a successful escape network.

Siebert lists four Underground Railroad agents active in Burlington County: John Coleman, Samuel Stevens, Robert Evans, and Enoch Middleton. He identifies Coleman and Stevens as being blacks.[60] Trusty says that Evans was also a free black man.[61]

The sources give evidence of seven major escape paths coursing through the Central Network. Four were the continuations of routes that began in southern New Jersey, and three originated in nearby Pennsylvania.

PHILADELPHIA LINE

Siebert describes the Philadelphia Line as an escape route that led from Philadelphia, through Camden, and eventually all the way to New York City. It was the most important Underground Railroad route in the entire state, because it not only guided fugitives coming from William Still in Philadelphia, but it also was the conduit for runaways coming from many of the southern escape paths that took them to New York.

This route began at Still's offices in Philadelphia. Still sent fugitives across the Delaware River to Camden, where they were met by Rev. Thomas C. Oliver, who was both an agent and a conductor, as was his father before him.[62] Oliver was born in Salem, New Jersey, in 1818. He attended a Quaker school for blacks in the town and received an education. His family moved to Philadelphia around 1833, and it was there that he became active in the Underground Railroad. He also became an A.M.E. minister and served in a number of New Jersey churches. During the 1840s, he was the pastor of the Macedonia A.M.E. Church in the black settlement of Fettersville, an area that is now part of the city of Camden. Established in 1832, the church is the oldest African-American church in the Camden area, located at 265 Spruce Street. Oliver used the church as a station where he would organize his fugitives into small groups before taking them northward.[63]

From Camden, Oliver guided the runaways over the road that ran along the river to the city of Burlington, about twenty miles from Philadelphia. He called his safe house in the city "Station A," and it was here that he got fresh horses.[64] The road he took to Burlington ran through the communities of Pennsauken, Westfield, and Cooperstown before reaching Burlington.[65]

The Burlington Pharmacy in Burlington City was used as a station for hiding fugitive slaves in the 1840s and 1850s. PHOTO BY KEVIN SWITALA

Pennsauken was also a destination for fugitives coming from Cape May and the Port Republic area.[66] The exact location of Oliver's "Station A" is not known; however, there are two other sites identified as Underground Railroad stations in the city. One was the pharmacy operated by the Quaker abolitionist William J. Allison, opened in 1831 at the corner of High Street and Union Street. Allison used the basement of the building as a hiding place for fugitives passing through Burlington. The second site was the estate of the

Grubbs family, located at Wood Street near the Riverfront Promenade. The family had constructed tunnels between buildings on their property and the riverbank, and according to local tradition, they hid runaways in the tunnels before sending them farther north.[67]

A possible alternate route for the Philadelphia Line was a major road that ran from Camden through Moorestown and Mount Holly, after which a major road branched off to Bordentown.[68] In 1765, the Quaker abolitionist Elisha Barcklow built a house in Moorestown near the main road from Camden. Local tradition has the house being used as an Underground Railroad station.[69]

The final stopover for the Philadelphia Line was the community of Bordentown, in the extreme northwest corner of Burlington County almost thirty miles to the north of Camden on the Delaware River. At this point, the route turns to the northeast and proceeds to New York City.[70]

Woodbury to Snow Hill Route

Siebert states that the usual manner of transporting runaways along the route from Salem to Woodbury was by wagon. Abigail Goodwin also had made use of the stage line that ran between the two towns.[71] In either case, the road taken would have run through Swedesboro, an identified Underground Railroad site. Other fugitives came to Woodbury from Mullica Hill, as in the description of the route from Cape May to Camden via Gravelly Run.

The town of Woodbury was strategically located at the juncture of roads coming from Salem, Bridgeton, Port Elizabeth, and Cape May. It was a natural place for an Underground Railroad station. It was also a station on the lines of both the Swedesboro and West Jersey Rrailroads.[72] Black workers on the Swedesboro Railroad hid runaways in railcars and sent them to Camden in this manner. In addition, Underground Railroad sites were also operating in the black Methodist Episcopal and Bethel A.M.E. churches in the town.[73]

Siebert has the Salem Line going from Woodbury to the town of Evesham Mount.[74] Before reaching this town, however, one of the escape routes passed through Snow Hill, a town at the confluence of routes coming from Port Elizabeth, Gravelly Run, Egg Harbor City, Port Republic, and Salem. The town was where William Still's parents settled and where he was born and raised.[75] Payne states that Snow Hill had an active A.M.E. church as early as 1822.[76] Attached to the town was a settlement of free blacks known as Free Haven, built on land originally purchased for blacks in 1840.[77] The two were finally merged into the community of Lawnside in 1907. One of the more famous Underground Railroad agents in New Jersey, Peter Mott, operated in Lawnside. Mott and his wife, Elizabeth, built a house there in

The home of Underground Railroad agent Peter Mott in Lawnside. PHOTO BY
KEVIN SWITALA

1844. It was from his home and the Mount Pisgah A.M.E. Church, in which
he later served as pastor, that he carried out his role as an Underground Railroad agent and conductor.[78] From Snow Hill, the freedom seekers had several
possible avenues of escape, with routes leading to Pennsauken, Haddonfield,
and Evesham Mount.

Snow Hill to Pennsauken
Pennsauken was one of the towns through which Siebert's Philadephia Line
passed on its way to Bordentown. The town was an Underground Railroad
destination for some freedom seekers who had reached Snow Hill from Cape
May or Port Republic.[79] On reaching Pennsauken, the fugitives would have
entered the Philadelphia Line and headed to Bordentown.

Snow Hill to Camden or Evesham Mount via Haddonfield
Haddonfield, now a suburb of Camden, was a small town located just a few
miles to the northeast of Snow Hill. Strategically placed on the main roads
and railroad coming from the Atlantic City area, it was the last major town

runaways reached before entering Camden proper. It was also linked by a series of roads to Evesham Mount, about eight miles to the northeast. Self-emancipators leaving Snow Hill went to Haddonfield, and from there they could go either directly to Camden or to Evesham Mount, by way of the town of Cherry Hill. Thomas Evans, an abolitionist and a Quaker, lived in Haddonfield. His family was active on the Underground Railroad in the nearby community of Cherry Hill, where Evans had purchased a home in 1816 that is still standing today. His son Josiah later owned the house, after Thomas had moved to Haddonfield around 1840. The house, which had been an Underground Railroad station under Thomas Evans, continued to operate as a station under Josiah Evans. Documentation shows that fugitives were hidden in the hayloft or attic before they were taken by covered wagon to the next station.[80]

EVESHAM MOUNT TO BORDENTOWN VIA MOUNT HOLLY
The large congregation of the A.M.E. church located in Evesham Mount indicates that the town had a fairly large free black population.[81] Siebert has the town as the beginning point of the final leg of the Salem Line running to Bordentown.[82]

Evesham Mount, now called Mount Laurel, was a town whose significance was great enough that it was on the stage line that ran through Camden to Philadelphia.[83] Payne lists an A.M.E. church as being in the community.[84] The church was most likely the one replaced by the Jacob's Chapel structure, built in 1859. A cemetery for blacks lies behind the church, and it is reported that the church was used as a sanctuary for fugitives.[85] The resident Underground Railroad agent in the town was a black man named John Coleman.[86] Benjamin Drew included the story of William Johnson in his collection of fugitive slave narratives. Johnson had escaped from Queen Ann County in Maryland, and after a brief stay in Philadelphia, he relocated in Evesham Mount. He liked the area and stayed there for nine years, working in a variety of occupations. He would have stayed much longer, but he was apprehended by some slave hunters, who then took him to Mount Holly for a hearing. He was released due to some legal technicalities, and fearing recapture, he went to Canada, where he settled in the town of St. Catharines in Ontario. He remained there until the end of the Civil War.[87]

In addition to having fugitives reach Evesham Mount from Snow Hill, some came from as far away as Port Republic by way of Batsto. These individuals would have passed through the town of Medford before reaching Evesham Mount. Dr. George Haines, a Quaker physician and abolitionist, had built a house in Medford in 1826, which was used as a shelter for runaways. Another doctor, Andrew E. Budd, later acquired the house and continued to use it as a safe haven for freedom seekers.[88]

The next stop on the route to Bordentown would have been the town of Mount Holly, only seven miles northeast of Evesham Mount. The town was originally settled by Quakers in 1681, and they still had a presence there in the 1800s.[89] Siebert includes Mount Holly in the Greenwich Line. He has this escape route coming from Greenwich through Swedesboro and Evesham Mount to Mount Holly, before it merged with the Philadelphia Line at Bordentown.[90] Roads led from Mount Holly to Burlington City in the east and Bordentown in the northeast.[91] Fugitives could have been taken by Underground Railroad agents to either site, and at those points they would have joined the Philadelphia Line. The great Quaker abolitionist John Woolman lived in Mount Holly.

In 1754, Woolman wrote the pamphlet *Some Considerations on the Keeping of Negroes,* which was one of the early publications against slavery in New Jersey.[92] The main agent in town, however, was a black man named Robert Evans, an active parishioner of the Mount Moriah A.M.E. Church there. The church was used as a safe haven for runaways passing through the area.[93] Evans would have taken his charges to Bordentown, either by the direct route or by way of Burlington City.

MINOR ROUTES FROM PENNSYLVANIA

Although most of the routes in the Central Network had their origins in southern New Jersey and the Philadelphia area, there were two other backup routes that had their origins in Pennsylvania. These were the escape paths that came from the towns of Yardley and Bristol.

Yardley to Trenton Route

Yardley was a small town on the Delaware River located about thirty miles to the north of Philadelphia. The town had an Underground Railroad station and was part of the Eastern Route of Pennsylvania's escape network. Fugitives essentially came from Norristown in Pennsylvania's Montgomery County to Yardley.[94] Although most of them continued northward through the network's system, some crossed the Delaware River and reached New Jersey just north of Trenton. After a short journey to Trenton, they entered the Philadelphia Line.

Bristol to Burlington Route

A second branch of Pennsylvania's Eastern Route also originated in Norristown, but instead of going to Yardley, it went to Bristol. This town was situated on the Delaware River about twenty-five miles from the heart of Philadelphia and was directly across the river from Burlington City. Bristol had a well-organized Underground Railroad system.[95] The agents here sent freedom seekers across the river to Burlington City, where they continued their journey on the Philadelphia Line.

NORTHERN NETWORK

New Jersey's Northern Network of Underground Railroad routes operated in an area bounded by a line extending from Bordentown to the Atlantic coast in the south to the northern limits of the state. Most of the activity was in the counties of Mercer, Middlesex, Monmouth, Somerset, and parts of Warren and Hudson.

The demographics of this area indicate a region that was conducive to an escape network. There were 8,319 free blacks living in these six counties in 1850. A number of Quakers lived there, as evidenced by the eight meeting-houses scattered throughout Mercer, Middlesex, Monmouth, and Warren Counties, according to the Federal Census of 1850, although their presence was not as extensive as was in the Central Network.[96] The A.M.E., A.M.E. Zion, and Colored Presbyterian Churches also had congregations along the main escape route in the towns of Trenton, Princeton, Crosswicks, Allentown, New Brunswick, Perth Amboy, and Jersey City.[97] Thus the conditions were quite favorable for the successful operation of an escape system taking freedom-seeking slaves from the heart of New Jersey northeastward to safety in New York.

Siebert lists a number of Underground Railroad agents in this network. In Mercer County, he lists Elias Conover, J. J. Earl, and B. Rush Plumly; in Middlesex, Jonathan Freedlyn and Adam Sickler; and in Hudson, John Everett, Dr. James Mott, and Peter J. Phillips.

The Northern Network contained seven different escape routes. Two channeled fugitive slaves from New Jersey proper to New York City, and five conducted runaways who had passed through Pennsylvania to the city.

PHILADELPHIA LINE

Siebert's Philadelphia Line reached its conclusion in the Northern Network. After reaching Bordentown, Underground Railroad conductors guided runaways to the next stop, the town of Princeton. According to Siebert, it was here that the horses used to pull the wagons in which the fugitives hid were changed again.[98] More recent research has shown that there were at least two

Underground Railroad stations in the town. One of them was the Monteith House, located at 344 Nassau Street, and the second station was across the street in an unnamed house.[99] From here, the freedom seekers were taken to New Brunswick, according to Siebert. The typical procedure was then to cross the Raritan River and go on to Jersey City. Cornelius Cornell lived just outside New Brunswick, and it was his job to keep a lookout for slave catchers who might be patrolling the area. If he spotted any, the conductors would take an alternate route to Perth Amboy. In either case, via Jersey City or Perth Amboy, the next stage of the journey was to enter New York City. A Quaker by the name of John Everett took runaways to the Forty-Second Street railway station, got them tickets, and put them on a through train to Syracuse.[100]

Perth Amboy and Jersey City were the last two stopovers in New Jersey before the fugitives were taken to New York. One of the main safe havens in Perth Amboy was the home of the Grimke sisters, famous abolitionists. Sarah Grimke and her sister Angelina Weld, as well as Angelina's husband, Theodore, operated an Underground Railroad station in their home, Eaglewood, near the town. From here, they would see to the safe transportation of their charges to New York City.[101] The Grimke sisters had been slaveowners years earlier in Charleston, South Carolina. After they came to the conclusion that owning slaves was immoral, they moved to Philadelphia and became ardent abolitionists. Between 1836 and 1838, they published a series of pamphlets addressed to Southern women attacking the institution of slavery, and they traveled widely, speaking out on the cause. After Angelina married Theodore Weld, a famous abolitionist in his own right, they moved to New Jersey and settled in Englewood.[102]

Most fugitives coming from New Brunswick went directly to Jersey City. When the direct route was too dangerous, however, some went by way of an alternate route that ran through the city of Newark. Newark had a sizable black community at this time, and they were a source of aid for the fugitives.[103] The runaways stayed in farmers' barns before entering Newark. During the night, conductors took them to Jersey City, where one of the main agents in the city, John Everett or Peter J. Phillips, received them. The agent then usually took them to the Hudson River Passenger Station, at the corner of Church Street and Chambers Street, where they were put on the night train for Albany. When that route was too risky, the freedom seekers went to the home of Lewis Tappan on West Broadway in New York City.[104]

Some fugitives arrived in Jersey City hidden in boats that had come over the Morris Canal. Opened in 1824, the canal brought coal from the Easton area of Pennsylvania. Underground Railroad agents hid runaways in underground brick tunnels near the Sugar House at the waterfront at the end of the canal.[105] At this point, some of them were hidden in the spaces between the cabins of boats heading north on the Hudson River to Albany and the Erie Canal.[106] Agents hired to carry the fugitives placed them in ferry boats and coal boats crossing the Hudson River to New York City. Some of the runaways may have purchased their passage by working for the ships and boat captains in the unloading of their cargoes.

Three Underground Railroad agents in Jersey City deserve mention. Rev. John Milton Holmes hid runaways in his Congregational Tabernacle Church, at the southeast corner of York Street and Henderson Street. David L. Holden used his home at 79 Clifton Place as an Underground Railroad station. And Dr. Henry D. Holt, a physician, provided his home at 134 Washington Street near the Morris Canal Basin as a safe house for fugitives.[107]

A possible alternate route may have run northwest from Newark to the town of Boonton. Underground Railroad sites existed in the town, as well as in Boonton Township. Going northwest from Boonton Township, there is some evidence that a line of other sites operated in the towns of Stockholm, West Milford, and Vernon.[108] Vernon was just a short distance from the New York border, and fugitives could have crossed it and entered the southern portion of the Underground Railroad escape network that ran through the eastern part of that state.

Philadelphia to New Brunswick via Trenton Route

Siebert describes another route that went from Philadelphia across central New Jersey, eventually reaching New York City. He learned of this route from Robert Purvis, the great black abolitionist and Underground Railroad agent in Pennsylvania. This escape path began in Philadelphia, but instead of crossing the Delaware River into Camden, it turned northward through Bucks County in Pennsylvania. Somewhere in the area of Morrisville, the fugitives crossed the Delaware and went into Trenton. From there they proceeded to Newtown and New Brunswick, New Jersey. At this point, they entered the Philadelphia Line and made their way to New York.[109]

Another possible means of following this route was to use the Camden & Amboy Railroad, a branch of which passed through Trenton and made its way to Jersey City.[110] Although there is no documented record of the line being used by fugitives, the possibility exists, especially considering the use of rail lines in the Southern Network. Trenton had a large A.M.E. congregation, and its main church was the seat of the group's Trenton Circuit in central New Jersey.[111] The free blacks living there surely helped the runaways on their way across New Jersey.

Three less frequently used escape routes that runaways had at their disposal led from Pennsylvania through New Jersey to New York City.

New Hope to Princeton Route

One minor route started at the town of New Hope in Pennsylvania. Fugitives came here from Philadelphia via Doylestown. After hiding in the A.M.E. church in New Hope, they received help from agents in crossing the Delaware River and making their way to Lambertville, New Jersey.[112] From here, they would travel fifteen miles eastward to Princeton and join the Philadelphia Line.

Easton to New Brunswick Route

Another minor route from Pennsylvania to New York ran from the border town of Easton to New York via New Brunswick, New Jersey. Some of the freedom seekers who traveled northward from the Philadelphia area went to the town of Bethlehem. At this point, the escape path split into three possibilities, one of which turned eastward to Easton on the Pennsylvania–New Jersey border.[113] Fugitives crossed the Delaware River at Easton and passed through the town of Phillipsburg, just across the river, on their way to New Brunswick. A stage line ran from Easton through Phillipsburg and followed two different routes, one going to Trenton and the other through Pohatcong Township and Somerville to New Brunswick. Local tradition has it that on the New Brunswick route, an Underground Railroad station existed at what is now the Springtown Stagecoach Inn on NJ Route 519 in Pohatcong Township in Warren County.[114]

Some of the freedom seekers took an alternate route to New Brunswick after reaching Somerville, going south for a few miles to Hillsborough Township and approaching New Brunswick from the southeast. Near the town of Hillsborough in the township, there existed a wooded area called the Sourlands Ridge. It was here that the fugitives hid and rested before making their entry into New Brunswick.[115]

Another possible means of escape from Phillipsburg was to hide on the cars of the Central New Jersey Railroad, which ran from that town, through Somerville and Newark, to Jersey City.[116] Fugitives also could have gone from Easton to Jersey City via the Morris Canal.

East Stroudsburg to Jersey City Route

A major escape route on Pennsylvania's Underground Railroad came from the southeastern part of the state and headed north to the town of Stroudsburg. Recent research has also unearthed an Underground Railroad site in the nearby community of East Stroudsburg that likely was used by runaways on one of New Jersey's minor routes. It was in the home of Robert Brown at the corner of Braeside Avenue and East Brown Street.[117] East Stroudsburg was only two miles from the Delaware River, and crossing into New Jersey would have been an option for the fugitives. Once they did so, they most likely followed the system of roads, which later became Interstates 80 and 280, all the way to Jersey City. This system would have passed through Boonton to the northwest of Jersey City. In this town, the Underground Railroad station was located in the Powerville Hotel, owned by the Hopkins family. As a young man, Charles Fern Hopkins, later a noted abolitionist and political figure, helped his father run the hotel and aid fugitives who passed through the area.[118] Another station was in the home of Dr. John Grimes, a Quaker abolitionist and active agent on the Underground Railroad. His father, Jonathan Grimes, had also been an agent.[119]

Another possible escape path could have started at Stroudsburg and headed east into northern New Jersey toward Stockholm. From Stockholm, an escape route ran through West Milford and Vernon into New York.[120]

SOUTH AND CENTRAL NEW JERSEY TO
NEW BRUNSWICK VIA BORDENTOWN ROUTE

On this route, fugitive slaves from the southern and central parts of New Jersey were conducted to freedom in New York City. It is this route that runaways, having passed through Woodbury, Snow Hill, and Evesham Mount, took to Bordentown on their quest for freedom farther north. According to tradition, an Underground Railroad station operated in a house on Burlington Street in the heart of Bordentown.[121] In addition to this site, there was an A.M.E. church in the town.[122] The congregation most certainly would have given fugitives assistance as they passed through the city.

The next stop on the escape path was the town of Crosswicks. It was only several miles from Bordentown and could be reached easily by a road that connected the two localities. In addition to the road, the Delaware & Raritan Canal, which had opened in 1834, passed through the region. This waterway joined the Delaware River in Bordentown with the Raritan River in New Brunswick, a short distance from New York City.[123] Canal boats were often used as hiding places for fugitives in their bid for freedom. Another option for fugitives could have been to hide in one of the cars of the Camden & Amboy Railroad trains that went from Bordentown to South Amboy on Raritan Bay.[124] More research needs to be done on this possibility, however.

Crosswicks was an important stopping place on the Northern Network. John Fabrino, citing an earlier work by Henry Charlton Beck, *Fare to Midlands: The Forgotten Towns of Central New Jersey* (1939), states that a number of Quakers were active in the area, chief of whom was Enoch Middleton. He operated a station out of his house, located on the north bank of Crosswicks Creek in the town. A retired merchant and abolitionist from Philadelphia, Middleton often corresponded with Lucretia Mott and William Still on matters of the Underground Railroad. His youngest son, Rudolph, helped him aid runaways. Fugitives would come to his home in small groups, ranging from three to five. Middleton or his son would take them to Allentown, Cranbury, or all the way to New Brunswick under the cover of darkness.[125]

Leaving Crosswicks, conductors took most of the fugitives to Allentown. The road that ran from Bordentown to Crosswicks also continued on to this town, where a house on Main Street was an Underground Railroad station. The house no longer exists, having been torn down some years ago. George Middleton was one of the main agents in Allentown, although he would never openly admit it.[126]

From Allentown, the freedom seekers made their way to Cranbury. Founded in 1697, this was one of the oldest towns in New Jersey. It had an A.M.E. church in the early 1800s.[127] The Cranbury Inn, at 21 South Main Street, was purported to have been an Underground Railroad station. Fugitives were brought to the inn from Crosswicks and Allentown, and then sent on to New Brunswick.[128]

Before reaching New Brunswick, however, the route ran through South Brunswick, where a farmhouse on Raymond Road, called the Red Maple Farm, was a stopover site. The house was built in 1740 by Joachim Gulick, whose family operated a stage line that ran along what is now NJ Route 27.[129] From here, the final leg in the journey to New Brunswick began. At this point, this route and the Philadelphia Line coincided, and the fugitives were guided to either Perth Amboy or Jersey City, before crossing into New York City.

Monmouth County Routes

Monmouth County was the first area in New Jersey where black slaves were used as a source of labor. In 1680, some seventy black slaves worked on a farm in Shrewsbury, and others labored at the ironworks in Tinton Falls, both in this county. In 1820, Monmouth County had one of the largest concentrations of slaves in New Jersey, with 1,248 that year.[130] It was to be expected, therefore, that some of those being held in bondage would try to gain their freedom by fleeing. Between 1726 and 1776, Colonial newspapers printed thirty-five advertisements for runaways from Monmouth County. Such notifications continued to be published throughout the 1800s. It is almost a certainty that many more had escaped, but their owners simply had not placed an advertisement in a paper for them.[131]

Aiding the freedom seekers in their efforts were fellow free blacks and Quakers. The tax rolls of the late 1700s show that free blacks were settling in the county.[132] Around 1840, a community of blacks arose in the western portion of Manalapan Township. Situated near the border with Middlesex County, it bore the name Africa and had an A.M.E. church.[133] The town would have been a safe haven for those heading north on an escape path. Tradition also has it that the Quakers in Upper Freehold Township used their homes as Underground Railroad stations.[134]

In addition to local slaves escaping from their masters, runaways from other locations also passed through the county. In 1765, two slaves, Pompey and Nero, escaped from their bondage in North Carolina. They followed the Appalachian mountain range all the way to Pennsylvania, and then crossed into New Jersey. They proceeded across the state, coming to the town of Shrewsbury in Monmouth County. The town apparently had a reputation as a stopover place for fugitives, though ironically, it was the same place where the first black slaves had been introduced into New Jersey. From here, Pompey and Nero, and others after them, made their way to Perth Amboy and then New York City.[135] Although more research needs to be done, it is logical that Monmouth County would have been a conduit for fugitives from the counties of eastern New Jersey, starting with Cape May.

New York—The
Backdrop

In the early 1600s, the Dutch East India Company had sent Henry Hudson to what would become the northern United States to find a passage through America to the East Indies. Reaching New York Bay in 1609, he sailed up the Hudson River for some distance, claiming the land on both sides of the river for the Netherlands. In 1624, the Dutch West India Company established a colony in the Hudson River valley, naming it New Netherlands. It was at this time, according to dubious legend, that they made the now famous purchase of Manhattan Island from the Native Americans for $24 worth of trinkets. The company appointed governors as directors general to manage the colony. Huge feudal-like estates, called patroonships, were given to those who could arrange for at least fifty people to settle the land there. The area around Albany made up the largest of these patroonships.

Eventually hostilities developed between the English colonists who had settled in Connecticut and the Dutch of New Netherlands. Another European power, the Swedes, also made an incursion in the Dutch-claimed lands of New Jersey, and war followed the friction. In 1664, Charles II of England granted to his brother, the duke of York, the lands held by the Dutch in America. The English attacked the Dutch capital of New Amsterdam, and, outgunned and outnumbered, the Dutch surrendered. The duke quickly renamed the city New York. English colonists soon arrived and absorbed the original Dutch inhabitants. The government of New York claimed all the land from the Hudson River west to Lake Erie, south to the border of the colony of Pennsylvania, and north to the Canadian border.[1]

The first black slaves made their appearance in New York in 1626. Eleven slaves were imported from the country of Angola in Africa.[2] They were employed to help build roads, houses, forts, and other infrastructure features in the colony of New Amsterdam.[3] A few years later, in 1629, the Dutch West India Company began to bring slaves on a regular basis from Angola, and then from Curacao, to the colony. They worked mainly at various agricultural pursuits on the farms in the Hudson Valley.[4] After 1647, black slaves began to work at various skill trades in the colony, serving as ship caulkers, blacksmiths, bricklayers, and stone masons.[5] The number of people in what became the colony of New York rose to 18,067 by 1698, and of this number, 2,170 were blacks, most of whom were slaves. In 1756, the number of adult slaves stood at 10,000. This was about 15 percent of the total population of New York. It also represented the largest slave population north of Maryland. Of those slaves, 2,278 resided in New York City, where they made up 16 percent of the population.[6] After the United States gained its independence and the state of New York was created, the number of free blacks living there increased steadily, as shown in Table 3.[7]

TABLE 3.
CENSUS DATA FOR NEW YORK, 1790 TO 1860

Year	Total population	Slaves	Free Blacks
1790	340,241	21,193 (6.2%)	4,682 (1.4%)
1800	586,613	20,613 (3.5%)	10,374 (1.8%)
1810	959,049	15,017 (1.6%)	25,333 (2.6%)
1820	1,372,812	10,124 (.74%)	29,163 (2.1%)
1830	1,918,608	75 (.004%)	44,870 (.02%)
1840	2,428,921	4 (.0002%)	50,027 (.02%)
1850	3,097,394	0	49,069 (.02%)
1860	3,831,590	0	49,005 (.01%)

The Dutch had treated the black slaves well, and there were no reports of brutality shown toward them, as there were later in American history. For the most part, they received the same treatment given to white indentured servants. The Dutch had no formal slave codes like the English did. They initiated a system called half-freedom, which allowed slaves a degree of personal liberty in exchange for occasional service at an annual fee of thirty schepels of wheat and one fat hog; however, their children had to remain slaves. Free blacks also began to appear in New Netherlands. Most of them had either purchased their freedom or been manumitted by their owners. They were treated in the same manner as whites. They could own property, legally marry in the Dutch Reformed Church, and pass on inheritances to their offspring.[8] The Dutch even armed their slaves during the Indian War of 1641–44.

The benevolent attitude toward black slaves changed when the English gained control of New Netherlands. All of the privileges granted by the Dutch ended for the blacks, both free and enslaved. The duke of York encouraged the slave trade in his colony, and 1684 saw the passage of a law in New York that recognized slavery as a legitimate institution.[9] Underlying the laws passed by the English was the principle that black slaves were property, and hence their enslavement would continue until they died or were manumitted. The law of 1664 stated that even the children of slaves were now slaves. Slaveowners in the colony had free rein when it came to the types of punishments they could inflict on their slaves, permitted to do anything short of killing or mutilating them. Even the free blacks lost many of the rights they had under the Dutch when the English gained control of New York.[10]

The Colonial government, and later the state government of New York, as well as several municipalities, passed twenty-five different laws that had an impact on the lives of enslaved and free blacks living there. Some were designed to exercise control over the lives of blacks in every detail, and others were passed to protect them. Laws enacted in 1680, 1702, and 1773 prohibited the sale of alcohol to blacks. The law of 1702 even forbade blacks to be present in a tavern on Sundays. Trade with a black slave without the consent of his or her master was prohibited by another law passed in 1702, and the New York City Council even enacted a law in 1740 forbidding blacks from selling agricultural products at public markets, in reaction to a fear that the blacks were selling whites diseased produce. Travel restrictions were included in the some of the laws. In 1705, Albany forbade slaves from being more than forty miles north of the town, out of fear that slaves might transmit information about Albany's defenses to the French in Canada. A slave could be executed for violating this law. The status of slavery, as stated in the law of 1664, was reinforced in a statute passed by the Colonial government in 1706, which stated that even being baptized a Christian did not change the fact that a slave was still a slave. New York City passed a law in 1710 that prohibited slaves from being on the streets at night without a torch or lantern.[11]

The most restrictive of the slave laws was passed by the New York City Council in 1731, in response to a general feeling of unease among the white population that there might be a slave insurrection. Earlier, in 1712, a plot had been carried out that resulted in the death of a number of whites at the hands of black slaves. On March 25 of that year, slaves plotted to murder all of the whites in the city. The plot was put into action on April 7, when two dozen armed slaves torched buildings and killed nine white people. The military eventually put down the insurrection, and most of the conspirators were executed. The ultimate consequence of this action was the passage in 1731 of a law that contained a number of harsh provisions regulating black slaves in many ways. One of these forbade the assembly of more than three blacks in the same place on a Sunday. Another denied the right of blacks to carry weapons. Blacks were forbidden to be on the streets at night unless in the company of their master. No more than twelve blacks could be in attendance at a funeral. The final provision was a vaguely worded statement that prohibited blacks from "using the streets in a disorderly manner."[12]

A decade later, another event took place that produced mass hysteria in the city. A robbery and arson occurred on February 28, 1741, and an indentured white servant named Mary Burton began to identify a group of black men as the perpetrators. Almost immediately after this, every fire and crime that occurred was blamed on blacks. By July, 102 black men had been arrested. Eighteen of them were hanged, fourteen were burned alive, and seventy were deported. In the end, it was discovered that Mary Burton had lied about everything, and no blacks had been involved in the crimes.[13] These events, however, lent credence to the harsh antislave codes enacted in the city.

Not all the laws passed in New York were antislave. As early as 1712, the New York Assembly enacted a law regulating manumission of slaves. It required masters to post a bond of £200 sterling to guarantee that their freed slaves could support themselves. In 1715, this law was repealed and another one passed requiring a far smaller bond.[14] In 1785, the law was changed once again. The new law stated that all slaves who were freed by their masters and were under the age of fifty did not require a security bond. All that was needed was a document that certified that the freed individuals could provide for themselves.

Other laws were enacted affecting the personal lives of blacks. In 1809, a state law legalized marriages of slaves and allowed free blacks to inherit property. A statute in 1810 required masters to teach the children of their slaves how to read the Bible. Two regiments of black soldiers were formed to fight in the War of 1812, and slaves could enlist if they had their masters' permission. The most interesting provision of this law was that black soldiers were to receive the same pay as whites.

In 1788, a state law passed that regulated slave trade, making it illegal for anyone purchasing a slave with the intention of selling him or her outside of New York. The penalty for this act was a fine of £100 and the freeing of the slave. There were laws that dealt with runaway slaves as well. Any runaways caught in New York could be returned to their owners, according to an 1817 law. By 1840, however, this law was amended by another statute that provided for a jury trial for a supposed fugitive slave. To help thwart the practice of kidnapping free blacks and selling them into slavery in the South, a law enacted that same year made it a duty for the governor of New York to return to New York all individuals who had been kidnapped or taken to another state for the purpose of enslaving them. An 1841 statute said that slaveholders from out of state could not keep their slaves in New York for more than nine months.[15]

The legislation that eventually led to the abolition of slavery in New York evolved over a period of years. The process began in January 1785, when seventeen outstanding citizens of the state formed the New York Manumission Society, whose goal was the abolition of slavery in the state. Among its members were such notables as John Jay, Alexander Hamilton, Gen. Philip Schuyler, James Duane, and Chancellor Robert Livingston. Jay served as the group's president. The society petitioned the state assembly to pass a bill that would gradually bring the practice to an end, but the bill failed to pass because of disputes over the wording of its provisions. The assembly did pass a bill that prohibited the importation of slaves and emancipated those who had been illegally brought into New York. It also provided for jury trials for slaves accused of capital crimes. When Jay became the governor of New York in 1795, he tried again to get the assembly to pass a gradual abolition of slavery bill. Once again, however, he failed.[16] It was not until 1799 that the drive to abolish slavery succeeded. In that year, the assembly passed a series of statutes stating that all slaves born after that year were freed. Children of slaves who had been born before 1799 were to remain in servitude until they reached the age of twenty-five for females and twenty-eight for males. In 1817, another gradual abolition statute was passed that said that as of July 4 of that year, all slaves born in New York before July 4, 1799, were to be freed. It contained a provision like that in the 1799 act, requiring male slaves to remain in bondage until age twenty-eight and females twenty-five. It was not until 1827 that slavery was completely abolished in the state. On July 4 of that year, 10,000 black men and women were granted their freedom.[17]

As in New Jersey, several conditions were necessary for the successful escape of enslaved people living in or passing through the state of New York. These included antislavery sentiment among the residents, with abolitionist societies, religious groups, or individuals, both black and white, who were willing to help fugitives pass through their areas. Also important was the existence of avenues of escape—roads, waterways, rail systems, and trails—that self-emancipators could use to reach freedom, as well as an Underground Railroad network to facilitate the escape of freedom seekers.

The great New York abolitionist, William Lloyd Garrison. HISTORICAL SOCIETY OF DELAWARE

ANTISLAVERY SENTIMENT

The antislavery sentiment in New York that made it possible for an Underground Railroad network to flourish took two forms: the actions of abolitionist and religious groups, and the existence of a large number of free blacks who were willing to help their fellow men and women escape bondage. One of the earliest antislavery societies in the state, the New York Manumission Society opened the African Free School to educate the children of manumitted black slaves. At its peak in 1822, the school had an enrollment of 800 students, drawn from a potential population of 2,000 to 3,000 black youngsters between the ages of five and fifteen who were eligible for attendance. A second early group was the New York Society for Mutual Relief, which was founded in 1810 by New York City's black community. Its goal was to aid recently manumitted and escaped blacks who had arrived in the city without much of an economic base.[18] The first major abolitionist organization in New York was the New York Committee for a National Anti-Slavery Society, formed by Arthur and Lewis Tappan of New York City in 1831. Two years later, the society merged with the larger American Anti-Slavery Society.[19]

According to Tom Calarco, by 1837 the state of New York had 274 antislavery societies operating within its borders.[20] The primary goal of these societies was the cessation of the practice of slavery in the United States.

Lewis Tappan, one of the leaders of the Underground Railroad network in New York City.
HISTORICAL SOCIETY OF DELAWARE.

Oswego County in New York was particularly active in sending petitions to Congress concerning slavery-related issues. On September 18, 1837, 139 men from the town of Mexico signed a petition that opposed the annexation of Texas, mainly because it would become a slave state:

> The undersigned, Inhabitants of The Town of Mexico in the State of New York respectfully pray your honorable body, promptly to reject all proposals for the annexation of Texas to this Union, from whatever source they may come.[21]

A second petition on this issue was signed by 88 men and 46 women from the town of Hannibal, also in Oswego County:

> The undersigned inhabitants of the town on Hannibal[,] County of Oswego and State of New York would respectfully represent that in their opinion the annexation of Texas to the United States would be attended with consequences detrimental to the interests[,] peace & prosperity of this country and would seriously endanger the capabilities of the Union. We would therefore earnestly protest against such annexation and would pray your honorable body to reject any proposal which may be made to that effect.[22]

A third petition, signed by 113 men from the town of Mexico, was directed against slavery and the slave trade in the District of Columbia and Florida:

> The undersigned petitioners, citizens of the town of Mexico, County of Oswego, New York, respectfully represent:
>
> That in the District of Columbia, over which Congress is vested, by the Constitution, with the right of exclusive legislation in all cases whatever, slavery exhists—subjecting a portion of the people of said District to every privation, disability & outrage: That the slave trade, that odious and hateful traffic in humanity, which nearly the whole civilized world has long since declared to be piracy when carried out within the limits of Africa, also exhists [*sic*] in said District & is carried on under protection & sanction of your honorable body thereby subjecting the people of the whole Union to the merited reproach & ignominy of that execrable system of unmitigated wrong and oppression.
>
> That in the Territory of Florida, Over which Congress exercises a like control a similar state of things prevail.
>
> Your petitioners, therefore respectfully ask the enactment of laws abolishing slavery & prohibiting slave trade in the said District of Columbia & also in the Territory of Florida.[23]

In addition to sending petitions and lobbying for the end of slavery, these high-minded individuals often rendered direct assistance to slaves who were seeking to emancipate themselves.

Religious groups also had a role in establishing a climate in which successful slave escapes could take place. The churches that were most active in this effort were the A.M.E. and A.M.E. Zion, Quaker, Presbyterian, Methodist, and Baptist. These religious denominations all spoke out against the practice, and some of their members were active in abolitionist causes. Many of these groups raised money and had clothing drives to help support the slaves who had managed to escape to New York. In some cases, they actively aided fugitive slaves on their quest for freedom. Church buildings were used as Underground Railroad stations, ministers and church members were agents, and the homes of many parishioners were stopover sanctuaries for weary self-emancipators.

The A.M.E. and A.M.E. Zion were by far the most active churches in directly assisting runaways in achieving their freedom. Founded in 1816 through the efforts of Rev. Richard Allen, the A.M.E. Church spread rapidly among the black population of the Atlantic states, so that by 1826 it had two bishops and 7,927 members.[24] In 1819, Allen sent Brother William Lambert to New York City to establish a branch of the A.M.E. there.[25]

The Society of Friends, or the Quakers, actively opposed the institution of slavery from the earliest days of the British colonies in America. The writings of George Keith in 1694, Ralph Sanford in 1729, Benjamin Lay in 1737, and John Woolman in 1754 established a theological and philosophical basis for the abolition of slavery among the Quakers. The earliest official condemnation of the institution occurred at the Philadelphia Yearly Meeting of the Quakers in 1754, and it affected the more than thirty thousand members of the denomination living in the eastern colonies at that time. In New York, there were Quakers among the settlers in the Dutch colony of New Amsterdam as early as 1657. Between 1774 and 1776, they were living in East Hoosack and Saratoga to the north on the Hudson River, as well as on Long Island, in Manhattan, and in the counties of Westchester and Dutchess along the southern portion of the Hudson. By 1789, they had spread to western New York and were centered near the town of Farmington in Ontario County. More than twenty thousand lived in the state by 1820.[26]

The federal census of 1850 showed that there were 133 Quaker meetinghouses in the state, scattered over thirty-three of the fifty-nine counties that existed in New York at that time. The largest concentrations of Quaker congregations were in Dutchess (nineteen), Westchester (sixteen), Queens (nine), Ulster (eight), Erie (seven), Cayuga (six), and Saratoga (five) Counties.[27] These counties played active roles in the operation of the Underground Railroad.

The Presbyterian, Methodist, and Baptist Churches also held antislavery positions in the late eighteenth and early nineteenth centuries in New York. The General Assembly of the Presbyterian Church in America condemned the institution of slavery in a pronouncement issued in 1787.[28] According to the federal census of 1850, there were 671 Presbyterian churches in the state of New York, which had the potential of providing an active base of support for Underground Railroad activities among the congregants.[29] In 1780, the National Conference of the Methodist Church had given a statement of its own on the topic.[30] The Methodist Church was the denomination with the largest number of congregations in New York in 1850, with 1,231 churches scattered throughout the state. Many of these were found on key routes of the Underground Railroad.[31] In the late 1780s and 1790s, the various general committees of the Baptist Church passed resolutions condemning slavery and urged for its abolition.[32] A core of dedicated supporters who would help self-emancipators in their journey northward likely could be found in the 781 Baptist churches operating in the state in 1850.[33]

However, not all members of denominations which condemned slavery shared this viewpoint or were willing to assist fugitives in their efforts to escape. Most likely, there was a core of dedicated supporters within each group who would have taken this radical step. The important point to remember is that, since these three groups are often mentioned in the context of helping runaways, where there were congregations of each, the potential existed for activists in the cause.

Individual members of these churches also became activists in the cause. In 1824, Rev. George Washington Gale, a Presbyterian revivalist who had preached mightily against slavery for years, retired to his farm in Whiteboro, in western New York. At this point in his career, he opened a divinity school in his home that became known as the Oneida Institute which taught an antislavery attitude supported by a strong religious conviction. Gale headed the school from 1827 to 1834.[34] Another Presbyterian revivalist, John Humphrey Noyes, settled in Rochester, New York. Like Gale, he was a dedicated abolitionist, and he helped create a strong abolitionist climate in that part of New York.[35] Rochester went on to become an important center on one of the major routes of the Underground Railroad in New York. The Methodist preacher Orange Scott traveled throughout the Burned-Over District in western New York in the 1830s and 1840s, preaching fiery antislavery sermons, especially in the area around Utica. This area of western New York earned this title because of the strong religious revivalism that swept through it in the period before the Civil War. New School Presbyterian, Mormonism, and the Millenial Church had their beginnings as a result of this renewed religious zeal.[36] Scott formed an antislavery group in Utica in 1843, calling it the Wesleyan Methodist Connection in America. Its members played a role in helping fugitives escape to Canada. The Baptist Church was also active in the antislavery cause in the 1830s and 1840s in the state. The Baptist preacher Elon Galusha preached abolitionism throughout his travels in western New York. In 1840, the National Baptist Anti-Slavery Convention was held in New York City.[37]

Free blacks also contributed to the antislavery sentiment in the state of New York. In many instances, it was they who gave critical assistance to fellow blacks in their journey to freedom. Table 4 shows the distribution of free blacks in New York during the critical years of the Underground Railroad's operation in 1840, 1850, and 1860.[38] The counties with the highest population densities were those most essential to the successful running of the Underground Railroad networks in the state.

TABLE 4.
THE NUMBER OF FREE BLACKS BY COUNTY
FOR 1840, 1850, AND 1860

County	1840	1850	1860
Albany	1,314	1,194	938
Allegany	142	128	264
Broome	223	431	464
Cattaraugus	38	102	151
Cayuga	435	543	451
Chautauqua	124	140	205
Chemung	113	286	572
Chenango	273	264	263
Clinton	86	112	128
Columbia	1,556	1,312	1,380
Cortland	46	42	16
Delaware	190	201	186
Dutchess	2,270	1,970	2,051
Erie	608	825	878
Essex	78	50	123
Franklin	3	62	19
Fulton	114	102	185
Genesee	115	77	84
Greene	893	895	819
Hamilton	3	2	3
Herkimer	287	203	251
Jefferson	141	191	209
Kings	2,843	4,065	4,999
Lewis	53	42	39
Livingston	140	209	184
Madison	223	298	300
Monroe	655	699	567
Montgomery	588	474	357
New York	16,358	13,815	12,574
Niagara	241	317	517
Oneida	644	672	638
Onondaga	477	613	555

TABLE 4.
THE NUMBER OF FREE BLACKS BY COUNTY
FOR 1840, 1850, AND 1860, *continued*

County	1840	1850	1860
Ontario	664	610	639
Orange	2,292	2,464	2,112
Orleans	69	108	131
Oswego	215	215	335
Otsego	222	175	207
Putnam	167	138	183
Queens	3,509	3,451	3,387
Rensselaer	1,190	1,019	1,058
Richmond	483	590	659
Rockland	432	596	549
Saratoga	649	618	691
Schenectady	410	388	241
Schoharie	493	478	484
Schuyler (created in 1854)	0	0	100
Seneca	199	181	213
Steuben	288	371	475
St. Lawrence	35	39	59
Suffolk	2,177	2,117	1,798
Sullivan	80	100	94
Tioga	162	197	248
Tompkins	253	325	297
Ulster	1,804	1,585	1,609
Warren	32	46	58
Washington	272	350	259
Wayne	222	268	270
Westchester	2,300	2,075	2,270
Wyoming (created in 1841)	0	64	52
Yates	134	165	157
Totals	50,027	49,069	49,005

These figures indicate that free blacks lived in all regions of New York. Some counties had much greater concentrations, and it was in these areas that major Underground Railroad routes flourished. Free blacks lived in cities and towns where they were tradespeople and craft workers. They lived in their own communities near towns and on isolated farms. Whatever their circumstances, they could be counted on to render aid to their brothers and sisters fleeing the bondage of slavery. Free blacks also expressed themselves in petitions to the various levels of government. After the passage of the Fugitive Slave Act of 1850, numerous meetings of free blacks were held throughout the state of New York. Major gatherings took place in Oswego and Buffalo, with petitions containing well-constructed resolutions that attacked the passage of the bill and the institution of slavery based on appeals to the ideas found in the Declaration of Independence, the U.S. Constitution, and tenets of Christianity.[39] New York also was the home of a number of black abolitionists, such as Sojourner Truth, Frederick Douglass, and James McCune Smith.

Support for abolitionism and the Underground Railroad was not, however, a universal sentiment shared by all citizens of New York. The state's rigorous antiblack and slave laws show that many feared the slave population and were in no mood to grant them freedom. In addition to legislative efforts to restrict black mobility and freedom, physical violence occasionally occurred in the form of antislave or antiabolitionist riots. Major antiabolitionist riots took place in New York City during 1833 and 1834, and a large mob in Utica on October 21, 1835, forced the individuals who were attempting to establish the New York State Anti-Slavery Society to move their meeting site from Utica to the estate of Gerrit Smith in Petersboro.[40]

AVENUES OF ESCAPE

New York was ideally situated to allow for several major Underground Railroad escape networks. It bordered Pennsylvania and New Jersey to the south; Connecticut, Massachusetts, and Vermont to the west; and Canada to the north. It was a natural conduit through which fugitive slaves had to pass in order to get from Pennsylvania and New Jersey to Canada, either directly or by way of Vermont, Massachusetts, or Connecticut.

Two of the Great Lakes, Erie and Ontario, separated the state from Canada and were natural highways over which fugitives could travel. New York also had numerous rivers that could help convey the self-emancipators toward their ultimate objective. Two of them, the Susquehanna and Delaware, crossed into Pennsylvania and New Jersey and were used with some regularity by Underground Railroad operatives. Other rivers flowed into Lake Erie or Lake Ontario and provided additional avenues of escape. New York City and Long Island had ready access to the Atlantic Ocean and water routes to the New England states. The Appalachian mountain range traversed the eastern portion of the state and contained innumerable ridges and valleys ideally suited for secret travel. The central and western parts of the state were located on the Allegheny Plateau, a land of rolling hills dotted with small towns and farmlands, also advantageous to weary travelers on their journeys to freedom.[41]

Three types of transportation played key roles in the successful operation of an escape system: a good road network, waterway transport, and railroad lines. The road system in New York was excellent and connected the many towns and cities, as well as rural areas, throughout the state. Beginning in 1812, a series of turnpikes ran from the border with Massachusetts through Albany to Lake Erie, near the town of Buffalo. Other roads fanned out from Albany and other points along the Hudson River.

Turnpike construction boomed in the state between 1812 to 1821, and by 1822, New York had more than four thousand miles of turnpikes. In the 1840s, plank roads became the vogue in the state and allowed for more efficient travel on a year-round basis. Later, these were replaced with all-weather macadam roads.[42] An 1844 map shows that all parts of the state were interconnected with roads, and many of them linked New York with Pennsylvania and New Jersey.[43] It was over this network of roads that many runaways headed northward toward Canada and freedom.

Fugitives traveled by waterway in several different ways. They could proceed along one of the many canals found in the state. Some hid on canal barges, and captains allowed others to travel on their craft in cooperation with Underground Railroad activities. The first and most important canal for escape possibilities was the Erie Canal. Authorized by the New York State Legislature in 1817, the canal connected the lower Hudson River with Lake Erie, linking Albany and Buffalo. It was completed in 1825, stretching for 364 miles along the northern portion of the state. Soon after this, several other major canals opened. The most important of these for the Underground Railroad were the Champlain Canal, which linked Albany to Lake Champlain and then the St. Lawrence River; the Olean to Rochester Canal; the branch of the Erie Canal that ran to the town of Rome; the canal from the Susquehanna River to the Erie Canal near Syracuse; the canal between Syracuse and Oswego on Lake Ontario; and the canal between the Delaware and Hudson

Rivers, which went from northeastern Pennsylvania, across New Jersey, to the town of Kingston, New York. By 1850, New York had 803 miles of canals within its borders.[44] Fugitive slaves used this system on many occasions to gain access to Canada.

Another type of water travel involved the use of the steamboats that both traversed the inland waterways of the state and linked New York with its neighbor states. The *Clermont* first sailed on the Hudson River in 1807. By 1812, a regular ferry service using steamboats opened in New York Harbor. By 1815, steamboats navigated on Long Island Sound, and there was regular traffic by steam between New York and Philadelphia. In the 1820s, the first of a long line of steamboats, the *Walk-in-the-Water*, built by the Erie Steamboat Company in Buffalo, began to sail all over Lake Erie, linking New York with western states and Canada.[45] Between 1848 and 1860, steamboats and sailing ships also began to traverse the waters along the Atlantic seaboard.[46] Goods and people, among whom were a number of freedom seekers, were transported from Southern states to New York in this manner.

By 1840, there also were 453 miles of rail lines scattered throughout New York State. In 1841, a railroad was completed that tied Boston to the Hudson River. Smaller lines connected many cities, such as New York City, Albany, Schenectady, Troy, Buffalo, Rochester, and Utica, in the 1840s. By 1850, the mileage of rail lines had increased to 1,409. The next year, two major lines linked the eastern and western parts of the state. The first was the New York and Erie Railroad.[47] A railroad map of New York from 1855 shows this line running from New York City across the southern portion of the state, through Binghamton, Oswego, Elmira, and Corning, to Dunkirk on Lake Erie. A spur of this line also went to Buffalo.[48] These towns appear as major Underground Railroad sites in the literature. A few years later, this railroad became known as the Erie Railroad, and it ran spur lines to a number of towns in northern Pennsylvania as well as additional connector lines to the New York Central Railroad, the other major rail system in the state.[49] One of the more important southern connectors was one that came from Harrisburg, Pennsylvania, and linked with the Northern Central Railroad. There is strong evidence that this line was used to convey fugitive slaves from the Harrisburg area to Elmira, New York, and from there to freedom in Canada.[50] The New York Central Railroad crossed the central portion of the state and connected Albany with Lake Erie near Buffalo. It had spur lines that ran to the northern reaches of the state as well as to the New York and Erie Railroad to the south.[51] Two of the major Underground Railroad escape networks active in the state can be traced along this rail system.

NEW YORK'S UNDERGROUND RAILROAD NETWORK

Enslaved black people sought their freedom in New York as early as the beginning of the 1700s. Advertisements for runaways appeared in the *New York Gazette* on a regular basis in the 1730s and 1740s. The following are some examples of these notices:

From the *New York Gazette,* of May 18, 1730:

Ran away, a Negro Man named Quash, from his master Cornelius DePeyster of New York City. The said negro has thick lips, and has lost a foretooth. Whoever can take up said Negro man and bring him to his maser, or secure and give Notice, so that this master can get him again, shall have forty shillings reward and all reasonable Charges.

From the *New York Gazette,* of January 30, 1732:

Run away about 10 o'clock on Thursday last, from John Cannon, New York City, three Negroes with a sloop belonging to said Cannon, burthen about 35 tons. Whoever takes up and returns said Negroe men and the sloop shall Receive Twenty Pounds and all reasonable Charges from John Cannon.

From the *New York Gazette,* of December 19, 1737

Ran away from John Bell, of New York City, a carpenter, one Negro woman named Jenney, 14-15 years, born in New York, speaks English and some Dutch. She has a flat nose, thick lips, and full faced; had on when she went away, a Bird's Eyed Waistcoat and Pettycoat of darkish colour, and a calico waistcoat with a large Red Flower, and a broad stripe, a calico petti-coat with small stripes and small red flowers. Whoever shall take up this said Negro Wench and Bring her to said John Bell, or secure her and give Notice, so that he can Have her again, shall have three pounds as a Reward, and all reasonable Charges.

From the *New York Gazette,* revived in the *Weekly Post-Boy* of July 10, 1749:

Run away the 21st Instant from William and Benjamin Hawxhurst, of Oyster-Bay on Long-Island, a negro Man named Tom, a middle sized Fellow and is pretty well cloth'd: Took with him a black Horse with a white Snip or Spot on his Nose. Whoever takes up and secures the said Negro and Horse, shall have a reasonable Reward paid by William and Benjamin Hawxhurst.[52]

Despite the evidence of such early attempts at self-emancipation, the formal operation of an Underground Railroad in New York State was a product of the 1800s. With the feeder routes coming from New Jersey and the Atlantic coast, as well as the extended border with Pennsylvania, the Underground Railroad appears to have had three major networks in New York. The Eastern Network proceeded, for the most part, north along the Hudson River valley toward Canada. This network had offshoots that carried fugitives into Vermont, Connecticut, Massachusetts, and Maine via the Atlantic coastline. The Central Network received freedom seekers from northeastern and north-central Pennsylvania, and guided them northward or northwestward to Canada by crossing either Lake Ontario or the Niagara River.

The Western Network operated through the western part of the state, and conveyed runaways to Niagara and from there across the river into Canada.

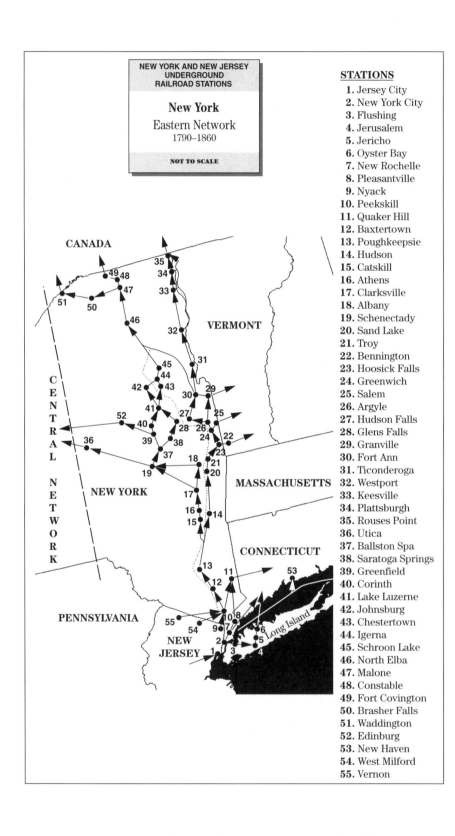

NEW YORK AND NEW JERSEY
UNDERGROUND
RAILROAD STATIONS

New York
Eastern Network
1790–1860

NOT TO SCALE

CANADA

VERMONT

CENTRAL NETWORK

NEW YORK

MASSACHUSETTS

CONNECTICUT

PENNSYLVANIA

NEW JERSEY

Long Island

STATIONS

1. Jersey City
2. New York City
3. Flushing
4. Jerusalem
5. Jericho
6. Oyster Bay
7. New Rochelle
8. Pleasantville
9. Nyack
10. Peekskill
11. Quaker Hill
12. Baxtertown
13. Poughkeepsie
14. Hudson
15. Catskill
16. Athens
17. Clarksville
18. Albany
19. Schenectady
20. Sand Lake
21. Troy
22. Bennington
23. Hoosick Falls
24. Greenwich
25. Salem
26. Argyle
27. Hudson Falls
28. Glens Falls
29. Granville
30. Fort Ann
31. Ticonderoga
32. Westport
33. Keesville
34. Plattsburgh
35. Rouses Point
36. Utica
37. Ballston Spa
38. Saratoga Springs
39. Greenfield
40. Corinth
41. Lake Luzerne
42. Johnsburg
43. Chestertown
44. Igerna
45. Schroon Lake
46. North Elba
47. Malone
48. Constable
49. Fort Covington
50. Brasher Falls
51. Waddington
52. Edinburg
53. New Haven
54. West Milford
55. Vernon

New York—The Eastern Routes

The Eastern Network of escape routes in New York ran essentially along the eastern portion of the state. For the most part, it followed the Hudson River valley northward to Canada. It was bounded to the north by New York's border with Canada; to the east by the borders with Connecticut and Massachusetts; to the south by the borders with New Jersey and the northeastern corner of Pennsylvania; and to the west by the Catskill and Adirondack Mountains, roughly along seventy-five degrees west longitude. The network involved twenty-four counties in eastern New York: Albany, Clinton, Columbia, Dutchess, Essex, Franklin, Greene, Hamilton, Herkimer, Montgomery, New York, Orange, Putnam, Queens, Rensselaer, Rockland, Saratoga, Schoharie, St. Lawrence, Suffolk, Sullivan, Ulster, Warren, and Westchester. Wilbur Siebert lists twenty-one Underground Railroad agents operating along this network in Albany, New York, Rensselaer, and Ulster Counties.[1] More recent research, however, shows that there were many more agents and conductors in this network than Siebert identifies.

Many factors, both natural and demographic, contributed to the formation and successful operation of the network. The geographic features of the area were well suited for a system of escape routes. The Hudson River provided an excellent pathway over which freedom seekers could travel. Barges of the Erie Canal, as well as other water traffic, plied these waters. The towpaths and trails along the shores of the river also presented opportunities for travelers to head northward. The area was crisscrossed by numerous roads and rail lines. The land was filled with farms and small towns providing means of support for a successful escape. The demographics of the Eastern Network were also supportive of an escape system. Table 5 paints a picture of potential assistance for freedom-seeking runaways[2]

TABLE 5.
DEMOGRAPHIC DATA FOR NEW YORK'S
EASTERN NETWORK IN 1850

County	Free blacks	Quaker meeting-houses	Methodist churches	Baptist churches	Presbyterian churches
Albany	1,194 (1.3%)	4	29	13	11
Clinton	112 (.27%)	2	16	2	7
Columbia	1,312 (3.0%)	4	19	10	9
Dutchess	1,970 (3.3%)	19	35	22	13
Essex	50 (.16%)	0	13	10	2
Franklin	62 (.25%)	0	4	2	0
Greene	895 (2.7%)	3	23	8	12
Hamilton	2 (.09%)	0	1	1	0
Herkimer	203 (.53%)	0	8	11	2
Montgomery	474 (1.5%)	1	13	4	10
New York	13,815 (2.7%)	4	41	24	41
Orange	2,464 (4.3%)	5	35	9	4
Putnam	138 (.98%)	1	11	7	5
Queens	3,451 (9.4%)	9	22	1	6
Rensselaer	1,019 (3.5%)	1	20	12	9
Rockland	596 (3.5%)	0	14	4	9
Saratoga	618 (1.4%)	5	29	21	13
Schenectady	388 (1.9%)	1	5	3	5
Schoharie	478 (1.4%)	0	26	14	7
St. Lawrence	39 (.06%)	0	30	14	15
Suffolk	2,117 (5.7%)	0	44	4	24
Sullivan	100 (.40%)	1	16	3	8
Ulster	1,585 (2.7%)	8	24	8	7
Warren	46 (.27%)	2	10	9	5
Washington	350 (.78%)	4	23	17	25
Westchester	2,075 (3.6%)	16	42	7	18
Totals	35,553 (2.3%)	90	553	240	267

These data reveal a climate most conducive to the successful operation of an Underground Railroad network, with a robust potential for aid. The large number of free blacks living in the region could provide not only shelter and guidance for those heading north toward Canada, but also an opportunity for the fugitives to blend into an existing black community and hide in broad daylight. Quaker congregations, many of which readily assisted runaways, were quite numerous along this network, and though not as committed to helping freedom seekers as the Quakers, the great number of Methodist, Baptist, and Presbyterian congregations in our area furnished sufficient members to help facilitate this escape network.

The Eastern Network of the Underground Railroad in New York may be divided into a number of components. New York City was a component in itself. A second escape branch consisted of a route through Long Island and a sea route to the New England states of Connecticut, Massachusetts, and Rhode Island. A third section ran from New York City either northward to the city of Albany or toward Syracuse. Several other routes left Albany and proceeded northeast to Vermont, directly northward toward Canada, or westward through New York.

NEW YORK CITY

Between 1790 and 1850, New York City grew to be the most prominent city in the United States. The population of the city in 1790 stood at 33,111, of which 1,119 were free blacks and 2,373 enslaved. By 1850, the total number of people living in the city was 515,547, and 13,815 of them were free blacks.[3] In 1850, as shown in Table 5, there were four Quaker meetinghouses and forty-one Methodist, twenty-four Baptist, and forty-one Presbyterian churches in the city. The literature describing the operation of the Underground Railroad in the state of New York clearly indicates that New York City was an integral part of that system.

Self-emancipators entered the city from several points. Most came from New Jersey, mainly the towns of Perth Amboy and Jersey City.[4] The Quaker Underground Railroad agent John Everett took fugitives from Jersey City into New York City and conducted them to the railway station on Forty-first Street, where he bought them tickets on the night train to Syracuse.[5] At times, he and a fellow agent, Peter J. Phillips, guided them to the Hudson River Passenger Station at the corner of Church Street and Chambers Street, where they purchased tickets for a night train going to Albany and saw that their charges safely boarded that train. When the Hudson River Station was guarded by slave catchers, they would take the freedom seekers to the home of Lewis Tappan on West Broadway.[6] Some fugitives, who had hidden in the tunnels on the Jersey City waterfront, were escorted by agents to the Erie Canal depot and secreted on board barges that were heading through New York City northward toward Albany.[7] Still others got assistance in boarding ferry boats and coal barges traveling from New Jersey to New York City.[8]

The fugitives who managed to reach the city could receive aid at a number of places. Many Underground Railroad agents and conductors maintained safe houses for runaways in New York City. Siebert lists nine active agents in the city: George T. Downing, Isaac Hopper, Oliver Johnson, Rev. Charles B. Ray, David Ruggles, Dr. McCune Smith, and three individuals for whom only surnames are given—Briggs, Gibbs, and Pennington.[9] Siebert frequently records only the last names of black agents on his list. Another black agent in the city was Henry H. Garnet.[10] George T. Downing operated an Underground Railroad station in his Oyster House restaurant at the corner of Broad Street and Wall Street, according to Charles Blockson.[11] Isaac T. Hopper was a Quaker abolitionist who had moved from Philadelphia to New York in 1829. He owned a store on Pearl Street where he hid freedom seekers. It was Hopper, along with David Ruggles, who gave aid to Frederick Douglass when he reached the city after his escape from Baltimore.[12] Rev. Charles B. Ray edited an abolitionist journal called the *Colored American*, and he was on the board that helped choose recipients of the land grants Gerrit Smith was giving to poor blacks in central New York.[13] David Ruggles, from Connecticut, moved to New York City at age seventeen and he worked in a number of small businesses. He became active in abolitionist circles, and in 1838, he edited the first black magazine, The *Mirror of Liberty.* Ruggles helped more than 1,000 fugitives gain their freedom from slavery and has been recognized by many as the most important Underground Railroad agent in the city.[14] Dr. James McCune Smith was another black person active in the African American Convention movement and one of the founders of the Radical Abolitionist Party. He owned two stores in the city and used both as safe houses for fugitives.[15] Henry Ward Beecher, one of the more famous abolitionist leaders in the country, opened his church in New York City, the Plymouth Church, to fugitives. Because of the large number of freedom seekers who passed through his church, it became known as the Grand Central Depot of the Underground Railroad in the city.[16]

Isaac Hopper, the leading Quaker Underground Railroad agent in eastern New York. LIBRARY OF CONGRESS

Another Underground Railroad agent who played an important role in the New York City system was Rev. Theodore Sedgewick Wright. Born in 1797 in Providence, Rhode Island, Wright was the first black person to receive a degree from the Princeton Theological Seminary. After graduating in 1828, he became a minister in the Presbyterian Church. Throughout his life, he was an outspoken critic of both the institution of slavery and the attempt to resettle freed blacks in Africa. After moving to New York City, he became the pastor of the First Colored Presbyterian Church and often used his church as a sanctuary for fugitives.[17]

Two other active participants in the system were Arthur and Lewis Tappan. William Still cites that Lewis Tappan hid runaways in the offices of the American Missionary Association, of which he was the treasurer. On another occasion, Lewis communicated to Still that he found fugitives seeking aid in the Sabbath school that his brother Arthur had started for the education of black people in the city. The Tappans spoke out against slavery and helped runaways at great risk. Still mentions that in the antiabolitionist riot of 1834 in New York City, a mob sacked the Lewis house, and there was an attempt to boycott the goods sold at Arthur's store.[18] Another agent in the city's escape system was Robert Hicks, the son of Isaac Hicks, a leading Underground Railroad figure on Long Island. The younger Hicks hid runaways in his home and sent them on to Long Island or to other relatives in Mamaroneck.[19]

There were several escape pathways that the Underground Railroad agents in New York City used to send their charges toward freedom in Canada. Some used the rail system or waterways to move them in a northwestern direction. Another system took them north to Albany. Still another conveyed the freedom seekers to Long Island, Connecticut, Massachusetts, or Rhode Island.

LONG ISLAND AND SEA ROUTES

Long Island had employed slave labor since the late 1600s. As was the case in so many other areas, when black slaves toiled in bondage, some of them sought their freedom by risking an escape. Richard S. Moss, in his analysis of newspaper accounts, discovered that between 1702 and 1825, 131 black slaves escaped from their bondage in Kings, Queens, and Suffolk Counties on Long Island. All but 23 of them were males in their twenties and thirties.[20]

Siebert mentions an escape route heading away from New York City that took fugitives to Boston, New Bedford, or Long Island. His map of the routes leading out of the city specifically shows one such pathway going over the Long Island Sound ultimately to Providence, Rhode Island; New Bedford, Connecticut; and Boston.[21] Blockson says that some freedom seekers traveled to New Haven, Connecticut, hidden on steamboats.[22] Steamboat traffic began to follow this course beginning in 1815, and New York City was connected to the four cities mentioned above early in the nineteenth century.

Long Island had a well-organized Underground Railroad that is often overlooked in discussions of slave escapes in and through the state of New York. Siebert does not list any agents on the island and mentions only in passing an alternate route from New York City that went through it.[23] That a route ran through Long Island should come as no surprise, as several of the factors needed for a successful escape operation were present there. First, the island had a large population of more than 5,000 free blacks living there in 1850.[24] Second, the Quakers had a strong presence on the western portion of the island. Third, waterway transportation existed in many places along the coast bordering Long Island Sound, where freedom seekers could cross by boat to reach Rhode Island, Connecticut, or northern New York State. Finally, a network was in place that aided runaways in their attempts to continue their journey northward.

Many black communities were scattered throughout Long Island. Most of them were near Quaker settlements, such as Westbury, Jericho, Flushing, and Jerusalem (North Bellmore). These communities provided a refuge for black slaves fleeing their bondage.[25] In some instances, the free blacks lived in Quaker towns along with whites. The old town of Flushing had a black citizenry that amounted to 25 percent of the entire population of the community. The A.M.E. Church had a presence on the island as early as 1811, with the founding of the Macedonia A.M.E. Church there.[26] Not all of the freedom-seeking blacks who came to the island continued on their journey. Many remained and blended into the numerous black communities there, and their descendants still live on the island today.[27]

The Quakers were extremely active in abolishing slavery on Long Island. As early as 1775–76, the members of the Westbury Friends Meeting manumitted 85 slaves. In 1776, they appointed Elias Hicks and Gideon Seaman to promote the freeing of slaves by all of the Quaker families living on the island. The effect of this was that 154 enslaved blacks were manumitted by 1791.[28]

The Underground Railroad network on Long Island was dominated by several families, chief among whom were the Hicks and Jackson families.[29] In addition, the families of Thomas Willis and Samuel Parson assisted in the effort to move fugitives northward to freedom.[30] The Hicks family route had its origins with Isaac Hicks, a Quaker who was trained to be a teacher and a tailor. In 1789, Hicks moved from his home in Westbury on Long Island to New York City, where he opened a grocery store on Water Street. In 1790, he married and moved to Brooklyn, where he became a partner in a lucrative whale oil business and grew quite wealthy. Hicks was active in abolitionist causes while he lived in New York. He was an original member of the Manumission Society and helped establish the African Free School in the city. After retiring from business in 1802, Hicks moved back to Westbury. He built a house and used it as a safe haven for runaways passing through Westbury. Another station in the town was located in the home of John and Lydia Hicks on Post Road, which they called the Old Place. From here, they guided freedom seekers to the Rosyln Mill at Hempstead Harbor, where they found passage on steamers and small boats crossing the sound to Westchester County, north of New York City.[31]

The Jackson family trail was an even more widely used escape path. John Jackson Jr., a Quaker, had settled in Jerusalem, Long Island, in 1687. His descendants freed their slaves between 1770 and 1830. Many of these freed people stayed in the area around Jerusalem and created a black community known as the Brush. An A.M.E. Zion church was built in the Brush in 1851 to tend to the spiritual needs of the growing community located there. The main safe house on this route operated out of the home of George Jackson, which was positioned next to Flushing Creek near Jerusalem. From this house, the route divided into two possibilities, based on avoidance of slave-catching patrols. The first path led to the Jackson mill in Jerusalem and the Brush. Fugitives reaching this area either stayed and blended into the Brush or continued on their journey. The other alternative consisted of transporting the runaways in small boats down Flushing Creek to Flushing Bay. From here, they would travel over Long Island Sound to Westchester County and the main Underground Railroad escape system that ran through the county heading northward.[32]

Two alternates to the Hicks and Jackson family routes were those operated by the Willis and Parsons families. Thomas Willis lived on a farm in Springfield near the old town of Jericho. He received fugitives sent by the Underground Railroad network in New York City. He and the other Quakers managed an escape route through Jericho by the 1840s.[33] Jericho was only six miles south of Oyster Bay, and from here, runaways were transported across the sound either to Westchester County, New York, or to Connecticut. Samuel Parsons moved to Flushing, Long Island, just before 1806. He purchased a farm and house there and moved in with his new bride, Mary

Bowne. The town of Flushing was on Flushing Creek, a waterway that was used extensively by the Underground Railroad conductors to move their charges to Long Island Sound. Parsons became very active in the Flushing Meeting of the Quakers there. He was an uncompromising opponent of slavery, in addition to helping fugitives passing through his area, he is most remembered for his work aiding those freed and self-emancipated blacks who resided in the Flushing area. It was through his efforts that a free school system, run by the Quakers, was established to educate the blacks in the region.[34]

NEW YORK CITY TO ALBANY ROUTE

The maps of Siebert and later Alexander C. Flick depict a major escape route from New York City to the state capital of Albany.[35] This leg of the journey essentially ran along the banks of the Hudson River from New York City to Albany, passing through Westchester, Rockland, Orange, Putnam, Dutchess, Ulster, Greene, and Columbia Counties. As indicated by the data in Table 5, this was an ideal stretch for an escape path, for it contained a population of 12,229 free blacks, 60 Quaker meetinghouses, 88 Baptist churches, 232 Methodist churches, and 88 Presbyterian churches in 1850. In addition, by 1812, New York City was connected to Albany by a major road and many other less-developed roads interlaced the area all along the Hudson River. The Erie Canal coursed between the two cities, with steamboats making regular runs, and finally the New York Central Railroad also linked the two major sites.[36]

Although Siebert outlines the route between New York City and Albany on his map of Underground Railroad routes, he does not give details of any stopping places along the pathway between the two cities. His map seems to assume that the fugitives were hidden or given passage on canal boats, steamboats, and railcars in New York City and sent directly to Albany in this fashion. Modern research, however, offers a more complete view of the escape system between the two cities, including land routes that freedom seekers would have taken.

From New York City, the first stop on one route to Albany appears to have been at the home of an agent named Joseph Carpenter, who operated an Underground Railroad station in New Rochelle, not too distant from the city. Most fugitives came to him from the city, although he did receive some from Long Island, as well. When it came time to send his guests on to the next point on their journey, there were two or three options. One was to send them eastward to Connecticut, where they would enter the New England system once they got across the state line. The second option was to forward them on to Joseph Pierce or Judge John Jay. Pierce was an agent who lived in the town of Pleasantville in northern Westchester County, and Jay was his brother-in-law. From either of these two safe houses, the fugitives would be guided to the home of David Irish in Quaker Hill.[37] A third possibility was that they simply went eastward for about a mile and crossed over into Connecticut.

Tom Calarco offers another variation on the route from New York City to Dutchess County. He has a path heading from the city to the town of Nyack, on the western banks of the Hudson in Rockland County. Edward Hesdra was the agent there, and he was assisted by a conductor named John W. Towot.[38] Freedom seekers were either led by Towot or came on their own, following directions given earlier, from the Hudson. They followed MacGregory Brook, near the town of Peekskill, to a safe house located on the brook. A secret room where runaways could hide was accessed by way of a secret staircase in the house. Peekskill was located in the northeastern corner of Westchester County, right on the Hudson River. The A.M.E. Zion Church in Peekskill, the oldest black church in the community and one of the oldest in the entire county, had a hiding place behind a secret panel behind the pulpit made to conceal fugitives. Local legend has William Sand offering his home as safe haven for fugitives, and an excape tunnel was supposed to have existed on the property of abolitionist Henry Ward Beecher. Harriet Tubman traveled through Peekskill while guiding fugitives to freedom in Canada. She used the A.M.E. Zion church in Peekskill as a stopping place.[39] An alternate to this route ran through Orange County, where there were many safe houses.[40] There were 2,464 free blacks living in the county in 1850, as well as a Quaker population with five meeting houses. More research needs to be done, however, to identify specific stations. Those freedom seekers who left Peekskill proceeded through Putnam County. Once again, more research is needed to identify the stopping places in that county, which certainly must have existed. After traversing Putnam County, the travelers would have entered Dutchess County, a region rich with Underground Railroad stations and agents.

Fugitives crossing into Dutchess County had several locales where they could find a safe haven. One of these was the home of David Irish in Quaker Hill, to the southwest of Poughkeepsie. Another possibility was to stay in the black community of Baxtertown, about a third of the way between the county line and Poughkeepsie. Upon reaching Poughkeepsie, the fugitives stayed with Uriah Boston, a black barber and abolitionist, or Rev. Charles Van Loon, the pastor of the First Baptist Church of Poughkeepsie.[41]

The route from Poughkeepsie appears to have divided at some point as it progressed northward toward Albany. Fugitives could stay in Underground Railroad safe havens on either side of the Hudson River before reaching the state capital. One route continued along the eastern side of the river through Dutchess County into Columbia County. Eventually it came to the town of Hudson, forty-five miles north of Poughkeepsie. Residing in the town were Joseph Peri, William Green, and C. Van Husen, who all were members of the Northern Star Association, an organization that provided financial support for two abolitionist papers, the *Northern Star* and the *Freeman's Advocate.* The association also played a role in the Underground Railroad by offering aid and comfort to fugitives passing through Hudson.[42] Because of the distance between Poughkeepsie and Hudson, there must have been other sites along that pathway. Fugitives on foot, or even those hidden in some conveyance by an Underground Railroad conductor, would have a hard time traveling that far without a stopping place along the way. From Hudson, the travelers appear to have gone either directly to Albany, thirty-four miles up the river, or to the town of Sand Lake, eleven miles west of Albany. From Sand Lake, they could have continued on to Albany or in some cases to Troy, about thirteen miles to the northwest. R. Johnson was an agent in Sand Lake, as was Abel Brown, who pastored the Sand Lake Baptist Church there.[43]

A second route ran along the western side of the Hudson River. Siebert lists two Underground Railroad agents active in Ulster County, a Colonel Colby and someone named Chase. In addition, Catskill and Athens, two towns in Greene County (to the north of Ulster County), had stations. Fugitives also could have accessed this route by crossing the Hudson River at some point north of Poughkeepsie but south of Hudson. In Catskill, a site was operated by the local agent there, Martin Cross.[44] In addition, the town had a large population of free blacks who could have given aid to runaways.[45] A few miles north of Catskill, the town of Athens, right across the river from Hudson, had a site in the home of William Thompson. Both Cross and Thompson were members of the Northern Star Association.[46] This route then most likely proceeded to Clarksville, in Albany County which had a resident agent named James C. Jackson.[47] From here, fugitives would have had two choices. They could go ten miles to the northeast, to the extensive escape network in Albany, or they could proceed fifteen miles to the north, to the town of Schenectady, which also had an Underground Railroad station.

THE ALBANY SYSTEM

Albany was the pivotal point in the Eastern Network of the Underground Railroad in New York. It is the northernmost station in the eastern portion of New York on Siebert's map, and the escape path splits into two major routes here. One goes east into Vermont, and the other west toward Buffalo.[48] However, the work of Paul and Liz Stewart, along with that of Tom Calarco, has shown that more options left Albany than Siebert imagined.

The town had more than two dozen sites and agents active in its Underground Railroad system. They were scattered throughout the city but tended to extend in a line from the southern part of town to its northern section. Siebert identifies Gen. William L. Chaplin, E. C. Delavan, E. W. Goodwin, Dr. James C. Jackson, Abigail and Lydia Mott, Stephen Myers, and a person named Williams as agents in Albany.[49] Chaplin was an activist who was arrested in Rockville, Maryland, for helping two men who had been enslaved by congressional members of Georgia. He spent time in a Washington, D.C., jail for his efforts and was eventually freed on a bail of $25,000. Delavan was a wealthy man who had helped finance the New York Temperance Union, built the Delavan House Hotel in Albany, and supported the antislavery settlers in Kansas. Goodwin served as one of the editors of the *Albany Patriot*, an abolitionist paper in the city, and was a member of the Albany Vigilance Committee. Jackson, an editor of the *Albany Patriot* and *Liberty Press*, was active in the Underground Railroad in Albany County and Oswego.[50] The Mott sisters were Quakers who regularly aided fugitives passing through the city from the late 1820s onward and were instrumental in forming the Albany Female Antislavery Society. They owned several businesses in Albany, including a linen goods store, boardinghouse, and clothing store that they operated at 524 Broadway.[51] Lydia tutored the nine-year-old daughter of Frederick Douglass in the late 1850s. Myers, a freed black man, began to help fugitives escape as early as 1831. He published two abolitionist newspapers, the *Northern Star* and the *Freeman's Advocate*, and he headed the Albany Vigilance Committee from the late 1840s to 1861.[52] Myers used his homes at 194 Livingston Avenue and on Third Street in Arbor Hill as safe havens for runaways passing through the city.[53] Calarco identified the Williams on Siebert's list as Chauncey P. Williams, a lumber merchant in Albany.[54]

Other individuals and sites have emerged since Siebert compiled his list. Three black churches in Albany were Underground Railroad sites. One was the African Baptist Church, on lower Hamilton Street between South Pearl Street and Grand Street. An early pastor, Rev. Nathaniel Paul, garnered support for refugee communities for runaways living in Canada in the 1830s. Another was the Israel A.M.E. Church, also on Hamilton Street, but farther up. This church was the oldest congregation still in operation in upstate New York. The Second Wesleyan Chapel, located on Third Street in Arbor Hill, also aided fugitives. Its pastor, Rev. John Sands, led an effort in the church to hide and assist freedom seekers passing through the city.

In 1842, Abel Brown, mentioned earlier in connection with Sand Lake, moved to Albany, where he helped start the Eastern New York Anti-Slavery Society. The society's offices were at 9 Exchange Street, in the heart of Albany, and runaways were hidden there at times. Brown also was instrumental in the creation of an abolitionist newspaper published in Albany called the *Tocsin of Liberty*. The paper had its offices at several locations in the city, including 56 State Street and 8 South Pearl Street.[55] These offices also served as hiding places for fugitives.[56] The Albany Vigilance Committee, located at 198 Lumber Street and headed by Stephen Myers, played a major role in the successful operation of the Underground Railroad system in this town. A key member of the committee was Thomas Elkins, a resident of the Arbor Hill section. Elkins was a black apothecary who served as the committee's secretary in 1856. Other participants in Underground Railroad activities sponsored by the committee were William Topp, a tailor who lived at 547 Broadway; a ferry boat captain named Abraham Johnson; William Gardner; James Wood; Richard Wright; Rev. J. J. Kelley; and Minos McGown, a lumber company owner whose business was on North Pearl Street. Although not listed as a member of the committee, William H. Johnson, a black barber in the city, was a member of Myers's Northern Star Association and hence an active member of the railroad.[57] Calarco completes the list of agents and conductors in the city with Richard Thompson, Mrs. Dilzey Dennison, Nathaniel Safford, Tappan Townsend, William Tweed Dale, Benjamin Cutler, William Matthews, and C. Brooks.[58]

Freedom seekers leaving the city of Albany essentially went in one of three directions: northeast to Vermont, north toward Canada, or west to Syracuse and ultimately Buffalo. To reach their goals on these three general routes, the fugitives passed through Rensselaer, Washington, Essex, Clinton, Schenectady, Saratoga, Warren, and Franklin counties. Table 5 shows that in this area, there were 2,645 free blacks, 15 Quaker meetinghouses, and 120 Methodist, 74 Baptist, and 66 Presbyterian congregations available to give possible assistance around the pivotal years of the late 1840s and early 1850s.

Three general escape paths existed, but they were not totally independent and intersected at times.

ALBANY NORTHEASTWARD ROUTE

Siebert's map depicts a route that left Albany and proceeded northeastward to Troy. From here, fugitives had two options: continue northeast and enter Vermont, with its extensive escape system, or turn north and head toward Canada along New York's eastern border.[59] Troy was only about six miles from Albany in Rensselaer County. In 1823, the Champlain Canal opened, running from Albany to Lake Champlain and passing through Troy. In 1841, the bond between the two towns was further solidified when a rail line ran between them.[60] It was only twenty-eight miles from Troy to the town of Bennington, Vermont.

Troy had a well-established Underground Railroad system with several prominent agents and conductors. Siebert cites two of them, John H. Hooper and Rev. Fayette Shipherd.[61] Hooper was a black worker who served as head of the Troy Vigilance Committee in the 1850s.[62] Shipherd was the pastor of the Free Congregational Church in the town. Another clergyman active in the cause in Troy was Henry H. Garnet, pastor of the Liberty Street Presbyterian Church.[63] Three other agents assisting fugitives passing through the town were James G. Stewart, William Rich, and a person named Willingham.[64] These individuals assisted the runaways on the next leg of their journey. Most of the freedom seekers continued to move eastward to Bennington. Another option was for them to head north, as outlined below.

ALBANY NORTHWARD ROUTES

Seibert's map clearly shows the route from Albany to Troy and Bennington, but also depicts the beginning of a northern route coming from Troy and proceeding up the Hudson Valley.[65] Calarco, Stewart, and Blockson have offered the possibility that several escape paths began in Albany and headed to the northern border of New York. Two lay east of Albany and one west. The two that began to the east of Albany are discussed first, and a description of the one to the west follows.

Albany–Troy–Lake Champlain–Rouses Point Route

Siebert describes a route that began in Albany, passed through Troy, and then, instead of going into Vermont, turned northward and proceeded to Lake Champlain, reaching the town of Rouses Point on the New York–Canada border. The fugitives then crossed into Canada and freedom.[66] This route essentially proceeded overland from Troy until it reached the Champlain Canal, which broke off from the Hudson River just below Hudson Falls and then went north to Lake Champlain. Steamboat traffic on the lake further facilitated the fugitives in their attempt to reach Rouses Point.[67] There is also the strong possibility that some freedom seekers reached Lake Champlain by hiding or being placed on canal boats leaving Albany and going up the Hudson directly to the Champlain Canal.

The first stopping place on the overland portion of this route was in the town of Hoosick Falls, in the northeastern corner of Rensselaer County, near the border with Washington County, about twenty-one miles from Troy.[68] The home of Garret Van Hoosen served as a safe house in the town.[69] From here, the pathway began to follow a zigzag pattern typical of Underground Railroad escape routes. The course cut back toward the Hudson River to the town of Union Village, now Greenwich. The fugitive was now in Washington County at this point. The route now divided into two possibilities. One path continued north for about ten miles to Argyle.[70] The second path went back northeastward, along what later became NY Routes 29 and 22, to the small town of Salem, forty miles north of Troy and only three miles from the Vermont border.[71]

At this juncture, some of the fugitives probably went the short distance into Vermont, others went on to Argyle, and still other proceeded northward to Granville. From Argyle, Underground Railroad agents guided the fugitives in one of two possible directions: either back toward the Hudson, to the town of Hudson Falls, or toward Vermont to Granville.[72] Those freedom seekers arriving at Hudson Falls could use the Champlain Canal, either by secretly boarding canal boats or by following the towpaths that ran alongside the canal, and continue their journey northward. The next stop for them was Fort Ann on the canal, where the overland and waterway routes merged into one. Those who had gone to Granville had two options: either cross into Vermont, as the town was on the border, or turn east again and head back to the canal and Fort Ann.[73]

This route then proceeded along the canal through Essex County into Clinton County. Once it reached Lake Champlain, there were several places where the freedom seekers could board steamboats and go north on the lake to Rouses Point. Two of the more prominent ones were Westport, on the southern end of the lake, and Plattsburgh, in the center of the eastern shore of the lake.[74] Calarco identifies another site, the town of Keeseville, which was a few miles from the lake between Westport and Plattsburgh. He also identifies the Bigelow family as offering assistance to fugitives in their home there.[75]

Albany–Troy–North Elba Route

Siebert alludes to another possible escape path from Troy up the Hudson Valley to the farm of John Brown, near the town of North Elba and Lake Placid.[76] He does not detail this route on his map, other than to have a line of march leaving Troy for a brief distance to the Hudson River, with the notation "TO ROUSES POINT." Farther up the map, he notes the location of John Brown's farm near North Elba.[77] In addition to the Brown farm, there was another settlement that would have given assistance to fugitives passing through the area. James McCune Smith, in a letter to Gerrit Smith dated February 6, 1850, reports on the disposition of 120,000 acres of land Gerrit had donated for the use of black settlers near North Elba. It was his job to promote the donation and screen potential settlers for the region. In the letter, James describes finding more than sixty black settlers in North Elba during a recent visit. He then gives a detailed report of their dwellings, occupations, and general positive attitude.[78] Flick's map of the Underground Railroad in New York also traces a route from Albany through Troy, northward to Westport on Lake Champlain, and from there to North Elba, and then back to Lake Champlain near Plattsburgh.[79]

A closer examination of the routes identified by more modern scholarship, coupled with the topography of the region, reveals the route's most probable course. As the earlier statements are in agreement that the route ran through Troy and then headed north to North Elba, in all likelihood it probably coincided with the overland route from Troy through Union Village (Greenwich), Argyle, Hudson Falls, and Fort Ann. From here, the escape path continued on to Westport and Lake Champlain. This is where Flick has his alternate route heading westward to North Elba, and then doubling back to the lake at Plattsburgh. Perhaps a better conjecture is that North Elba was an objective on a route that began in Albany and ran up the western side of the Hudson River. North Elba lies directly in the route's line of march to sites in Schroon Lake and Malone. From North Elba, instead of turning eastward to Plattsburgh, it seems more likely that the route would have followed the natural terrain of the region and followed the roads (now NY Routes 86 and 30) going to Saranac Lake and the town of Malone, not far from the Canadian border.

Albany–Schenectady–Ballston Spa–Constable Route

Another escape path proceeded from Albany and headed north by way of Schenectady. Schenectady lay only twelve miles to the northwest of Albany and was a major staging area for the route that ran west all the way to Buffalo.

*The famous abolitionist John Brown. He operated an Underground Railroad
station in his farm in North Elba, New York.* LIBRARY OF CONGRESS

Some fugitives, however, turned north at Schenectady and took a route that ran almost directly to Canada. The first stop on this route was the town of Ballston Spa in Saratoga County, only fifteen miles north of Schenectady. A. White was the Underground Railroad agent in the town.[80] From here, runaways had two possibilities for the next leg of their journey: They could go to Saratoga Springs or Glens Falls. In Saratoga Springs, six miles to the northeast, they would be in the care of John Van Pelt.[81] They could then travel to Greenfield, where Underground Railroad agent Mason Anthony took care of them. There were two alternate routes from Greenfield. Anthony could forward them west to the home of John Barker in Edinburg, where they would enter the Central Network of New York's Underground Railroad, or continue to send them northward to Lake Luzerne.[82]

Freedom seekers going from Ballston Spa to Glens Falls, located across the Hudson River from Hudson Falls, could stay at a number of safe houses in the town, most of which were operated by Quakers. Calarco states that the route turned back westward at this point toward Lake Luzerne.[83] A case could be made, however, for an alternate that took fugitives the short distance across the Hudson to Hudson Falls. From there, they would have headed toward Lake Champlain. On leaving the Lake Luzerne region, the fugitives went to either Johnsburg or Chestertown, where two Wesleyan Methodist ministers operated stations—Rev. Enos Putnam in Johnsburg, and Rev. Thomas Baker in Chestertown. Whether the runaways stayed in Johnsburg or Chestertown, the next leg of the journey had them converging on the town of Igerna, where they stayed at the home of the Perry family. They then headed north through Schroon Lake and North Elba in Essex County to the town of Malone in Franklin County. The Harison family and the Malone Presbyterian Church offered sanctuary to weary travelers at this point. The final stage of the journey on this route went from Malone to Canada, traveling ten miles north through Constable or fifteen miles northwest through Fort Covington.[84] An alternate route left Malone and headed westward to Brasher Falls. From here, it proceeded to the Central Network.

ALBANY WESTWARD ROUTE

Another route began in Albany and went twelve miles northwest to Schenectady. The lines of communication between these two cities were very strong. The Erie Canal linked the two early in the 1800s, and in 1841, a railroad ran between them. The New York Central Railroad later joined the two even more strongly in 1851.[85] Both of these transportation systems further linked

Albany with Buffalo on Lake Erie, not far from Niagara and the Canadian border. The main agent in Schenectady was Francis Dana.[86] Dana sent most of the freedom seekers who passed through the city westward and into the Central Network, although some were sent northward to Ballston Spa. In either case, Schenectady served as a critical marshaling point in the operation of the Eastern Network.

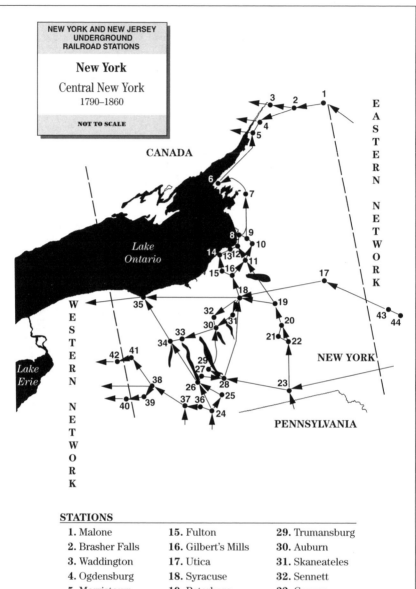

CANADA

E
A
S
T
E
R
N

N
E
T
W
O
R
K

Lake
Ontario

Lake
Erie

W
E
S
T
E
R
N

N
E
T
W
O
R
K

NEW YORK

PENNSYLVANIA

STATIONS

1. Malone	15. Fulton	29. Trumansburg
2. Brasher Falls	16. Gilbert's Mills	30. Auburn
3. Waddington	17. Utica	31. Skaneateles
4. Ogdensburg	18. Syracuse	32. Sennett
5. Morristown	19. Peterboro	33. Geneva
6. Cape Vincent	20. Lebanon	34. Canandaigua
7. Watertown	21. Plymouth	35. Rochester
8. Port Ontario	22. Norwich	36. Big Flats
9. Pulaski	23. Binghamton	37. Corning
10. Richland	24. Elmira	38. Hornellsville
11. Mexico	25. Spencer	39. Alfred
12. New Haven	26. Watkins Glen	40. Scio
13. Scriba	27. Burdett	41. Mt. Morris
14. Oswego	28. Ithaca	42. Perry

New York—The Central Routes

The Central Network of New York's Underground Railroad consisted of a large portion of the state, stretching roughly from seventy-five to the seventy-eight degrees west longitude. Pennsylvania bordered it to the south and accounted for the majority of entry points into the network. Lake Ontario, with Canada on its northern shore, lay to the north. The area was an extension of the Appalachian ridges and valleys that ran through Pennsylvania northward. This terrain, filled with valleys, mountains, rivers, and streams, made for an ideal setting with many natural escape paths.

Twenty-four counties lay within this network, some of them also overlapping with the Eastern and Western Networks. Most of these counties were not as well populated as the ones in the Eastern Network, but they still had pockets where freedom seekers could find aid. Several cities of reasonable size, such as Syracuse and Rochester, existed there, as well as numerous small towns, villages, and farms. Table 6 provides a picture of the demographics of this network.[1]

These data reveal some interesting characteristics of the makeup of the population of the Central Network. The number of free blacks is far lower than the 35,553 that existed in the Eastern Network, although there were many free blacks and former fugitives who were instrumental in the successful operation of the escape routes through this part of the state. The number of Quakers living here also was much smaller. There were only twenty-eight meetinghouses in the central portion of the state, whereas the eastern region had ninety. Because of this, there were far fewer Quaker agents and conductors here. The number of Methodist congregations was basically the same as in the Eastern Network, but there were more Presbyterian churches and nearly twice as many Baptist. The region that made up the Central Network was largely agricultural, so it should come as no surprise that it had a smaller overall population.

As far as direct participation in the Underground Railroad, Siebert lists sixty-two agents scattered among ten of the twenty-four counties found in

TABLE 6.
DEMOGRAPHIC DATA FOR NEW YORK'S
CENTRAL NETWORK IN 1850

County	Free blacks	Quaker meeting-houses	Methodist churches	Baptist churches	Presbyterian churches
Allegany	128 (.34%)	0	16	14	12
Broome	431 (1.4%)	0	20	16	12
Cayuga	543 (.98%)	6	23	22	20
Chemung	286 (.99%)	0	9	7	7
Chenango	264 (.65%)	1	28	38	12
Cortland	42 (.17%)	0	15	14	5
Delaware	201 (.50%)	0	22	10	18
Herkimer	203 (.53%)	0	8	11	2
Jefferson	191 (.28%)	2	33	22	13
Lewis	42 (.17%)	0	12	8	4
Livingston	209 (.51%)	0	21	13	23
Madison	298 (.69%)	4	22	23	8
Monroe	699 (.80%)	0	23	22	19
Oneida	672 (.67%)	4	43	29	23
Onondaga	613 (.71%)	0	33	24	20
Ontario	610 (1.4%)	3	21	15	11
Oswego	215 (.35%)	0	21	15	13
Otsego	175 (.36%)	4	31	29	16
Seneca	181 (.71%)	0	15	11	7
Steuben	371 (.58%)	0	31	22	22
St. Lawrence	39 (.06%)	0	30	14	15
Tioga	197 (.79%)	0	12	7	3
Tompkins	325 (.84%)	1	31	18	13
Wayne	268 (.60%)	3	23	17	13
Totals	7,203 (.62%)	28	543	421	311

the network: Allegany (one); Chemung (two); Chenango (one); Livingston
(one); Madison (two); Monroe (thirty-six); Oneida (one); Onondaga (eight);
Oswego (eight); and Steuben (two).[2] The work of Judith Wellman, Tom
Calarco, and the material on the websites at Oswego and Rochester Uni-

verisities has shown many more individuals were involved in the escape network than Siebert had been aware of.

The Central Network had excellent lines of communication. The Erie Canal traversed the entirety of the network, stretching from Albany to Buffalo. In addition, smaller canals linked the town of Rome to Lake Ontario by way of Watertown, Syracuse, and Oswego; the Susquehanna River near Elmira to the Erie Canal just west of Syracuse; and this same river from Binghamton to the Erie Canal just east of Rome. In addition to the canal network, rail lines linked New York City to Albany, Schenectady, Troy, Buffalo, Rochester, and Utica by 1841. These lines were all tied together with the creation of the New York Central Railroad, which also expanded, by way of spur lines, into most of the towns of central New York in 1851. The southern counties of the Central Network were further tied together with the inception of the Erie Railroad, which took passengers to Buffalo.[3] Maps from the period show that all of the towns and cities in the region were connected with an extensive road system.

The system of escape paths running through the Central Network was fairly complex. Siebert's map shows three entry and five exit points in the system. It also depicts routes that are essentially straightforward and simple to follow.[4] In reality, however, the system was much more complicated. It had at least seven entry points, five of which came from towns in northern Pennsylvania—Montrose, Friendsville, Towanda, Springfield, and Williamsport—and two from eastern New York, Schenectady and Malone. The network also had at least nine escape path systems. Each one of these was also much more complicated than Siebert's map depicts, and many involved towns and locations that do not appear on his map. The picture of the Central Network that has now emerged is one of an interwoven system of pathways moving back and forth through the region and involving a great number of people, both black and white.

SCHENECTADY TO SYRACUSE AND POINTS WEST

There were two routes that freedom seekers used coming from eastern New York. The first began in Albany and headed west through the town of Schenectady. Siebert quotes Frederick Douglass as saying that this was one of the main escape systems that ran from Philadelphia through New York and Albany to Rochester by way of Syracuse, and eventually Canada.[5] It was also one of the two routes that Harriet Tubman later revealed she had used to get to Buffalo.[6]

Harriet Tubman, seated on the far right, shortly before her death at her home in Auburn, New York, that she also kept as an Underground Railroad station.
SCHOMBURG CENTER FOR RESEARCH IN BLACK CULTURE, NEW YORK PUBLIC LIBRARY

Schenectady lies only twelve miles to the northwest of Albany, and both the Erie Canal and a rail line connected the two towns. Francis Dana was the chief Underground Railroad agent in Schenectady, and he sent freedom seekers passing through his station either westward to Utica or northward to Ballston Spa. Utica lay eighty-one miles northwest of Schenectady and was connected to that town by the Erie Canal, the New York Central Railroad, and a road that eventually became Interstate 90. Utica had a strong Anti-Slavery Society and was to be the site of the organizational meeting of the New York Anti-Slavery Society in 1835 until an antiabolitionist mob forced transfer of the meeting elsewhere. It was the site of the successful rescue of two fugitive slaves who were apprehended by the local police and being held in the Utica jail. A force of black and white abolitionists broke into the jail and set them free in January 1837.[7] An A.M.E. congregation formed in the town as early as 1828, giving testimony to a black community there.[8] Siebert also lists an agent named Alvan Stewart operating in the area.[9] From Utica, the escape course went to Syracuse.

Syracuse lies in Onondaga County and was a major hub of the Underground Railroad. Several routes converged on the town, and freedom seekers had at least five major options when leaving. It was only fifty-four miles from Utica and shared the same lines of communication that linked Utica to

Schenectady. References to its importance appear on Siebert's map and in the text of his work. He cites Rev. Jermain W. Loguen as the chief Underground Railroad agent in Syracuse, with six other agents and conductors working with him there. Loguen escaped from bondage in the South, and came to Syracuse in 1841, finding that the town possessed an antiabolitionist attitude that was promoted by local political and religious figures. An Onondaga County Anti-Slavery Society, formed in 1835, functioned in the area, but it faced strong opposition by the establishment in Syracuse. But a number of people, mostly members of the Presbyterian, M.E., and Congregational churches in the town, were abolitionists at heart. When Loguen arrived, he stayed with a Doctor Adams for a while, until he purchased his own house. In Syracuse, he immediately got involved in activities to aid other fugitives and their families. He opened a school for the children of the blacks living there, in which he taught them how to read and write. He also applied for and was granted a license as an elder in the A.M.E. Church. Loguen quickly became an effective speaker against slavery. The Church sent him to work in the towns of Cortland, Bath, and Ithaca for a total of five years, before he returned to minister in a church in Syracuse. After a two-year stay in that town, he was sent to Troy, where he preached until 1850. Returning to Syracuse, he helped establish the Syracuse Vigilance Committee to aid fugitives fleeing under the Fugitive Slave Act of 1850.[10]

A famous antislavery event took place during Loguen's stay in Syracuse. It has become known as the "Jerry Rescue." On October 1, 1851, a fugitive slave named Jerry was captured by some marshals and their posse and brought to the local commissioner's office in Syracuse for arraignment. The famous Gerrit Smith and Leonard Gibbs were his legal representatives. Word quickly spread throughout the city, and a huge crowd descended on the office. When the hearing adjourned for dinner, Jerry managed to run from the room, despite the fetters on his feet and hands. He was caught only half a mile away and taken to the local police department. The people following these events determined to set Jerry free and stormed the building. The marshal in charge petitioned a captain of the state militia for help, but before the militia could be organized, the colonel in charge of the troops countered the order and refused to give the marshals any aid. The mob then broke into the building, causing many of the posse members to flee and wounding those that stayed. They freed Jerry, guided him to safety in Oswego, and put him on a boat for Canada. Warrants were issued for the arrest of the mob's leaders as they had violated the law by participating in the rescue.

Pressed by his friends, Loguen went to the town of Skaneateles to avoid being arrested. He stayed there with a Mrs. Lydia Fuller. From there, he was taken to Rochester and the home of Samuel D. Porter, who saw to it that Loguen boarded a boat for Lewiston, where he crossed the bridge into Canada. He settled in St. Catharines and preached in the local A.M.E. church. In the spring of 1852, he returned to Syracuse, determined to face the charges lodged against him. While on a train to Skaneateles to retrieve his horse and carriage, which he had left there in his earlier escape, he encountered the marshal and some of the posse from the Jerry incident. He boldly sat with them and even engaged them in conversation. A few women also traveling on the train thought Loguen had been arrested and was being transported south. They spread word, and a huge crowd materialized at Auburn, the next station of the route. Back in Syracuse, another large crowd formed when word reached them of what was happening. But the women had misunderstood what was taking place, for no attempt was made to arrest Loguen, and he returned to Syracuse to a joyous reception. Loguen continued to speak out against slavery and aid fugitives right to the end of that institution. His fame as an Underground Railroad leader spread far and wide, and he received financial aid from individuals and groups in places as distant as Great Britain.[11] He reported that he had helped a total of fifteen hundred freedom seekers as they passed through Syracuse.[12]

Siebert also refers to several other agents in the Syracuse area: Abner Bates, Rev. Luther Lee, Rev. Samuel J. May, Rev. Ovid Minor, and two individuals he simply calls Barbour and Carson.[13] A tanner with a shop in town, Bates was a member of the Congregational Church. Lee was a Wesleyan Methodist minister, May a Unitarian minister, and Minor a Congregational minister.[14] Further testimony to the Underground Railroad activity in Syracuse comes from William Still, who cites three letters he received from fugitives, John Thompson, William Cooper, and Manual T. White, who had passed through the city.[15] The following letter from Loguen to Still gives a glimpse of the Underground Railroad system in Syracuse and the human side of leaving all behind in order to gain one's freedom.

SYRACUSE, Oct. 5, 1856

Dear Friend Still:—I write to you for Mrs. Susan Bell, who was at your city some time in September last. She is from Washington city. She left her dear little children behind (two children). She is stopping in our city, and wants to hear from her children very much indeed. She wishes to know if you have heard from Mr. Biglow, of Washington city. She will remain here until she can hear from you. She feels very anxious about her children, I will assure you. I should have written before this, but I have been from home much of the time since she came to our city. She wants to know if Mr.

Biglow has heard anything about her husband. If you have not written to Mr. Biglow, she wishes you would. She sends her love to you and your dear family. She says that you were all kind to her, and she does not forget it. You will direct your letter to me, dear brother, and I will see that she gets it.

Miss F. E. Watkins left our house yesterday for Ithaca, and other places in that part of the State. Frederick Douglass, Wm. J. Watkins and others were with us last week; Gerritt Smith with others. Miss Watkins is doing great good in our part of the State. We think much indeed of her. She is such a good and glorious speaker, that we are all charmed with her. We have had thirty-one fugitives in the last twenty-seven days; but you no doubt, have had many more than that. I hope the good Lord may bless you and spare your long to do good to the hunted and outraged among our brethren.

Yours truly,   J. W. Loguen
Agent of the Underground Railroad.[16]

A letter to Still from Manual White sheds more light on the operation of the Syracuse network and Loguen's role in it.

SYRACUSE, July 29, 1857

My Dear Friend Mr. Still:—I got safe to Syracuse, and found the house of our friend, Mr. J. W. Loguen. Many thanks to you for your kindness to me. I wish to say to you, dear sir, that I expect my clothes will be sent to Dr. Landa, and I wish, if you please, get them and send them to the care of Mr. Loguen, at Syracuse, for me. He will be in possession of my where-abouts and will send them to me. Remember me to Mr. Landa and Miss Millen Jespan, and much to you and your family.

Truly Yours,   Manual T. White.[17]

Freedom seekers had five options. They could go west to Rochester and continue on to Niagara; they could head to Oswego and cross Lake Ontario at that point; or they could proceed by one of three different routes to the southwest and go to Auburn or Ithaca, and from there to Niagara by a southern route.[18]

SYRACUSE TO ROCHESTER

Rochester was the largest town in Monroe County. It had strong canal, rail, and road links with Syracuse, ninety-seven miles to its east. Being a port city across Lake Ontario from Canada, it was an ideal setting for an Underground Railroad station. Siebert has thirty-six active agents listed for Monroe County, most of whom operated in Rochester. The chief of them was the great anti-slavery figure Frederick Douglass. Of these, fourteen were most prominent: Asa, Daniel, and Amy Anthony, the uncle, father, and sister of the famous activist Susan B. Anthony; George A. Avery, who founded the Monroe County Bible Society and used his shop at 12 Buffalo Street (now Main Street) as a station; William Bishop, a minister at the town's A.M.E. Zion Church; William Bloss, who lived on Lower East Avenue and published the abolitionist paper *Rights of Man* in the 1830s; Drs. L. C. Dolley and Sarah Adamson, physicians who lived on East Avenue next to Bloss; William S. Falls, a foreman at the *Daily Democrat*, in the same building as the offices of the famous abolitionist paper *North Star*, who hid fugitives in the press room; former slave Thomas James, pastor of the Rochester A.M.E. Church, which also served as an Underground Railroad station; Lindley M. Moore, a teacher who was the first head of the Rochester Anti-Slavery Society; Samuel D. Porter, the first secretary of the Rochester Anti-Slavery Society, who used his barn as a hiding place for runaways; Ashley S. Sampson, whose house on Brooks Avenue was a safe house; and Edward C. Williams, who hid freedom seekers in the sail loft of his ship equipment business on Buffalo Street.[19] The other active agents and conductors—Nelson Bostwick, Rhoda Degarmo, Benjamin Fich, Grove S. Gilbert, George H. Humphrey, Joseph Marsh, Amy Post, and Henry Quinby—were not as prominent.[20] Another source of assistance for fugitives in the city came from the A.M.E. church, which dated back to 1828.[21] From Rochester, fugitives could go by way of Lake Ontario directly to Canada or continue overland and enter the Western Network with Niagara as their goal.

Syracuse to Oswego

Oswego was only forty miles north of Syracuse. The Oswego River and Oswego Canal ran between the two towns. Oswego was a port on Lake Ontario and the largest city in Oswego County. Siebert identifies it as an Underground Railroad site and lists George L. Bragdon, Edward Fox, someone named French, James C. Jackson, George Salmon, William Layman Salmon, Ard. H. Stevens, and Asa S. Wing as the principal activists in the county's system.[22] Jackson first served as an operative in Albany County and the town of Mexico. He came to Oswego at the urging of Gerrit Smith and lived near him in the town of Petersboro. Jackson became the editor of the abolitionist papers *Albany Patriot* and *Liberty Press*.[23] Still reports that he received two letters from a fugitive who stayed in Oswego, Oscar D. Bell.[24]

The findings of Siebert along with more recent scholarship reveal that in addition to the town of Oswego, the county also had Underground Railroad stations in Fulton, Gilbert's Mills, Pulaski, New Haven, Richland, Schroeppel, Scriba, and Mexico, each of which had its own agents and conductors.[25] Fugitives left Syracuse and most likely followed either the Oswego River or Canal northward. After about fifteen miles, near the town of Phoenix, they had two alternatives. One took them farther down the river to the town of Fulton, from which they continued onward to Oswego. The other went northeast to the town of Gilbert's Mills, where fugitives faced two more options: continue to Oswego on a route that paralleled the river or go farther to the northeast and follow the road (now NY Route 3) to Mexico.

Mexico lay sixteen miles east of Oswego and thirty miles north of Syracuse. This town was quite active in the abolitionist cause and sent letters to the U.S. Congress opposing the admission to the Union of slave states. Several families here opened their homes to freedom seekers heading north. Asa and Caroline Wing lived on the north side of NY Route 69, near the intersection with U.S. Route 11. They aided fugitives who came from Syracuse in their home, then sent them either to Oswego or farther north up NY Route 3 to Cape Vincent, by way of Richland and Pulaski. George Bragdon was the agent in Richland. In addition to receiving freedom seekers from Gilbert's Mills, he also hid those who came from Petersboro.[27] Those going to New Haven would have stopped at the Kilburne residence. D. Kilburne attended meetings of the Mexico Anti-Slavery Society, where he admitted in August 1836 that he had helped fugitives who had come to his home.[28] Starr and Harriet Clark also aided fugitives in Mexico. Clark had a tin shop on Main Street in New Haven and hid fugitives there from the 1830s to the beginning of the Civil War.[29] He sent his visitors on to the farm of Asa and Mary Beebe outside Oswego. Orson Ames also lived on Main Street of New Haven and had a tannery across the street from his home. He operated a sawmill and a shoemaker's shop as well. He was quite active on the Mexico Vigilance Committee and used his many buildings as hiding places for runaways. From New Haven, fugitives passed through a station in Scriba before entering Oswego.[30]

The town of Oswego had a number of agents active in the cause. Charles and Flora Ann Smith, Tudor and Marie Grant, John B. and Lydia Edwards, and Asa and Mary Beebe offered aid and comfort to freedom seekers passing through the town. Charles Smith had come to Oswego as a fugitive slave. He had escaped from Maryland in 1840, and after spending some time in Canada, he returned to Oswego and opened a barbershop in the basement of a building on the corner of West First Street and Bridge Street in the 1850s.[31]

Tudor Grant was also a former slave who had fled from Maryland. He came to Oswego in 1832, and like Smith he opened a barbershop. Grant was very active on the Oswego Vigilance Committee.[32] John B. Edwards lived in a house on West Third Street. He was a construction supervisor for Gerrit Smith's many building projects in Oswego. Edwards was Smith's main agent in the town, and he coordinated most of the departures of fugitives from the city. The main method he used was to put them on ships sailing across Lake Ontario to Canada.[33] The Beebe family, who lived on a farm just outside Oswego, hid fugitives in their barn and then drove them into town, hidden in a wagon loaded with wheat. The Beebes received runaways coming from Petersboro and sent them on to Port Ontario.[34] A black man, James W. Seward, resided in Schroeppel and was the Underground Railroad agent in that town.[35]

Freedom seekers had two alternatives when they left Oswego. One was to board a ship and directly cross Lake Ontario to Canada. The other was to cross into Canada by heading northeast to one of several jumping-off places along the eastern shore of the lake. Flick describes a route that went to Port Ontario, to the northeast of Oswego but still in Oswego County. A crossing of the lake to Canada could be made at this point, or the journey could continue on the road, which later became U.S. Route 11, to Watertown. From here, there were three options: go to Cape Vincent in Jefferson County, or Morristown or Ogdensburg in St. Lawrence County. Fugitives could enter Canada from any of these locales.[36]

SYRACUSE TO AUBURN OR ITHACA

Flick lists another escape path that left Syracuse but, instead of heading directly west, went southwest to the town of Auburn in Cayuga County. Siebert's version of this route passes through Skaneateles (Glen Haven) before it reaches Auburn.[37] Skaneateles was a hamlet just eight miles east of Auburn. That it was a stopover on this route is further supported by the fact that Still received letters from two fugitives, Theodicia Gilbert and Edward Lewis, who had stayed in the town during their flight north.[38] The letter from Lewis details this route more specifically and adds a personal touch from someone who left all to escape bondage.

SKANEATELES, Dec. 17, 1857

Dear Sir:—As I promised to let you hear from me as soon as I found a home, I will now fulfill my promise to you and say that I am alive and well and have found a stopping place for the winter.

When we arrived at Syracuse we found Mr. Loguen ready to receive us, and as times are rather hard in Canada he thought best for us not to go there, so he sent us about twenty miles west of Syracuse to Skaneateles, where George Upshur and myself soon found work. Henry Grimes is at work in Garden about eight miles from this place.

If you should chance to hear any of my friends inquiring about me, please direct them to Skaneateles, Onondaga county, N.Y.

If you can inform me of the whereabouts of Miss Alice Jones I shall be very obliged to you, until I can pay you better. I forgot to ask you about her when I was at your house. She escaped about two years ago.

Please not to forget to inquire of my wife, Rachel Land, and if you should hear of her, let me know immediately. George Upshur and myself send our best respects to you and your family. Remember us to Mrs. Jackson and Miss Julia. I hope to meet you all again, if not on earth may we so live that we shall meet in that happy land where tears and partings are not known.

Let me hear from you soon. This from your friend and well wisher,

> Edward Lewis
> Formerly, but now William Brady.[39]

Auburn sat the head of Owasco Lake, one of the Finger Lakes. The town was also a stopover on a route that came from Pennsylvania to the south. A letter to William Still from Rev. L. D. Mansfield identified him as an agent in the town. Still also received two letters from a fugitive who stayed there, Nat Ambie, thus further confirming the role the town played on this escape path.[40] An alternate route appears to have existed from Syracuse to Auburn that involved the town of Sennett. This small town, only five miles northeast of Auburn, was on a road that ran directly from Syracuse to Auburn, to the north of the road that went from Syracuse through Skaneateles to Auburn. The argument that Sennett was a station and on an alternate route rests on three letters Still received from Harriet Eglin, a freedom seeker who stopped there while fleeing from enslavement. The following is one of those letters.

> SENNETT, June 1856
>
> Mr. William Still:—Dear Sir:—I am happy to tell you that Charlotte Gildes and myself have got along thus far safely. We have had no trouble and found friends all the way along, for which we feel very thankful to you and to all our friends on the road since we left. We reached Mr. Loguen's in Syracuse, on last Tuesday evening & on Wednesday two gentlemen from this community called and we went with them to work in their families. What I wish you would do is to be so kind as to send our clothes to this place if they should fall into your hands. We hope our uncle in Baltimore

will get the letter Charlotte wrote to him last Sabbath, while we were at your house, concerning the clothes. Perhaps the best would be to send them to Syracuse to the <u>care of Mr. Loguen</u> and he will send them to us. This will more certainly ensure our getting them. If you hear anything that would be interesting to Charlotte or me from Baltimore, please direct a letter to us to this place, to the care of Rev. Chas. Anderson, Sennett, Cayuga Co., N.Y. Please give my love and Charlotte's to Mrs. Still and thank her for her kindness to us while at your house.

> Your affectionate friend,
> Harriet Eglin.[41]

From Auburn, the route continued westward to Geneva, at the head of Seneca Lake where it connected with the Eastern Network of escape routes and led to Niagara.[42] An alternate route seems to have existed, based on Loguen's letter to William Still dated October 5, 1856, in which he tells Still that he has sent a Miss F. E. Watkins on an escape path that took her to Ithaca and "other places in that part of the State."[43] Ithaca was on the escape routes coming from southeastern New York.

MALONE TO LAKE ONTARIO ROUTE

A second escape path coming from the Eastern Network ran from the town of Malone to Lake Ontario. An Eastern Network route ran north from North Elba and John Brown's farm to the town of Malone in Franklin County, and from there northward to Canada. This was probably the main direction of this escape path, as well, but there appears to have been an alternate route that turned westward from Malone. The Ogdensburg and Lake Champlain Railroad had a line that ran from Malone through Brasher Falls to Ogdensburg in St. Lawrence County. Fugitives reportedly followed the tracks from Malone to Ogdensburg. Brasher Falls would have offered them something of a haven, as an Underground Railroad agent named Calvin T. Hubbard had a station in the town. In Brasher Falls, the route split into two paths. One continued on to Ogdensburg, and the other went to Waddington on the St. Lawrence River. In Waddington, the Chamberlain and Ogden families provided assistance to the travelers. Another option was to go to Morristown, also on the shore of Lake Ontario.[44] Whether they went to Ogdensburg, Waddington, or Morristown, the next stop for freedom seekers was Canada.

BINGHAMTON TO OSWEGO AND
PORT ONTARIO ROUTE

Siebert depicts a route on his map that came from the Pennsylvania town of Waverly, passed through Montrose, and headed north across the New York border to Plymouth. He shows another pathway nearby from Waverly to the small Quaker community of Friendsville. Siebert does not say where it went from this point.[45] A look at the geographic terrain running from both Montrose and Friendsville shows that a natural passageway leads across the border of Pennsylvania and into New York, to the larger town of Binghamton in Broome County. Binghamton was originally known as Chenango Point, because it was at the confluence of the Susquehanna and Chenango Rivers. Until the late 1700s, it was the site of a Native American settlement. After the Revolutionary War, white settlers moved into the area and renamed the site Binghamton in honor of a wealthy banker in Philadelphia, William Bingham. In the 1830s, the Chenango Canal that ran northward to the Erie Canal provided the town with a link to Albany and western New York. During the next decade, a line of the New York & Erie Railroad ran through Binghamton.[46] An old Indian trail known as the Great Owego Warriors Trail came from the Native American village of Tioga (Athens), just across the border in Pennsylvania, and followed the Susquehanna River into the area around Binghamton. It was an offshoot of another Indian trail, the Great Warriors Trail, which came from Towanda, south of Tioga.[47]

Although Siebert does not list Binghamton as an Underground Railroad site, Flick does. On his map of the route coming from Montrose, an escape trail passes right through Binghamton.[48] From here, the freedom seekers could have followed the Chenago Canal or the road that ran northward (now NY Route 12) toward Norwich, about thirty-four miles away. From Norwich, it was a short trip to an Underground Railroad site in Plymouth. This town lies in Chenango County, and Siebert names a Colonel Berry as an agent active in that county. The escape path then goes into Madison County, to the town of Lebanon. This twelve-mile journey could have been made in a single night. From Lebanon, the fugitives went another twelve miles north to Petersboro, a major site on the Underground Railroad in the same county.[49]

An examination of a period map showing the railroad connections coming from Binghamton reveals the possibility of other Underground Railroad escape opportunities. The New York & Erie Railroad had a line that ran from Binghamton northward to the New York Central Rail line south of

Oswego. There were also spur lines going to Ithaca and Elmira. It is known that fugitives were hidden in baggage cars and sent on this railroad to Rochester and then Niagara.[50]

Petersboro was one of the key nodes in the Underground Railroad system coming from northeastern Pennsylvania through southern New York. It was also the home of the great abolitionist figure Gerrit Smith. The town was the site of the January 1842 convention of the Liberty Party. At the convention, the participants encouraged slaves to escape and pledged to aid them in every way possible. The town also had a black settlement in which freedom seekers could have been hidden for some time.[51] Another abolitionist in Petersboro was Samuel Ringgold Ward, an avid opponent of slavery who was a well-known speaker on the subject and active in the Underground Railroad. In a letter to Nathaniel P. Rogers dated June 27, 1840, Ward criticizes a number of white abolitionists for preaching abolitionism but showing prejudice toward blacks in a number of ways, such as supporting proslavery laws that kept blacks from voting, excluding them from social circles, and segregating them during church services. He does however, praise some white abolitionists in central and western New York, including Gerrit Smith, Lysander Spooner, William Goodell, and James G. Birney, for living what they preached.[52]

Two alternative escape paths left Petersboro. According to Siebert, Smith would convey his charges along either one of these routes. One went to Syracuse; the other led in a slightly more northerly direction to the town of Mexico, and then on to Port Ontario or Cape Vincent, both departure points along the shore of Lake Ontario. Assisting Smith in these activities was a Dr. Jarvis.[53]

ELMIRA TO THE NORTHEAST ROUTES

Elmira is a town in Chemung County, a few miles from the border with Pennsylvania. The area in which it is located was settled in the late 1700s, like Binghamton. The name of town originally was Newtown, but in 1828 it was changed to Elmira. By the 1840s, Elmira had become a transportation center with the arrival of canals, particularly the Chemung Canal, and railroad lines.[54] Its location at the confluence of a number of river valleys helped in its development as a transportation center possessing strong links with a great deal of New York and Pennsylvania. All of these factors contributed to its becoming an attractive destination for fugitives passing through central Pennsylvania on their way to freedom in Canada.[55]

In addition to these more modern transportation elements, several Indian trails merged at Elmira. These trails later became major roads, such as NY Route 14 and U.S. Route 220. One trail came north from the town of Towanda in north-central Pennsylvania. Towanda was an Underground Railroad site from which freedom seekers went to either Binghamton or Elmira.[56] One of the trails, the Sheshequin Path, came from Towanda and merged with the Forbidden Path at Tioga (Athens) before turning northwest to Elmira. The Forbidden Path then continued westward through Corning and across the southern tier of New York. Another trail, the Horsehead's Path, also came north from the Sheshequin Path, leaving it at the town of Grover, Pennsylvania, just north of Williamsport, which was a major Underground Railroad center in north central Pennsylvania.[57]

Elmira figured prominently as an Underground Railroad clearing center on Siebert's map. He shows an escape path coming directly from Harrisburg, Pennsylvania, to Elmira and states that this route was most active between 1850 and 1860. Freedom seekers traversing the distance between Harrisburg and Elmira mainly used the Northern Central Railroad. They would be hidden in baggage cars by agents in Harrisburg on early-morning trains to Elmira.[58] This was also the second of the two alternate routes that Harriet Tubman used when she took fugitives to Canada from Maryland.[60] Siebert cites John W. Jones as the chief Underground Railroad agent in Elmira between 1844 and 1864, with Jervis Langdon as his friend and aide in this venture.[60] Jones had escaped from slavery in Leesburg, Virginia, and settled in Elmira in 1844. With the help of Langdon, Simeon Benjamin, Sylvester G. Andrus, Rev. Thomas K. Beecher, and Ariel S. Thurston, all prominent citizens in the town, Jones ran an effective escape network.[61]

In a letter to William Still, Jones makes mention of his use of the railroad to send fugitives to the north.

ELMIRA, June 6th, 1860

Friend Wm. Still:—All six came to this place. The two men came last night, About twelve o'clock; the man and woman stopped at the depot, and went east on The next train, about eighteen miles, and did not get back till to-night, so That the two men went this morning, and the four went this evening.

O, old master don't cry for me,
For I am going to Canada where colored men are free.

P.S. What is the news in the city? Will you tell me how many you have sent over to Canada? I would like to know. They all send their love to you. I have nothing new to tell you. We are all in good health. I see there is a law

passed in Maryland not to set any slaves free. They had better get the consent of the Underground Rail Road before they passed such a thing. Good
night from your friend,   John W. Jones.[62]

To facilitate his operation, Jones received financial assistance from James
M. Robinson, William Yates, and Riggs Watson. He aided more than 800
fugitives in their journey northward to freedom. Jones served as the sexton at
the Elmira First Baptist Church and hid runaways in his home next to the
church. He made use of the Northern Central Railroad by hiding fugitives
on board its baggage cars during the 4:00 A.M. run northward.[63] There were
several options for sending freedom seekers northward from Elmira.

ELMIRA TO ROCHESTER VIA WATKINS GLEN
The train on which John Jones hid fugitives in baggage cars headed north
from Elmira. It passed through Watkins Glen in Schuyler County and went
northwest to the town of Canandaigua in Ontario County.[64] From here, the
railroad line had two tracks going northward, one to Rochester and the other
to Niagara.[65] Once in Rochester, the next stop for the travelers would have
been Canada.

ELMIRA TO BUFFALO OR NIAGARA VIA HORNELLSVILLE
The main line of the New York & Erie Railroad left Elmira and went westward through the town of Corning to Hornellsville (Hornell) in Steuben
County. At this point, it split into two lines, one going farther west to
Dunkirk and the other northwest to Buffalo. Both of these towns were in the
Western Network of New York's Underground Railroad.[66] Siebert lists two
agents working in Steuben County on this escape pathway, a Judge Balcom
and Judge Otis Thacher.[67] In addition to sending fugitives to Rochester via
the Watkins Glen line, John Jones also would have put them on trains heading in this direction. Flick's version of this route runs from Elmira to Hornellsville and then to the town of Warsaw in Wyoming County and the
Western Network. From Warsaw, the escape path goes to Niagara instead of
Buffalo.[68] Siebert has a curious route on his map related to Warsaw. A brief
route begins in Mount Morris in Livingston County and goes to Warsaw. It
does not have any beginning and just suddenly appears in Mount Morris. He
also includes a Col. Reuben Sleeper as an agent working in Livingston
County.[69] Sleeper was the president of the Livingston Anti-Slavery Society,
but there is some question whether he actually was involved in helping runaways escape.[70] In all likelihood, Mount Morris was a stopover on the route
from Hornellsville to Warsaw that began in Elmira.

Elmira to Lake Ontario or Niagara via Ithaca

Yet another escape route left Elmira with either Lake Ontario or Niagara Falls as its ultimate goal. This pathway went to the northeast toward the town of Ithaca. Flick's map shows the route going directly to Ithaca, but more recent research has identified Underground Railroad sites at the towns of Spencer in northwestern Tioga County and Burdett, eighteen miles west of Ithaca, near the southern shores of Seneca Lake in Schuyler County.[71] This route follows the classic zigzag pattern seen in many escape pathways. From Ithaca, the route proceeded northward to Trumansburg, in northwestern corner of Tompkins County near the southern shore of Cayuga Lake. The next safe haven was found in the town of Auburn, situated at the northern end of Owasco Lake. From here, fugitives had two options. One alternative was to continue northward, possibly to Oswego and Lake Ontario, probably by way of Syracuse.[72] The other choice was to leave Auburn and go west, through Geneva and Canandaigua, to the Western Network and ultimately Niagara.[73] Flick also posits an overland route that ran along the western side of Seneca Lake, following a road (now NY Route 14) from Elmira, through Watkins Glen, directly to Geneva.[74]

Elmira Westward via Corning

A fourth possible route headed westward from Elmira, through an Underground Railroad station in Big Flats, to the town of Corning.[75] With the route passing through Big Flats, it was probably an overland escape path. A strong argument for this route is also supported by an escape path that came from Williamsport in Pennsylvania, going overland via Trout Run along the old Indian trail called the Tioga Path, which intersected with the Forbidden Path near Corning. Just south of Corning at the Pennsylvania border, the Putnam family operated a safe house for freedom seekers.[76] From Corning, fugitives could have boarded one of the trains carrying other runaways coming from Elmira or continued overland to Hornellsville and the Western Network.

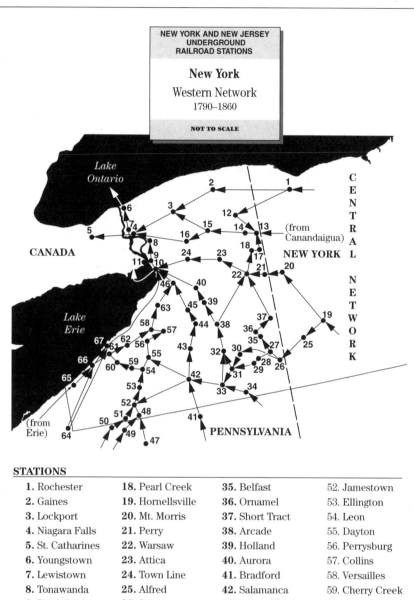

NEW YORK AND NEW JERSEY
UNDERGROUND
RAILROAD STATIONS

New York
Western Network
1790–1860

NOT TO SCALE

Lake Ontario

CANADA

Lake Erie

(from Canandaigua)

NEW YORK

CENTRAL NEW YORK NETWORK

(from Erie)

PENNSYLVANIA

STATIONS

1. Rochester	**18.** Pearl Creek	**35.** Belfast	52. Jamestown
2. Gaines	**19.** Hornellsville	**36.** Ornamel	53. Ellington
3. Lockport	**20.** Mt. Morris	**37.** Short Tract	54. Leon
4. Niagara Falls	**21.** Perry	**38.** Arcade	55. Dayton
5. St. Catharines	**22.** Warsaw	**39.** Holland	56. Perrysburg
6. Youngstown	**23.** Attica	**40.** Aurora	57. Collins
7. Lewistown	**24.** Town Line	**41.** Bradford	58. Versailles
8. Tonawanda	**25.** Alfred	**42.** Salamanca	59. Cherry Creek
9. Black Rock	**26.** Scio	**43.** Ellicotville	60. Cassadaga
10. Buffalo	**27.** Belmont	**44.** Riceville	61. Fredonia
11. Fort Erie	**28.** Friendship	**45.** Springville	62. Forrestville
12. Elba	**29.** Nile	**46.** Orchard Park	63. Eden
13. LeRoy	**30.** Cuba	**47.** Warren	64. Wattsburg
14. Morgansville	**31.** Hinsdale	**48.** Frewsburg	65. Ripley
15. Pembroke	**32.** Ischua	**49.** Sugar Grove	66. Westfield
16. Clarence	**33.** Olean	**50.** Bear Lake	67. Dunkirk
17. Covington	**34.** Ceres	**51.** Busti	

New York—The Western Routes

The Western Network of New York's Underground Railroad operated in the area roughly from seventy-eight degrees west longitude to the western boundaries of the state. Lake Erie and the Niagara River bounded the network to the west, Pennsylvania to the south, and Lake Ontario to the north. Nine counties were involved in the Western Network: Allegany, Cattaraugus, Chautauqua, Erie, Genesee, Livingston, Niagara, Orleans, and Wyoming. Table 7 provides some interesting demographics for this area.[1]

These data show that the number of potential allies for fugitives passing through the Western Network was not as great as in the other two networks. Of particular note is the fewer number of Quaker congregations found in the region. Nevertheless, the intensity and density of support were still very high in the Western Network.

Siebert lists thirty-eight Underground Railroad agents and conductors active in the seven counties of the Western Network: Allegany (one), Cattaraugus (three), Chautauqua (seven), Erie (six), Genesee (four), Niagara (four), and Wyoming (thirteen).[2] Christopher Densmore expands the total number to 113 agents in eight counties: Allegheny (fifteen), Cattaraugus (seven), Chautauqua (thirty-nine), Erie (twenty-six), Genesee (five), Niagara (ten), Orleans (one), and Wyoming (ten).[3] In addition to the individuals identified as agents and conductors, there was a strong base of abolitionist support in western New York. This is readily seen by the number of branches of the American Anti-Slavery Society located in the counties of the area in the late 1830s: Allegany (fourteen), Cattaragus (ten), Chautauqua (thirteen), Erie (twenty-three), Genesee (twenty-four), Niagara (twelve), Orleans (three), and Wyoming (four). This totals 103 branches of the society, each having dozens of members.[4] The A.M.E. Church also was present in western New York and adjacent Canada. Bishop Payne, in his work on the history of the Church, states that as early as 1828, A.M.E. congregations and churches were active in Buffalo and the Canadian town of Niagara.[5] Thus despite the fewer number of free blacks, Quakers, Methodists, Baptists, and Presbyterians in

TABLE 7.
DEMOGRAPHIC DATA NEW YORK'S
WESTERN NETWORK IN 1850

County	Free blacks	Quaker meeting-houses	Methodist churches	Baptist churches	Presbyterian churches
Allegany	128 (.34%)	0	16	14	12
Cattaraugus	102 (.26%)	0	12	14	5
Chautauqua	140 (.28%)	0	23	30	14
Erie	825 (.82%)	7	23	23	16
Genesee	77 (.27%)	1	13	11	16
Livingston	209 (.51%)	0	21	13	23
Niagara	317 (.75%)	4	16	9	10
Orleans	108 (.37%)	1	14	12	9
Wyoming	64 (.20%)	1	15	19	15
Totals	1,970 (.49%)	14	153	145	120

western New York, the Underground Railroad network there still had a significant population base of sympathizers from which to draw and be effective.

The transportation grid in the Western Network was also more than adequate for the efficient operation of an escape system. As early as 1812, turnpikes linked Albany with Buffalo. A decade later, more than 4,000 miles of turnpikes tied together the majority of towns in the state. The main line of the Erie Canal ran from Albany to Buffalo, through Rochester, and a smaller canal went from Olean to Rochester.[6] Early railroad maps show rail lines running from Rochester to Buffalo by 1841, and a decade later, the New York Central and the New York & Erie Railroads had established lines connecting most of the key places in the state with Buffalo and Niagara.[7] In the 1860s, the Erie Railroad, the renamed version of the New York & Erie line, had spur lines that tied together the vast majority of towns that held Underground Railroad stations of the Western Network.[8] Steamboats began to operate on Lake Ontario in 1816, carrying people and products between Canada and New York. In 1829, the Welland Canal was completed, linking Lake Erie and Lake Ontario.[9] Eber Pettit, an early writer about the Underground Railroad from western New York, reports that steamboats on Lake Erie were used regularly to transport fugitives from Buffalo and Cleveland to Canada.[10]

Freedom seekers using carriages to travel to Canada. HISTORICAL SOCIETY OF
DELAWARE

The escape system in the Western Network had a degree of complexity
that reflected the dangers inherent in being so close to the final destination of
Canada. Fugitives entered the network from about twelve entry points, coming from the northeast, southeast, and southwest. The northeastern access
routes entered the Western Network at Gaines, Morganville, and LeRoy.
Those from the southeast entered at Scio, Perry, Warsaw, Olean, and Salamanca. Runaways coming from northwestern Pennsylvania into southwestern New York passed through Busti, Frewsburg, Jamestown, and Westfield.
Exit points into Canada from this network were at Dunkirk and in the
region between Buffalo and Youngstown.

ROUTES FROM THE NORTHEAST

Two major escape paths in the Western Network came from the northeast,
originating in Rochester and Elmira. Both made use of railways, roads, and
canals to move fugitives from one safe house to another. Their ultimate

destinations in New York were the towns of Niagara and Youngstown, as well as the region along the Niagara River that lies between the two.

ROCHESTER TO THE NIAGARA REGION VIA LOCKPORT

Siebert and Flick both describe a route that proceeded from Rochester through Lockport to Niagara.[11] Rochester and Niagara were connected by a series of roads that ran through Gaines and Lockport. The main line of the New York Central Railroad went from Rochester to Lockport, and then on to Niagara.[12] Gaines must have been a small Underground Railroad station, because it had only one agent, Robert Anderson. Lockport, on the other hand, had an established Underground Railroad presence, as witnessed by the number of agents and conductors active in the town. Siebert lists Thomas Binmore, M. C. Richardson, and Lyman Spauling aiding fugitives in the town, identifying M. C. Richardson as Moses Richardson.[13] Densmore includes a Spaulding on his list, probably the same person that Siebert identifies as Spauling. In addition to also having Binmore on his list of agents in Lockport, Densmore adds the names of Darius Comstock, Francis Hichens, Moses Richardson, and a Dennis W.[14] A citation from a local newspaper, the *Lockport Journal and Courier*, dated November 17, 1859, supports the contention that Lockport was an important stopover on the Underground Railroad: "U.G.R.R.—Fugitive slaves are continually finding their way through to land of refuge, by means of the underground R.R. Two of them passed through here day before yesterday and are now safe in Canada."[15] Eber Pettit identifies Dennis W. as an Irishman who lived on a farm between Canal and Ridge Roads, about four miles from Lockport. He took runaways across the Niagara River into Canada.[16] From Lockport, fugitives went another fifteen miles to the Niagara district.

The Niagara district stretched from Tonawanda, between Buffalo and Niagara, to Youngstown, at the point where the Niagara River enters Lake Ontario. It included the towns of Tonawanda, Black Rock, Niagara, Lewiston, and Youngstown, as well as the Suspension Bridge spanning the Niagara River, connecting New York with Canada. Freedom seekers passed into Canada across the Suspension Bridge near Niagara Falls and on ferry boats from Black Rock, Lewiston, and Youngstown. Once across, they made their way to Rev. Hiram Wilson in St. Catharines, Canada.[17]

The town of Niagara was strategically placed at the end of several escape paths. The Suspension Bridge provided direct entrance into Canada. Accesses to small boats above and below the town also facilitated crossing to freedom. W. H. Childs was an agent in the town, along with Ben Jackson and a person simply known as "P."[18] Further attesting to the town's importance, William

Still received five letters from James H. Forman, Thomas F. Page, and Stepheney Brown, freedom seekers who were waiting to enter Canada from there.[19]

CANANDAIGUA TO NIAGARA VIA MORGANVILLE

The second route that came from the northeast passed through Canandaigua in Ontario County and headed west to Morganville in Genesee County. From here, it went through Pembroke and Clarence to Niagara, according to Siebert's and Flick's maps. This route came from a combination of escape paths that originated in Elmira and Syracuse but merged at the town of Geneva, also in Genesee County and fourteen miles east of Canandaigua. At the town of Pembroke, Siebert has an alternate route proceeding northeast to Lockport, joining the Lockport to Niagara route.[20]

ROCHESTER AND WARSAW TO NIAGARA VIA LEROY

LeRoy, a small town strategically located between Rochester and Warsaw in the southeastern corner of Genesee County, had Underground Railroad escape paths converging on it from both of these larger sites. The route from Rochester reached LeRoy from the northeast, passing through Elba. Another path came from Warsaw after going through Pearl Creek. Because the trail from Warsaw ran through Covington Township in northern Wyoming County, it was referred to as the Covington Connection. The Pearl Creek agent, High Brooks, hid fugitives who had come from Warsaw in his home, and then guided them through Pavilion Center, up the Bernd Road, to the home of Daniel McDonald, who lived on the outskirts of LeRoy. Whether fugitives came from Rochester or Warsaw, they followed the roads from LeRoy that went west to Niagara.[21]

ROUTES FROM THE SOUTHEAST

Several escape routes proceeded from the southeast to the towns of Dunkirk, Buffalo, and the Niagara region. They had their origins in Scio, Olean, Perry, Warsaw, and Salamanca.

SCIO TO DUNKIRK

This route began in Corning, a town on the main line of the New York & Erie Railroad coming from Elmira. Fugitives who hid in the baggage cars of early-morning trains on that line passed through Corning en route to Hornellsville. Corning was also the entry point for self-emancipators who came overland from central Pennsylvania via Indian trails in the region. These freedom seekers were secreted on the trains from Elmira to Hornellsville as well. Pettit states that fugitives arrived in Dunkirk hidden on freight cars from Corning. These trains had to have passed through Hornellsville and Scio, so a spur line of the New York & Erie Railroad left Hornellsville, ran through Alfred, and headed for Dunkirk.

The rail line entered the Western Network at the town of Scio in Allegany County. From Scio, the track went westward to Belmont, Cuba, and Hinsdale before reaching Olean. At this point, it went northwest, making connections with Salamanca, Dayton, and Perrysburg before arriving at Dunkirk.[22] Another probable escape path ran overland for a short distance, paralleling the rail line from Scio to Olean. It proceeded from Scio through Belmont, Friendship, Nile, and Hinsdale before reaching Olean. The evidence for this route consists of the listing of Underground Railroad agents active in each of these towns and the existence of roads connecting them.[23]

The tale of one fugitive that Pettit relates provides a glimpse into the workings of this segment of the Western Network. A fugitive named Dan arrived in Dunkirk hidden in a freight car and was then put aboard a train of the Buffalo & Erie Railroad going to Buffalo. Unfortunately for Dan, his master was also on board the same train. The conductor of the train, also an Underground Railroad sympathizer, put Dan off at the next station, Silver Creek. An unnamed agent then took him to one of the key operatives in the area, a Deacon Andrews. Andrews also appears on Siebert's list of agents in Chautauqua County. Andrews sent Dan to the town of Arkwright, and from there a black conductor named John Little took him to a farm near Forestville owned by the Cranston family. They took Dan to Black Rock in the Niagara region, where he boarded a boat and crossed over into Canada.[24] The story is an excellent example of the quick thinking of agents and the complicated nature of alternate routes to aid freedom seekers in attaining their goal.

OLEAN TO DUNKIRK OR NIAGARA

Olean, like Corning, was a focal point for fugitives coming overland from Pennsylvania, as well as for freedom seekers traveling on the New York & Erie Railroad from Elmira. In the first instance, runaways came across the border from the town of Coudersport, Pennsylvania, through Ceres in Allegany County to Olean. These fugitives had passed through the Pennsylvania town of Williamsport and followed the Shamokin and Sinnemahoning Indian Trails into New York and Olean.[25] In Olean, they could have joined other freedom seekers who were on the trains coming from Elmira and Corning, heading for the Underground Railroad operation in Dunkirk. Another possibility for those reaching Corning on foot from Pennsylvania would have been to follow the Forbidden Indian Trail from Corning to Olean. This trail dips back into northern Pennsylvania east of Corning, but then turns north and passes by Olean before heading to Salamanca, about twenty-five miles due east of Jamestown in Cattaraugus County.[26] These fugitives most likely would have continued overland to Jamestown, an important Underground Railroad center. Yet another option for the travelers was the Forbidden Trail, which turned north at Salamanca through Cattaraugus County and could have taken them to the vicinity of Dunkirk. Further research needs to be conducted on these options.

Another option for freedom seekers reaching Olean was to travel overland north through stations in Hinsdale and Ischua, following Ischua Creek to Arcade in Wyoming County. At this point, there were two divergent escape paths. One went northeast to Warsaw and ultimately to Buffalo. The second also reached Buffalo but proceeded northwest from Arcade, passing through stations in Holland and Aurora. All of these towns had Underground Railroad agents. The fact that Arcade had three active agents indicates its importance in the overall escape system.[27]

PERRY OR WARSAW TO BUFFALO

Siebert depicts a route on his map that begins suddenly in Mount Morris in Livingston County, goes west for about ten miles to Warsaw in Wyoming County, and then turns northwest, ending at Attica, also in Wyoming County. He shows no beginning or end for this path.[28] Eber Pettit attested to a station in Attica operated by an agent named Col. Charles O. Shepard, who was also active in the Arcade station. Shepard was a member of the New York senate and the Liberty Party.[29] Flick's map provides a more comprehensive view of the route, showing its origin and destination. Flick's version of this route, beginning in Elmira, passes through Hornellsville and reaches Warsaw. The Mount Morris connection may actually have been a stopover on the Hornellsville to Warsaw route. Fugitives leaving Hornellsville would have entered the Western Network at Perry before going on to Warsaw. Flick shows the escape path going from Warsaw to an unidentified town to the northwest, where it connected with the route coming from Geneva and Canandaigua. He does not have Attica as part of this pathway, however.[30] An examination of railroad maps from the period reveals that the New York & Erie Railroad had a major line extending from Elmira through Hornellsville to Warsaw, and running from there through Attica to Buffalo.[31] Fugitives were transported on this line hidden in baggage cars. This would indicate that both Siebert's and Flick's maps are correct, when the two are merged.

Wyoming County had a strong base of support for freedom seekers passing through the region. Densmore further identifies the individuals on

Siebert's list, specifying Allen Y. Breck, Dr. Augustus Frank, Seth M. Gates, F. C. D. McKay, Frank Miller, and Andrew W. Young as agents in Warsaw, and Josiah Andrews, Willard J. Chapin, Rev. Ellin Galusha, and Samuel F. Phoenix in the nearby town of Perry. He also mentions Ralston W. Lyman, Col. Charles O. Shepard, and H. N. Waldo as agents in Arcade, in the southwest corner of Wyoming County.[32]

SALAMANCA AREA TO BUFFALO AND THE NIAGARA REGION

Pettit made a passing reference to a route that came from the town of Bradford in northern Pennsylvania. Fugitives coming from this direction would have arrived in the region of Salamanca, New York. From here, the route led about ten miles almost directly north to Ellicottville. From this town, the fugitives would have followed a natural valley that stretched into Erie County through Riceville to Springville. Pettit places a station in Springville, and he names the agent there simply as Deacon E., who conveyed his visitors northward to Buffalo and the Niagara area.[33] Salamanca was also on the rail route from Elmira to Dunkirk.

ROUTES FROM THE SOUTHWEST

Two major systems of escape routes came from northwestern Pennsylvania into southwestern New York. One passed through Jamestown and the other through Westfield.

BUSTI–FREWSBURG–JAMESTOWN TO BUFFALO
AND THE NIAGARA REGION ROUTE

Jamestown was a strategically located town in southern Chautauqua County only ten miles from the border with Pennsylvania. It was a major entry point for fugitives who came from Warren, Bear Lake, and Sugar Grove in Pennsylvania. Those coming from Warren took a major road (now U.S. Route 62) directly to Jamestown or may have gone to Frewsburg, which was about two-thirds of the way from Warren to Jamestown and a little east of Route 62. The agents in the town were George Washington Fenton and Hiram Thayer.[34] Runaways who came from Bear Lake and Sugar Grove followed a road that ran through the town of Busti before reaching Jamestown.[35] Busti must have been a major site, as ten agents and conductors lived in and around the town: Norman Backus, Jabez Broadhead, Rev. John Broadhead, Dr. Brown, Alvin Plumb, Humphrey Pratt, William Storum, Ed Wells, and two individuals simply referred to as Curtis and Green.[36]

Once freedom seekers came to Jamestown, they received aid from a number of people. Phineas Crossman, Katherine Harris, Dr. William Hedges, Addison A. Page, Addison Price, Silas Sherman, Clinton Windsor, and Frank Van Dusen gave shelter to weary travelers.[37] Of these, Katherine Harris, freeborn in 1809 in the Pennsylvania town of Meadville to a black father and white mother, was the most famous. After she married, she moved to Buffalo with her husband. He died in 1828, and she and her daughter moved to Jamestown three years later. She married a man named John Harris in 1835, and they lived in the black section of Jamestown, a community known as Africa or Old Jamestown that became a haven for fugitives in the 1840s and 1850s. Harris was the chief agent there and often cared for groups of runaways ranging from three to seventeen in number. Silas Sherman regularly brought fugitives to her from his house on Pine Street. She also received runaways directly from Dr. Brown in Busti and Dr. Caitlin in Sugar Grove.[38]

Agents could take or send freedom seekers leaving Jamestown in two directions. The first, and apparently the more popular, alternative was northeast to Fredonia and Dunkirk, on the shores of Lake Erie. The second was to Buffalo and the Niagara region by way of Cattaraugus and Erie Counties.

Jamestown to Buffalo or the Niagara Region via Leon or Fredonia

Pettit outlined an escape path that left Jamestown and went through Falconer, on the outskirts of Jamestown, northeast for about ten miles to Ellington. There was an agent in Falconer named Edward Work.[39] Ellington had an active Ladies' Anti-Slavery Society, which sent clothing and bedding to William Still in Philadelphia.[40] Still preserved some of the missives he received from the society, and letters like the following give a picture of the dedication of these ladies to the cause.

ELLINGTON, Nov. 21st, 1859

MR. WILLIAM STILL:—Dear Sir:—In the above-named place, some five years since there was formed a Ladies' Anti-slavery Society, which has put forth its feeble endeavors to aid the cause of "breaking every yoke and letting the oppressed go free," and we trust, through our means, others have been made glad of heart. Every year we have sent a box of clothing, bedding, etc., to the aid of the fugitive, and wishing to send it where it would be of most service, we have it suggested to us, to send to you the box we have at present. You would confer a favor upon the members of our society, by writing us, giving a detail of that which would be the most service to you, and whether or no it would be more advantageous to you than some nearer station, and we will send or endeavor to, that which would benefit you most.

William Wells Brown visited our place a short time since, recommend-
ing us to send to you in preference to Syracuse, where we sent our last box.
Please write, letting me know what most is needed, to aid you in your glorious work, a work which will surely meet its reward. Direct, Ellington,
Chautauqua county, N.Y.   Your sister, in the cause,
                                                    Mrs. M. Brooks[41]

From Ellington, the path proceeded to Leon in Cattaraugus County. At
this point, it seems to have split into two divergent routes. One alternative
went through Cattaraugus and Erie Counties, continued through Dayton
and Perrysburg to Versailles, where Eber Pettit kept a station. Pettit had
moved to Versailles in 1837, where he opened a tannery and later a "botanic
mill" that grew herbs and plants for medicinal uses. His father, James Pettit,
operated an Underground Railroad station in Cordova, just outside of Fredonia. His father also sent fugitives on to him in Versailles by another route.
Eber forwarded his charges to a conductor he simply called "Friend Andrew,"
who lived about six miles away. Andrew took the fugitives to the region
between Buffalo and Niagara, usually Black Rock, and put them on a boat
for Canada across the Niagara River. Pettit states that in some cases, probably
to throw off slave catchers, fugitives were taken first to the small town of
Collins or Collins Center, to the southeast of his station, before they reached
Versailles.[42] From Collins Center, Lorenzo and Anna Mabbett transported
fugitives northward in their wagon.[43]

The second option from Leon was to turn to the northwest and head for
Fredonia. Leaving Leon, the travelers passed through Cherry Creek and Cassadaga (Cassadaigua). Both towns had agents: George Frost, Oliver Lee, and
Holman Vail in Cherry Creek, and Benjamin Miller and Joseph Sackett in
Cassadaga.[44] Another reason that these two towns likely were safe havens is
that the distance between Leon and Fredonia, more than twenty miles, was
too great for fugitives traveling secretly and cautiously to cover in a single
day. On reaching Fredonia, the freedom seekers came into the care of Dr.
James Pettit, who then sent them on through the town of Forestville in
northern Chautauqua County to his son in Versailles. From here, they went
or the Niagara Region.[45]

Westfield to Buffalo or the Niagara Region Route
The second major route taken by freedom seekers from northeastern Pennsylvania began at the town of Westfield, New York. Escape paths originating
in Erie and Wattsburg, Pennsylvania, converged on this town, which was
located near the shore of Lake Erie only eleven miles from the border.[46] Fugi-

tives coming from Erie passed through the town of North East, crossed the state line, and went to Ripley, three miles away. Hervay Hall had a safe house in the town, and after runaways stayed with him, he forwarded them to Westfield.[47] Those passing through Wattsburg entered the southwest corner of New York, and most headed to Westfield, although some went directly to Dunkirk. With the proximity of Lake Chautauqua, some fugitives who had come from Wattsburg may have followed the shores of the lake eastward to Jamestown, but more research needs to be done on this possible route.

A Mr. Knowlton operated the station in Westfield, according to Pettit. Knowlton forwarded fugitives on to Fredonia and nearby Cordova, where Dr. James Pettit received the travelers.[48] Flick has another route that ran from Westfield to Dunkirk, only a short distance from Fredonia.[49] In all of the sources, the route then follows the coast road to the city of Buffalo.

Buffalo was the major city in western New York, the end point of the Erie Canal, Erie Railroad, and New York Central Railroad and an important abolitionist center. Its antislavery sentiment went back to 1838, when the Buffalo City Anti-Slavery Society was formed. The census of 1840 showed that 350 free blacks lived within the city. In 1843, the National Convention of Colored Men took place at the Vine Street A.M.E. Church in Buffalo, and the major topic was ways to end slavery in America. The Michigan Street Baptist Church, at 511 Michigan Street, was also an active antislavery congregation.

Pettit speaks of steamboats transporting fugitives from Buffalo to Canada on a regular basis.[50] Drew includes a story of a freedom seeker named James Adams, who escaped from the Kanawha Valley of Western Virginia. Adams made his way to Cleveland, where he boarded a schooner and sailed over Lake Erie to Buffalo.[51] Densmore mentions ten agents active within the city.[52]

The traffic of fugitives to Buffalo apparently was a year-round activity. Siebert records an interview conducted in 1893 with Prof. Edward Orton of the Ohio State University. The professor recalled that in 1838, when he was a boy in Buffalo, he saw two sleighs containing fugitives coming to his house at night all the way from the Western Reserve region of Ohio. Not all the freedom seekers went to Canada from Buffalo. Siebert states that a number of them chose to settle in the Buffalo area. After the passage of the Fugitive Slave Act of 1850, however, large numbers of blacks living in Buffalo fled the city and moved to Ontario.[53]

The nearby town of Black Rock was generally used by the Underground Railroad in Buffalo as the main site from which to take freedom seekers into Canada. Roderick Park, at the foot of Ferry Street and the Black Rock Canal, was the place where fugitives boarded boats or ferries to cross the Niagara River and into Canada.[54]

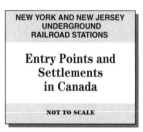

NEW YORK AND NEW JERSEY UNDERGROUND RAILROAD STATIONS

Entry Points and Settlements in Canada

NOT TO SCALE

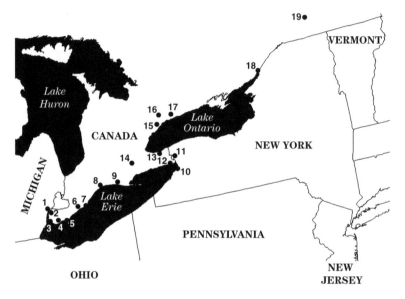

STATIONS

1. Detroit
2. Windsor
3. Colchester
4. Amherstburg
5. Gosfield
6. Buxton
7. Pelee's Point
8. Port Stanley
9. Port Burwell
10. Buffalo
11. Niagara
12. Fort Erie
13. St. Catharines
14. Brantford
15. Hamilton
16. Yorkville
17. Toronto
18. Kingston
19. Montreal

Canada

Canada was the primary destination for most slaves fleeing their bondage in the eastern United States. The major reasons for this were Canada's easy access from slave states in the East, its laws guaranteeing freedom for any slave crossing the border into the country, and its network of support for freedom seekers reaching its territory.

The first black person mentioned in Canada was Mathieu de Costa, who appeared in French records from 1608 as being a "Negro servant" to the governor of Port Royal. In 1632, Oliver Le Jeune was the first black African brought from that continent to Canada and sold as a slave in the colony of New France.[1]

The number of African slaves grew, and in 1705, slavery was legalized in New France in conformity with a law called the Code Noir. Most slaves who toiled in New France came there from Africa after spending some time in French possessions in the Caribbean. They worked in manor houses, on farms, and on the frontier.[2]

After the war ended, many loyalists moved to Canada along with their black slaves. Among them was a group called the Black Pioneers, an all-black regiment who had fought for the British Army during the war. They moved to the Maritime Provinces in 1783 and settled in Birchtown, Nova Scotia. They numbered about 3,000 individuals, counting their families. They experienced a degree of hostility from the white population there, however, and their lot was not a happy one. One reaction to the influx of so many blacks was to attempt to resettle them in Sierra Leone. Those who reached this African territory were met with hostility by the native Africans residing there, however, and the resettlement attempt came to an end.

A radical change in the attitudes of Canadians toward slavery began in 1793. In that year, the lieutenant governor of Upper Canada, John Graves Simcoe, had to deal with a case involving the beating and transportation across the Niagara River of a slave girl named Chloe Cooley by her master, William Vrooman. Simcoe was a sympathizer of the English abolitionist

William Wilberforce, who was on a crusade to abolish slavery in the British Empire. Simcoe could not do anything in the Cooley case, because Canadian law sided with Vrooman. This factor motivated him to have a law passed in 1793 entitled An Act to Prevent the Further Introduction of Slaves and to Limit the Term of Enforced Servitude within This Province. Although it did not end slavery in Canada, it did have an impact on it. The children of slaves would be set free by the law when they reached the age of twenty-five, and it put an end to the importation of new slaves into Upper Canada. With this improved atmosphere in Upper Canada, one of the immediate results was that slaves from the United States began to escape and cross through the Northwest Territories into Canada, settling in the region. By 1800, there were forty small settlements of former slaves engaged in farming in Upper Canada.

While these events were taking place in Upper Canada, the cause of abolition was gaining ground in Lower Canada. The various newspapers in that region backed the ending of the institution of slavery and printed stories of slave abuse in graphic detail. In 1803, the chief justice of Lower Canada, William Osgood, ruled that slavery was a practice that was "incompatible with British law." Although it did not abolish the practice initially, it did free more than 300 men and women being held in bondage.[3]

Freedom seekers headed north from the United States across the border into Canada in small numbers in the late 1700s and early 1800s. It was not until after the War of 1812, however, that this flow became heavier. During the war, nearly 2,000 fugitives managed to reach Halifax. The reaction on the part of the whites there was not favorable. They feared the economic impact of so many people willing to work for low wages and needing governmental assistance, and in 1815, Nova Scotia passed an ordinance forbidding any further black immigration into the province. But the opposite sentiment was expressed in Upper Canada, where the current lieutenant governor, Sir Peregrine Maitland, sought black immigrants and made an effort to find them work. He also saw to the awarding of land grants for blacks who were veterans of the war.[4]

Tales of freedom for those reaching this "promised land" began to filter throughout the South when black veterans of the U.S. Navy returned home. These sailors had served on the ships of the American fleet fighting on the Great Lakes. Siebert states that by 1815, fugitives were crossing the Western Reserve in Ohio, and regular stations of the Underground Railroad were lending them assistance.[5] Evidence of the impact of this phenomenon can be seen in a petition that the General Assembly of Kentucky sent to the U.S. Congress in 1827, protesting the official reception of fugitive slaves by the

Canadian government. The petition requested that Congress negotiate a treaty with Canada that would require the immediate return of all fugitives to their rightful masters. The British government refused to enter into negotiations on this matter.[6]

The issue of slavery in Canada was finally resolved when the Emancipation Act, passed in 1833 by the British government, became effective on August 1, 1834. This law abolished slavery in all of the British Empire, including Canada.[7] Now reaching Canada was an even more desirable goal for enslaved people in the United States. In 1838, a legal case in which the United States requested the extradition of a fugitive slave named Jesse Happy further reinforced the concept of Canada as a place of freedom for runaway slaves. In the Happy case, the Canadian government denied the request on the grounds that no evidence was presented that Happy had committed a crime that Canada recognized. Since slavery did not then exist in Canada, the accusation that Happy had broken the law by running away had no merit under Canadian law.[8]

Siebert writes that between 1828 and 1838, the number of freedom seekers attempting to reach Canada increased dramatically. The area of Canada along the Great Lakes from New York to Michigan and pathways running along the coastline of New England became the main entry routes for fugitives to follow into the land of freedom. Realizing that this phenomenon was increasing, a number of private individuals began to make a serious attempt to help the newcomers. One of the early efforts in this area was a mission school for the children of runaways operated in the 1840s by Isaac J. Rice. A Presbyterian minister who had come to Canada from Ohio, Rice opened his school in Amherstburg, Ontario. The main goal of the school was to provide the next generation of black children with the skills necessary to survive in a competitive economic environment. Another example of the Canadian government's effort to help former slaves find meaningful employment, and hence not be a burden on society, was a land acquisition program it instituted. Fugitives could obtain a fifty-acre parcel of land for farming at the price of $2.00 per acre. They then had ten years to pay off the debt. Abolitionist groups in the United States also sent large amounts of clothing and other necessities to the freedom seekers now settling in Canada.[9]

The fugitives were naturally drawn to black settlements, where they received support from their compatriots. Freedom seekers settled in Ontario at Welland and St. Catharines near the Niagara River; Colchester, Windsor, and Amherstburg near Detroit; London, Chatham, and Dresden; and Oro, Toronto, and the Queen's Bush.[10] Among the many settlements, three emerged as major black colonies in the 1840s, attracting the largest numbers of fugitives: the Dawn Settlement at Dresden, the Elgin Settlement at Buxton, and the Refugees' Home in Windsor.

The Dawn Settlement was the idea of two of the most famous Underground Railroad figures in Canada: Rev. Hiram Wilson and Josiah Henson. Wilson was a white minister from the United States whose name appears frequently in escape stories from the Niagara-Buffalo area of New York. Henson was a former slave who had fled from bondage with his wife and children after he learned he was going to be sold to another master in New Orleans. The Hensons went first to Ohio and then on to Canada, where Josiah became an outspoken critic of slavery in the United States. He traveled to England three times, delivering numerous speeches on the brutality of that institution. His life story was purported to have inspired Harriet Beecher Stowe in the writing of *Uncle Tom's Cabin*.[11]

In 1842, Wilson and Henson established the British and American Manual Labor Institute for Colored Children in Upper Canada. The purpose of the school, built on 300 acres of land, was to train boys and girls in the practical arts so that they might become self-sufficient members of Canadian society. Wilson served as director of the institute for the first seven years of its existence. The area around the school quickly became colonized by blacks, and the whole complex became known as the Dawn Settlement. By 1852, there were 60 students at the institute and 500 settlers on the property. Eventually, Native American, white, and adult students were also admitted to the institute. Land for fugitives arriving from the United States became available around the property of the institute at a rate of $2.50 per acre for a parcel of fifty acres. This could be paid off in twelve annual installments. By 1862, more than 1,000 people were living in the settlement.[12]

Rev. William King, a Presbyterian minister from Louisiana, had freed fifteen slaves in the 1840s and brought them to Upper Canada. In 1849, the Elgin Association, a group formed for the purpose of settling black fugitives from the United States on government land in Upper Canada, acquired a large tract of land near the area where King had brought his charges. It was called the Elgin Society after Canada's governor general, Lord James Bruce Elgin. The community that formed there was generally known as the Elgin Settlement. The Buxton Mission School was opened here to help educate the new arrivals and their children. It was named in honor of Thomas F. Buxton, a well-known philanthropist. Each black family that settled in the community received twenty-five acres of land, of which five acres were free if they cultivated the land for a period of three years. The other twenty acres were sold to them at a price of $2.00 per acre, which could be paid in nine installments.[13]

The Refugees' Home Society, an organization formed by abolitionists in 1851, established a settlement for freedom-seeking blacks from the United States in 1851–52. Land was made available at a reduced rate for settlers, and a school was established for educating children in the skills necessary for their survival in this new economic environment.[14] The main source of funding for this venture came from abolitionists in the United States, who purchased land and resold it to black settlers at a reduced rate. Within three years of the founding of the home, they had distributed more than 2,000 acres to 150 people. Two of the key agents in obtaining donations for this effort were Henry and Mary Bibb. Henry, a former slave, had escape from his bondage but was recaptured when he returned to free his family. Eventually, after many attempts, he was successful and they all were able to reach Canada. The Bibbs settled in a home in the town of Sandwich in Upper Canada. They spent endless hours speaking out against slavery and aiding fugitives who had recently come from the United States, and they started a newspaper for the black community in Canada called the *Voice of the Fugitive.*[15]

The 1850s saw an increase in the number of freedom seekers arriving in Canada, and the effort to aid them was stepped up. The Anti-Slavery Society of Canada came into existence in Toronto in 1851. Both blacks and whites were active members of this group, and within a short time, branches of the society appeared all over Ontario. That same year, Harriet Tubman relocated the center of her efforts to free slaves in Maryland and Delaware from New York to St. Catharines in Canada, where she operated until 1858. The North American Convention, involving abolitionists from both Canada and the United States, met in St. Lawrence Hall in the city of Toronto in 1851. One of the major topics of discussion was how to help the fugitives arriving in Canada. In 1852, W. H. Merritt, along with Harriet Tubman and Elias Adams, formed the Refugee Slaves' Friend Society, whose efforts centered on assisting freedom seekers reaching and living in Canada.[16]

The year 1853 witnessed the emergence of another notable figure in the antislavery cause in Canada. Mary Ann Shadd, a freeborn black from Delaware, had moved in 1851 to Windsor, Canada, where she was an impassioned advocate of education and equality for blacks in Canadian society. One of her major objectives was the complete integration of blacks into all aspects of Canadian society. This flew in the face of the contemporary view at that time, even among many abolitionists, that separate but equal opportunities in education, housing, and other aspects of life was the more desirable approach. To promote her views, she founded an abolitionist newspaper, the *Provincial Freeman*, in Windsor. She later moved the operations of the paper to Toronto and then to Chatham. Her strong views on the need for education led her to study law, and at age sixty, she became the first black female lawyer in all of North America.[17]

Religious bodies also played a key role in helping freedom seekers coming to Canada. As early as 1828, an A.M.E. church opened its doors in Amherstburg to serve the spiritual needs of blacks living in that area. Not too many years later, a small log church opened its doors in the crucial Underground Railroad center of St. Catharines, near the border with the United States. It was the first A.M.E. church in the area. In 1855, a much larger and better-constructed building replaced the log church. It had a large seating capacity, and Harriet Tubman often attended services there while on her rescue missions. The Salem Chapel sill exists today at 92 Geneva Street in St. Catharines.[18]

By 1856, there were A.M.E. churches throughout the province of Ontario as more and more blacks came to the region. At an ecclesiastical convention in Chatham that year, the leaders of the A.M.E. Church decided to change the name of the Canadian branch to the British Methodist Episcopal Church of Canada (B.M.E.), to acknowledge the debt of gratitude its members had to the British government in Canada for providing sanctuary and support for freedom seekers fleeing from the United States.

The Baptist Church also was active in assisting blacks in Canada. The Amherstburg Baptist Association and the Canadian Anti-Slavery Baptist Association were particularly active in Ontario. In order to consolidate their efforts, the two merged in 1856.[19] One of the more outstanding figures among the Baptist clergy was Rev. Anthony Burns. Burns had escaped slavery and fled to Boston, where slave catchers caught him on May 24, 1854. After a rescue attempt failed to free him, he was brought before the courts in Boston and ordered returned to his owner in Virginia. But an abolitionist group then purchased his freedom, and he returned to Boston. Later, he went to Oberlin College in Ohio, and then to Fairmount Theological Seminary in Cincinnati. He became a Baptist minister and went to Ontario, where he worked among the black populace.[20]

Freedom seekers coming into Canada from New York, Pennsylvania, Ohio, and Michigan passed through a number of entry points. Siebert's map shows these as being Kingston, on Lake Ontario; St. Catharines and Port Erie, across the Niagara River; Port Stanley, Port Burwell, Pelee's Point, Gosfield, and Colchester, on Lake Erie; and Sandwich, Windsor, and Sarnia, across the Detroit River. Siebert gives the major settlement areas for freedom seekers as Amherstburg, Windsor, Port Stanley, Port Burwell, St. Catharines, Hamilton, Toronto, Kingston, and Montreal.[21]

Several Underground Railroad stations still exist in Ontario, among them three well-preserved sites. The Griffin House is at 733 Mineral Springs Road in Ancaster. It was owned by Enerals and Pricilla Griffin. Enerals was an escaped slave who settled in the Ancaster area and farmed the land on which the house sits today. The couple are buried in the local St. Andrew's Presbyterian Church Cemetery.[22] Bertie Hall, at 657 Niagara Parkway in Fort Erie, was built in 1830 by William Forsythe Sr. The house purportedly had a secret tunnel that connected its basement with the riverbank not too far away. Fugitives came through the tunnel into the house and found refuge there. Bertie Hall now houses the Mildred Mahoney Silver Jubilee Doll's House Gallery.[23] At 8 Navy Street in Oakville is the Oakville Museum on the Erchless Estate. The town of Oakville was a harbor for ships traveling over the Great Lakes. Many of the captains aided fugitives in their escape attempts. James Wesley Hill was the conductor in Oakville who helped these freedom seekers get from the ships to safe havens farther inland. Hill was reported to have aided more than 700 fugitives in this effort. The exhibits at the museum recall the town's participation in the Underground Railroad.[24] Another excellent museum is the St. Catharines Museum at the Welland Canals Centre, which celebrates the role this important town played in the Underground Railroad movement.[25]

The letters written by fugitives living in Canada contained in William Still's work support Siebert's findings and also add a few more settlements to his total. Still has twenty-four letters from St. Catharines, thirteen from

The town of Hamilton in Ontario Province was a key destination for freedom-seeking slaves. LIBRARY OF CONGRESS

Hamilton, one from Kingston, one from Montreal, thirty from Toronto, five from Brantford, one from Salford, and one from Yorkville, a town near Toronto. They cover the years 1853 to 1861, with the majority being written between 1855 and 1859.[26]

It is not known exactly how many freedom seekers reached Canada from the United States. A report on this topic given to the Freedmen's Inquiry Commission in Washington, D.C., in 1864 estimates that 30,000 to 40,000 fugitives reached Canada between 1800 and 1864. The report also states that in the year 1852, the Anti-Slavery Society of Toronto determined that the black population in Canada stood at 30,000 persons.[27] Gara rejects these numbers, however, citing that the Canadian census of 1860 listed only 11,000 blacks as living in the country.[28] Samuel Ringgold Ward, himself an escaped fugitive, supports the contentions of the Freedmen's Commission when he states in his autobiography that in 1855, there were between 35,000 and 40,000 "coloured people" in Canada. Of these, he says, about 3,000 were freeborn and the others were fugitives from the United States.[29] In his work, Siebert comments on the confusion over the exact number of fugitives who had reached the safety of Canada. He cites the census of 1850, which listed 2,502 male and 2,167 female blacks as living in Upper Canada, but he makes a footnote to these numbers stating that there were "about" 8,000 more living in Western Canada. He also quotes Dr. Howe, who had written the Freedmen's Inquiry Commission report, as saying that the census of 1860, which listed 11,223 blacks, contained many discrepancies and had grossly undercounted the actual number of black people living in Canada at that time. Howe also said that after his tour of the land in 1863, he had concluded that as many as 20,000 were living there. At the opposite end of the population numbers is Rev. Hiram Wilson, who puts the population figure at closer to 60,000 black individuals, based on his direct involvement with helping fugitives reach and settle in Canada.[30]

Blacks living in Canada worked at a variety of occupations. Farming was the main pursuit of most of those living in the black settlements scattered across the land, but others found work in skilled and semiskilled trades. Some were adept at plastering, painting, blacksmithing, and carpentry; others pursued work as builders or mill workers. A group became shopkeepers and clerks, which eventually gave rise to a middle class among the black citizenry.[31] At Amherstburg, the main occupation of the 600 blacks living there was the cultivation of tobacco. Near Niagara Falls, many freedom seekers became waiters in hotels. Others began to farm the rich land along the Conestogo River, between Waterloo and Guelph.[32]

Some former fugitives became entrepreneurs and started businesses that became very successful. One such individual was Thornton Blackburn. Thronton and his wife, Lucie, left Kentucky and traveled to Toronto in 1833. While working as a waiter at Osgoode Hall, Blackburn noticed that Toronto did not have any form of public transportation. After obtaining the pattern for a horse-drawn carriage from a Montreal businessman, he had a carriage maker build one and painted it a distinctive yellow and red. In 1837, Blackburn began to operate the carriage, which he called "the City," providing the first taxicab service in Upper Canada. His cab business became a success, and over time, Blackburn and his wife became two of the more prominent members of the black community in the city.[33]

The many letters that William Still received from successful escapees in Canada paint a detailed picture of what life was like for them in their new home. The following are a few of these portrait.

St. Catharines, Feb. 20th, 1854

Mr. Still—Dear Sir:—It is with great pleasure that I have to inform you, that I have arrived safe in a land of freedom. Thanks to kind friends that helped me here. Thank God that I am treading on free soil. I expect to go to work to-morrow in a steam factory.

I would like to have you, if it is not too much trouble, see Mr. Minhett, the steward on the boat that I came out on, when he gets to Norfolk, to go to the place where my clothes are, and bring them to you, direct them to the care of Rev. Hiram Wilson, St. Catharines, Niagara District, Canada West, by rail-road via Suspension Bridge. You mentioned if I saw Mr. Foreman. I was to deliver a message—he is not here. I saw two yesterday in church, from Norfolk, that I had known there. You will send my name, James Henry, as you knew me by that name; direct my things to James Henry. My love to you and your wife and children.

Yours Respectfully, Solomon Brown.[34]

The writer of this letter had changed his name from James Henry to Solomon Brown. This was a common practice in an effort to start a new life with a new identity and thereby thwart recapture attempts. The letter also reveals that the writer has obtained employment in a steam factory and that Rev. Hiram Wilson gave him assistance. Wilson helped many newcomers adjust to life in their new environment. The use of the railroad crossing of the Suspension Bridge is also mentioned as a line of communication for freedom seekers.

The next letter, also from St. Catharines, gives more insights as to why so many fugitives decided to stay there. It details several support institutions, such as a black Masonic lodge, churches, and other organizations that gave emotional, social, and material support to the newly settled self-emancipators.

St. Catharine, April 16, 1855

MR. WILLIAM STILL, Dear Sir:—Your letter date April 7th I have just got, it had been opened before it came to me. I have not received any other letter from you and can get no account of them in the Post Office in this-place. I am well and have got a good situation in this city and intend staying here. I should be very glad to hear from you as soon as convenient and also from all of my friends near you. My Brother is also at work with me and doing well.

There is nothing here that would interest you in a way of news. There is a Masonic Lodge of our people and two churches and societys here and some other institutions for our benefit. Be kind enough to send a few lines to the Lady spoken of for that mocking bird and much oblige me. Write soon and believe me your obedient Servt

Love & respects to lady and daughter   Joseph Robinson[35]

The following letter, signed by four individuals, came from Toronto and gives a picture of life in that city for the new residents. Of particular interest is the listing of the relatively low wages that blacks were paid for the work they did in that city.

Toronto, C. W., Aug. 17th, 1856

Mr. Still:—Dear Sir—These few lines may find you as they leave us, we are well at present and arrived safe in Toronto. Give our respects to Mrs. S.— and daughter. Toronto is a very extensive place. We have plenty of pork, beef and mutton. There are five market houses and many churches. Female wages is 62½ cents per day, men's wages is $1 and york shilling. We are now boarding at Mr. George Blunt's, on Centre street, two doors from Elm, back of Lawyer's Hall, and when you write to us, direct your letter to the care of Mr. George Blunt, &c. [Signed], James Monroe, Peter Hines, Henry James Morris, and Matthew Bodams.[36]

The key to the success of the newcomers was in education. At first, those reaching the black settlements received schooling there. As they became more established and decided to send their children to established public schools, they began to experience discrimination. Although most white

Canadians were tolerant to the presence of blacks, they did take issue with mixed schools.[37] The children of black parents were barred from many schools, and this provoked much anger and agitation among the black community. To help rectify the situation, the Canadian government passed the Common Schools Act, which established schools for all across the country. The schools were segregated, however, foreshadowing the school crisis in the United States prior to its own civil rights movement. As would be the case later in the United States, the schools for blacks did not have sufficient staffing, books, or materials, and many closed not long after opening.[38]

Although Canada certainly was a haven to which freedom-seeking enslaved people fled, the attitude of many Canadians toward the newcomers changed over the years. In the 1820s and 1830s, the freedom seekers generally were well received in most of Canada. After the 1840s, however, the reception began to cool. As the numbers of fugitives began to increase during the late 1840s and early 1850s, tensions began to rise. In addition to the schooling situation, the fact that new residents were willing to work for wages far below those of the white Canadians caused great friction with those being displaced from their occupations by the new workers. During the 1850s, a "casual" type of segregation began to develop in Canada. Blacks were not as well received as they had been earlier.[39]

Canada did not remain a land of freedom for blacks after the Civil War had concluded. Following the War and the period known as the Reconstruction Era in American history, many blacks left Canada and returned to the United States. The official line of the Canadian government on this exodus was that the hope of reuniting with lost families, the more suitable weather conditions and the familiarity of the land were the major reasons for this departure. However, there were a number of factors in Canada that also contributed to this choice on the part of black people living there. The problem with the segregated schools, the substandard pay in many jobs, the prejudicial slant of many newspaper editorials, and the neglect on the part of the government to addressing many of these issues, led to a migration south from Canada. This migration continued throughout the decades after the Civil War to the point that, by 1900, only 18,000 black citizens still resided in Canada.[40] Canada had served a vial purpose at a time of need for many enslaved blacks, but it did not fulfill the role of a "promised land" for the years that followed the operation of the Underground Railroad.

NOTES

THE STORY OF JOHN HENRY HILL

1. William Still, *The Underground Railroad: A Record of Facts, Authentic Narratives, Letter, &c.* (Philadelphia: Porter & Coates, 1872; repr., New York: Arno Press and the *New York Times*, 1968), 191.
2. Ibid.
3. Ibid.
4. Ibid., 191–92.
5. Ibid., 192.
6. Ibid.
7. Ibid.
8. Ibid., 194.
9. Ibid., 193.
10. Ibid., 195.
11. Ibid.
12. Ibid., 200.

THE SETTING

1. Stanley M. Elkins, *Slavery: A Problem in American Institutional and Intellectual Life* (New York: Grosset & Dunlap, 1963), 38.
2. *The Statistical History of the United States from Colonial Times to the Present* (Stamford, CT: Fairfield Publishers, 1965), 11–12.
3. *1790, 1850, and 1860 County Level Census Data—Sorted by State/Counties—New Jersey* (fisher.lib.virginia.edu/cgi-local/censusbin/census/cen.pl).
4. *1790, 1850, and 1860 County Level Census Data—Sorted by State/County—New York.*
5. Samuel Eliot Morison, *The Oxford History of the American People* (New York: Oxford University Press, 1965), 295.
6. Catherine Drinker Bowen, *Miracle at Philadelphia: The Story of the Constitutional Convention, May to September 1787* (New York: Book-of-the-Month Club, 1966), 201–4.
7. Henry Steele Commager, ed., *Documents in American History* (New York: Appleton-Century-Croft, 1958), 128–32.
8. Ibid., 197–98.
9. John A. Munroe, *Federalist Delaware, 1775–1815* (New Brunswick, NJ: Rutgers University Press, 1954), 20, 158, 218.
10. Morison, *Oxford History,* 295.
11. Commager, *Documents,* 37–38.

12. Ira V. Brown, *The Negro in Pennsylvania History* (University Park: Pennsylvania Historical Association, 1970), 3.

13. Louis Tiller, *The Crusade against Slavery, 1830–1860* (New York: Harper & Brothers Publishers, 1960), 13–14.

14. Wayland F. Dunaway, *A History of Pennsylvania* (Englewood Cliffs, NJ: Prentice-Hall, 1948), 185.

15. Mary Stoughton and A. M. Locke, *Anti-Slavery in America from the Introduction of African Slaves to the Prohibition of Slave Trade, 1618–1808* (Boston: Ginn & Company, Publishers, 1907), 146–47.

16. Tiller, *Crusade against Slavery,* 122–23.

17. David Christy, *Pulpit Politics; or, Ecclesiastical Legislation on Slavery in Its Disturbing Influences on the American Union* (New York: Farran & McLean Publishers, 1862; repr., New York: Negro Universities Press, 1969), 343.

18. Stoughton and Locke, *Anti-Slavery in America,* 41.

19. Ibid., 216, 224.

20. William W. Sweet, *The Story of Religion in America* (New York: Harper & Brothers, Publishers, 1930), 421–22.

21. Wilhelmina S. Robinson, *Historical Negro Biographies* (New York: Publishers Company, 1967), 5–6.

22. David Brian Davis, ed., *Ante-Bellum Reform* (New York: Harper & Row, Publishers, 1967), 29.

23. Ibid., 30.

24. Ibid., 31–32.

25. Ira V. Brown, *Pennsylvania Reformers: From Penn to 1848* (Philadelphia: Temple University Press, 1988), 49.

26. Elkins, *Slavery,* 179–80.

27. Brown, *Pennsylvania Reformers,* 8.

28. Tiller, *Crusade against Slavery,* 67.

29. Julie Winch, *Philadelphia Black Elite Activism, Accommodation, and the Struggle for Autonomy, 1787–1848* (Philadelphia: Temple University Press, 1988), 49.

30. Robinson, *Historical Negro Biographies,* 120.

31. Ibid., 72.

32. Ibid., 119.

33. Ibid., 74, 82, 108.

OPERATION OF THE RAILROAD

1. Larry Gara, *The Liberty Line: The Legend of the Underground Railroad* (Lexington: University of Kentucky Press, 1967), 2.

2. Ibid., 3.

3. Ibid., 166, 171.

4. Letter to Robert Morris, April 12, 1786, in *The Writings of George Washington from the Original Manuscript Sources, 1745–1799,* ed. John C. Fitzpatrick (Washington, DC: U.S. government Printing Office), vol. 28, 407–8.

5. Letter to William Drayton, November 20, 1786, in ibid., vol. 29, 78–79.

6. W. J. McKnight, *A Pioneer History of Jefferson County, Pennsylvania, and My First Recollections of Brookville, Pennsylvania, 1840–43, When My Feet Were Bare and My Cheeks Were Brown* (Philadelphia: J.B. Lippincott Company, 1898), 273.

7. Robert C. Smedley, *History of the Underground Railroad in Chester and the Neighboring Counties of Pennsylvania* (Lancaster, PA: Office of the Journal, 1883; repr., New York: Arno Press and the *New York Times*, 1969), 25.

8. Wilbur H. Siebert, *The Underground Railroad: From Slavery to Freedom* (New York: Macmillan Company, 1898; repr., New York: Russell & Russell, 1967), 34.

9. Ibid., 45.

10. Smedley, *History of the Underground Railroad*, 34–35.

11. Rev. Calvin Fairbanks, *During Slavery Times* (New York: Patriotic Publishing Co., 1890; repr., Negro Universities Press, 1969), 61–62.

12. Martin Duberman, ed., *The Antislavery Vanguard: New Essays on the Abolitionists* (Princeton, NJ: Princeton University Press, 1965), 303.

13. Samuel Ringgold Ward, *Autobiography of a Fugitive Negro: His Anti-Slavery Labours in the United States, Canada & England* (London: John Snow, 1855; repr., New York: Arno Press and the *New York Times*, 1968), 292–93.

14. S. G. Howe, *Report to the Freedmen's Inquiry Commission, 1864: The Refugees from Slavery in Canada West* (Boston: Wright & Potter, Printers, 1864; repr., New York: Arno Press and the *New York Times*, 1969), 9.

15. Tiller, *Crusade against Slavery*, 91.

16. Siebert, *Underground Railroad*, 27–28.

17. Letter Book, undated entry, in Fitzpatrick, *Writings of Washington*, vol. 30, 481.

18. Howe, *Freedmen's Report*, 9.

19. Ibid.

20. Marion Gleason McDougall, *Fugitive Slaves, 1619–1865* (Boston: Fay House Monographs, 1891; repr., New York: Bergman Publishers, 1967), 25.

21. Levi Coffin, *Reminiscences* (Cincinnati: Robert Clarke Company, 1898; repr., New York: Arno Press and the *New York Times*, 1968), 111.

22. Ibid., 20, 111–13; and Smedley, *History of the Underground Railroad*, 28–29.

23. Smedley, *History of the Underground Railroad*, 270.

24. Fairbanks, *During Slavery Times*, 11.

25. Coffin, *Reminiscences*, 111.

26. Fairbanks, *During Slavery Times*, 10.

27. Ibid., 20–23.

28. Still, *Underground Railroad*, 106–7.

29. Fairbanks, *During Slavery Times*, 15–19.

30. Frederick Douglass, *Narrative of the Life of Frederick Douglass, an American Slave, Written by Himself* (New York: Penguin Books USA, 1986), 124.

31. Still, *Underground Railroad*, 98.

32. Ibid., 165–67.
33. Ibid., 54–55.
34. Ibid., 81–84.
35. Ibid., 282–83, 607–10.
36. Norman R. Yetman, ed., *Voices from Slavery: 100 Authentic Slave Narratives* (Mineola, NY: Dover Publications, 2003), 33–34.
37. McDougall, *Fugitive Slaves, 1619–1865*, 25.
38. Commager, ed., *Documents of American History*, 321–23.
39. Siebert, *Underground Railroad*, 122–23.

NEW JERSEY—THE BACKDROP

1. Thomas A. Bailey, *The American Pageant: A History of the Republic* (Boston: D. C. Heath and Company, 1961), 36–38.
2. Morison, *Oxford History*, 77.
3. Ibid., 79.
4. Giles R. Wright and Edward Lama Wonkeryor, *"Steal Away, Steal Away . . .": A Guide to the Underground Railroad in New Jersey* (Trenton: New Jersey Historical Commission, n.d.), www.state.nj.us/state/history/underground_rr.pdf.
5. *New Jersey Slave Laws Summary and Record*, www.slaveryinamerica.org/geography/slave_laws_NJ.htm.
6. Clement Alexander Price, *Freedom Not Far Distant: A Documentary History of Afro-Americans in New Jersey* (Newark: New Jersey Historical Society, 1980), 2.
7. "The Underground Railroad in Bucks, Burlington and Montgomery County," *Burlington County Times*, May 5, 2004, wysiwyg://42/http://www.phillyburbs.com/undergroundrailroad/NJabolition.shtml.
8. *New Jersey Slave Laws.*
9. Philip S. Foner, *History of Black Americans: From Africa to the Emergence of the Cotton Kingdom* (Westport, CT: Greenwood Press, 1975), 238.
10. Ibid.
11. *1790 to 1860 County Level Census Data—New Jersey.*
12. "New Jersey and Slavery," *New Jersey before the Civil War*, zorak.monmouth.edu/~njhist/NJTheCivilWar1.html.
13. Interracial Committee, *Negro in New Jersey*, 15.
14. *1790 to 1860 County Level Census Data—New Jersey.*
15. *New Jersey Slave Laws Summary and Record,* www.slaveryinamerica.org/geography/slave_laws_NJ.htm; *New York Slave Laws Summary and Record*, www.slaveryinamerica.org/geography/slave_laws_NY.htm; and, *Pennsylvania Slave Laws Summary and Record*, www.slaveryinamerica.org/geography/slave_laws_PA.htm.
16. *Virginia Slave Laws Summary and Record*, www.slaveryinamerica.org/geography/slave_laws_VA.htm.
17. Ibid.

18. *An Act for Regulating of Slaves*, intranet.rutgers.edu/~clemens/slavelaw1714 .html.
19. *New Jersey Slave Laws.*
20. *An Act Respecting Slaves, Acts of the General Assembly*, chapter DCCXYVV, intranet.rutgers.edu/~clemens/slavelaw1798.html.
21. *An Act for the Gradual Abolition of Slavery (1804)*, intranet.rutgers.edu/ %7Eclemens/slavelaw1804.html.
22. *Certificate of Abandonment, Piscataway Township, New Jersey, 1806*, www.scc .rutgers.edu/njwomenshistory/Period_2/abandonment.htm.
23. *A Manumission of Abigal, 1808*, www.scc.rutgers.edu/njwomenshistory/ Period_2/manumission.htm.
24. *An Act for the Gradual Abolition of Slavery, and Other Purposes Respecting Slaves*, intranet.rutgers.edu/~clemens/slavelaw1820.html.
25. Foner, *History of Black Americans*, 271.
26. Ibid., 370.
27. *First Federal Congress: Petitioning the Federal Government*, www.gwu.edu/~ffcp/ exhibit/p11/p11_4.html.
28. William J. Jackson, *New Jerseyans in the Civil War for Union and Liberty* (New Brunswick, NJ: Rutgers University Press, 2000), 16–17.
29. Foner, *History of Black Americans*, 371.
30. Jackson, *New Jerseyans in the Civil War*, 5.
31. Foner, *History of Black Americans*, 372.
32. Sweet, *Religion in America*, 203–4.
33. Jackson, *New Jerseyans in the Civil War*, 5.
34. *1860 County Level Census Data—New Jersey—Churches.*
35. Sweet, *Religion in America*, 143–44.
36. *1860 County Level Census Data—New Jersey—Churches.*
37. Tiller, *Crusade against Slavery*, 13–14.
38. Dunaway, *History of Pennsylvania*, 185.
39. Sweet, *Religion in America*, 417.
40. Daniel A. Payne, *History of the African Methodist Episcopal Church* (Nashville: Publishing House of the A.M.E. Sunday-School Union, 1861; repr., New York: Arno Press and the *New York Times*, 1968), 33.
41. Emma Marie Trusty, *The Underground Railroad: Ties That Bound Unveiled: A History of the Underground Railroad in Southern New Jersey from 1770 to 1861* (Philadelphia: Amed Literary, 1997), 67.
42. *1840, 1850, and 1860 County Level Census Data—New Jersey.*
43. *Life Pictorial Atlas of the World* (New York: Time, 1961), 210–11.
44. George Rogers Taylor, *The Transportation Revolution, 1815–1860* (New York: Harper & Row, 1951), 58–59.
45. *The State of New Jersey Compiled from the Most Authentic Information*, mapmaker.rutgers.edu/HISTORICALMAPS/NJ_1753%20copy.jpg.
46. Taylor, *Transportation Revolution*, 23, 30, 31.

47. Ibid., 79.

48. Ibid., 89.

49. Trusty, *Underground Railroad*, 96–97, 160, 354.

50. George Fishman, *The African American Struggle for Freedom and Equality: The Development of a People's Identity, New Jersey, 1624–1850* (New York: Garland Publishing, 1997), 61, 63.

51. *Runaway Slave Advertisements*, www.runet.edu/~shepburn/web/Runaway%20 Slave%20Advertisements.htm.

NEW JERSEY ROUTES

1. Siebert, *Underground Railroad*, 124–25.

2. Ibid., 113.

3. Ibid., 113, 124–25.

4. Jeffrey M. Dorwart, *Cape May County, New Jersey: The Making of an American Resort Community* (New Brunswick, NJ: Rutgers University Press, 1992), 15–16, 18, 36–38, 63–64.

5. Ibid., 67, 82, 83.

6. Siebert, *Underground Railroad*, 413.

7. Still, *Underground Railroad*, 528–30.

8. Dorwart, *Cape May County*, 83.

9. Wright and Wonkeryor, *"Steal Away,"* 10.

10. Dorwart, *Cape May County*, 83.

11. *Map of New Jersey, 1826*, mapmaker.rutgers.edu/NJ_1826.jpg: *Map of New Jersey, 1856*, mapmaker.rutgers.edu/NJ_1856.jpg.

12. Trusty, *Underground Railroad*, 102.

13. *Map of the Rail Roads of New Jersey and Parts of Adjoining States, 1869*, mapmaker.rutgers.edu/HISTORICALMAPS/RAILROADS/rr_NJ_PA_NY.jpg.

14. Trusty, *Underground Railroad*, 214

15. Ibid., 188, 193–94.

16. Ibid., 214.

17. *Map of New Jersey, 1856*.

18. Trusty, *Underground Railroad*, 149, 177.

19. Ibid., 247.

20. Ibid., 236, 247, 249.

21. *Map of New Jersey, 1856*.

22. Trusty, *Underground Railroad*, 202.

23. *Map of New Jersey, 1826*.

24. Payne, *African Methodist Episcopal Church*, 33.

25. Trusty, *Underground Railroad*, 83, 98, 102.

26. Ibid., 213.

27. Ibid., 103.

28. *1830, 1850, and 1860 County Census Level Data—New Jersey*.

29. Payne, *African Methodist Episcopal Church*, 33.

30. *Map of New Jersey, 1753*, mapmaker.rutgers.edu/HISTORICALMAPS/NJ_1753%20copy.jpg; and *Map of New Jersey, 1856.*
31. *Map of the Rail Roads, 1869.*
32. Ward, *Autobiography*, 19, 22–26.
33. Still, *Underground Railroad*, 37–38.
34. Siebert, *Underground Railroad*, 124, 125, 413.
35. Ibid., 15.
36. Wright and Wonkeryor, *"Steal Away,"* 7.
37. Siebert, *Underground Railroad*, 125.
38. Federal Writers' Project, *New Jersey: A Guide to Its Present and Past* (New York: Viking Press, 1939), 611.
39. Siebert, *Underground Railroad*, 413.
40. *1850 County Level Census Data—New Jersey.*
41. Payne, *African Methodist Episcopal Church*, 33.
42. Wright and Wonkeryor, *"Steal Away,"* 7.
43. Siebert, *Underground Railroad*, 125.
44. Trusty, *Underground Railroad*, 96.
45. *Map of the Rail Roads, 1869.*
46. Trusty, *Underground Railroad*, 93, 96, 97, 160, 161.
47. *Map of New Jersey, 1856.*
48. *1850 County Level Census Data—New Jersey.*
49. Payne, *African Methodist Episcopal Church*, 33.
50. Siebert, *Underground Railroad*, 413.
51. Wright and Wonkeryor, *"Steal Away,"* 7.
52. Still, *Underground Railroad*, 256, 257, 617–22.
53. Siebert, *Underground Railroad*, 124.
54. *Map of New Jersey, 1753.*
55. Payne, *African Methodist Episcopal Church*, 33.
56. Trusty, *Underground Railroad*, 247–49, 254.
57. Ibid., 260.
58. *1850 County Level Census Data—New Jersey.*
59. Payne, *African Methodist Episcopal Church*, 33.
60. Siebert, *Underground Railroad*, 413.
61. Trusty, *Underground Railroad*, 19.
62. Siebert, *Underground Railroad*, 123–24.
63. Wright and Wonkeryor, *"Steal Away,"* 8, 10.
64. Siebert, *Underground Railroad*, 124.
65. *Map of New Jersey, 1856.*
66. Trusty, *Underground Railroad*, 177.
67. *Burlington, N.J.*, 08016.com/allison.html and 08016/grubb-estate.html.
68. *Map of New Jersey, 1856.*
69. Wright and Wonkeryor, *"Steal Away,"* 8.

70. Siebert, *Underground Railroad*, 124.

71. Ibid.; Still, *Underground Railroad*, 257.

72. *Map of New Jersey, 1856; Map of Railroads of New Jersey and parts of the Adjoining States 1869.*

73. Trusty, *Underground Railroad*, 352, 354.

74. Siebert, *Underground Railroad*, 124.

75. *Abolitionism in New Jersey*, www.njtimes.rutgers.edu/abolt.htm.

76. Payne, *African Methodist Episcopal Church*, 33.

77. Federal Writers' Project, *New Jersey*, 600.

78. National Park Service, *Aboard the Underground Railroad—Peter Mott House*, www.cr.nps.gov/nr/travel/underground/nj2.htm.

79. Trusty, *Underground Railroad*, 177.

80. Wright and Wonkeryor, *"Steal Away,"* 8.

81. Payne, *African Methodist Episcopal Church*, 33.

82. Siebert, *Underground Railroad*, 124.

83. "19th Century Mount Laurel," *Mount Laurel Township*, http://www.mount laurel.com/hist19chtm.

84. Payne, *African Methodist Episcopal Church*, 33.

85. "Jacobs Chapel," *Mount Laurel Township*, www.mountlaurel.com/jacob.htm.

86. Trusty, *Underground Railroad*, 369.

87. Benjamin Drew, *A North-Side View of Slavery: The Refugee; or, The Narratives of Fugitive Slaves in Canada* (Boston: John P. Jewett and Company, 1856; reprinted in *Four Fugitive Slave Narratives* (Reading, MA: Addison-Wesley Publishing Company, 1968), 22–25.

88. Wright and Wonkeryor, *"Steal Away,"* 8.

89. William McMahon, *South Jersey Towns* (New Brunswick, NJ: Rutgers University Press, 1973), 98.

90. Siebert, *Underground Railroad*, 125.

91. *Map of New Jersey, 1856.*

92. Price, *Freedom Not Far Distant*, 21–26.

93. Trusty, *Underground Railroad*, 368.

94. Charles L. Blockson, *The Underground Railroad in Pennsylvania* (Jacksonville, NC: Flame International, 1981), 48.

95. Ibid., 36.

96. *1850 County Level Census—New Jersey.*

97. Payne, *African Methodist Episcopal Church*, 33; Trusty, *Underground Railroad*, 67, 374.

98. Siebert, *Underground Railroad*, 124.

99. David Learn, "Journey to Africa via Princeton," *Princeton Packet*, June 26, 1998, www.pacpubserver.com?new/news/6-27-98/slaves.html.

100. Siebert, *Underground Railroad*, 124.

101. Federal Writers' Project, *New Jersey*, 363.

102. Paul Goodman, *Of One Blood: Abolitionism and the Origins of Racial Equality* (Berkeley: University of California Press, 1998), 101, 177, 178.

103. Fishman, *African American Struggle*, 157.

104. Alexander Maclean, *The Underground Railroad in Hudson County, part 11,* 2002, www.cityofjerseycity.org/ur/undergroundrailroadinhudsoncountyeleven.shtml.

105. "Downtown Jersey City Homes for Sale in Hudson County, New Jersey," *Downtown Jersey City,* www.downtown-jerseycity-homesforsale.com/cityprofile.htm.

106. Federal Writers' Project, *New Jersey,* 275.

107. Carmela Karnoutsos, "The Underground Railroad in Jersey City," *Jersey City Past and Present,* www.njcu.edu/programs/jchistory/pages/U_Pages/Underground_Railroad.htm.

108. Wright and Wonkeryor, *"Steal Away,"* 3.

109. Siebert, *Underground Railroad,* 125.

110. *Map of the Rail Roads, 1869.*

111. Payne, *African Methodist Episcopal Church,* 33.

112. Charles L. Blockson, *The Underground Railroad* (New York: Berkley Publishing Group, 1987), 216.

113. William J. Switala, *Underground Railroad in Pennsylvania* (Mechanicsburg, PA: Stackpole Books, 2001), 152.

114. Wright and Wonkeryor, *"Steal Away,"* 9.

115. Jack Baney, "Hillsborough Backs Effort to Protect Ridge," *Packet Group,* June 22, 2000, www.pacpubservice.com/new/news/6-22-00/sourlands.html.

116. *Map of the Rail Roads, 1869.*

117. Christine Magnotta, "Dream House Sours for Couple," *Pocono Record,* July 6, 1998, www.poconorecord.com/1998/local.tjd70360.html.

118. Wright and Wonkeryor, *"Steal Away,"* 10.

119. "Grimes Homestead," *Aboard the Underground Railroad,* www.cr.nps.gov/nr/travel/underground/nj1.html.

120. Wright and Wonkeryor, *"Steal Away,"* 3.

121. Scott Morgan, "Shiloh Baptist Church Members Celebrate Black History Month at Their Bordentown City Church," *Register-News,* February 12, 2004, www.pacpub.com/site/news.cfm?newsid=10957492&BRD=1091&PAG=461&dept...

122. Trusty, *Underground Railroad,* 67.

123. Lea Kahn, "Canal's Past Revisited through Pictorial," *Lawrence Ledger,* January 17, 2002, www.pacpub.com/site/news.cfm?newsid=3012543&BRD=1091&PAG=461&dept_i...

124. *Map of the Rail Roads, 1869.*

125. John Fabiano, "Recrossing Crosswicks," part 2 of 4, *Messenger-Press,* July 15, 2004, www.pacpub.com/site/news?cfm?newsid=12335558&BRD=1091&PAG=461&dept_...

126. John Fabiano, "Historically Speaking: A Look at the Allentown-Upper Free-hold of the Past," *Messenger-Press*, August 23, 2001, www.pacpub.com/site/news?cfm?newsid=2254354&BRD=1091&PAG=461&dept_i...

127. "History of Cranbury," *Early History—Cranbury, N.J.*, www.cranbury.org/history/earlhist.html.

128. Wright and Wonkeryor, *"Steal Away,"* 9.

129. "South Brunswick Riding the 'Railroad' through Red Maple Farm," *Home News Tribune*, June 1, 2003, nl.newsbank.com/nl-search/we/Archives?s_site=thnt&f_sitename=Hom...

130. *1820 County Level Census Data—New Jersey.*

131. Graham Russell Hodges, *Slavery and Freedom in the Rural North: African Americans in Monmouth County, New Jersey, 1665–1865* (Madison, WI: Madison House, 1997), 58, 177.

132. Ibid., 123.

133. Franklin Ellis, *History of Monmouth County, New Jersey*, (Philadelphia: R. T. Peck & Co., 1885), 692.

134. Hodges, *Slavery and Freedom*, 182.

135. Ibid., 61–62.

NEW YORK—THE BACKDROP

1. Bailey, *American Pageant*, 36–39, 131.

2. Foner, *Blacks in America*, 232.

3. Ross W. Higgins and Margaret Vetare, "Establishing Slavery in Colonial New York," *Historic Hudson Valley*, 1, www.hudsonvalley.org/web/phil-slav.htm.

4. Foner, *Blacks in America*, 234.

5. Higgins and Vetare, "Establishing Slavery," 1.

6. Foner, *Blacks in America*, 235, 256.

7. *1790 to 1860 County Level Census Data—New York.*

8. Higgins and Vetare, "Establishing Slavery," 2.

9. Foner, *Blacks in America*, 234, 235.

10. *New York Slave Law Summary and Record,* www.slaveryinamerica.org/geography/slave_laws_NY.htm.

11. Ibid.

12. Foner, *Blacks in America*, 269–70.

13. Ibid., 274–75.

14. Ibid., 238.

15. *New York Slave Law.*

16. Foner, *Blacks in America*, 366–68.

17. *New York Slave Law.*

18. Foner, *Blacks in America*, 574, 557.

19. Fairbanks, *During Slavery Times*, 10, 20–23.

20. Still, *Underground Railroad*, 106–7.

21. *Against the Annexation of Texas,* www.oswego.edu/Acad_Dept/a_and_s/history/ugrr/anti4.html.
22. Ibid., www.oswego.edu/Acad_Dept/a_and_s/history/ugrr/anti3.html.
23. *Against Slavery and the Slave Trade in the District of Columbia and Florida,* www.oswego.edu/Acad_Dept/a_and_s/history/ugrr/anti5.html.
24. Robinson, *Historical Negro Biographies,* 5–6.
25. Payne, *African Methodist Episcopal Church,* 34.
26. Christopher Densmore, "The Society of Friends in Western New York," *Quakers in Western New York,* ublib.buffalo.edu/libraries/units/archives/urr/Quakers_in_Western_New_York.html.
27. *1850 County Level Census Data—New York*
28. Christy, *Pulpit Politics,* 343.
29. *1850 County Level Census Data—New York.*
30. Stoughton and Locke, *Anti-Slavery in America,* 41.
31. *1850 County Level Census Data—New York.*
32. Sweet, *Religion in America,* 421–22.
33. *1850 County Level Census Data—New York.*
34. Louis Filler, *The Crusade against Slavery, 1830–1860* (New York: Harper & Brothers, 1960), 32.
35. Ibid., 33.
36. *The Burned-Over District,* history.acusd.edu/gen/civilwar/01/burned.html.
37. Ibid., 123–25.
38. *1840, 1850, and 1860 County Level Census Data—New York.*
39. "Meeting of Colored Citizens," *Oswego Palladium,* June 1, 1850, www.oswego.edu/Acad_Dept/a_and_s/history/ugrr/palla3.html; "Mass Meeting of Colored Citizens, October 3, 1850," *Buffalo Daily Republic,* October 4, 1850, and "Mass Meeting of Colored Citizens, October 17, 1850," [Rochester, NY], *North Star,* October 24, 1850, ublib.buffalo.edu/libraries/units/archives/urr/Mass_Meeting_of_Colored_Citizens,_1...1/13/2004.
40. Filler, *Crusade against Slavery,* 63, 72, 76, 294.
41. *Life Pictorial Atlas,* 212–13.
42. Taylor, *Transportation Revolution,* 23, 28, 30.
43. J. Calvin Smith, *Map of the State of New York, Cities, Towns and Villages, 1844,* digital.nypl.org/images/w/434731w.jpg.
44. Taylor, *Transportation Revolution,* 33–35, 79.
45. Ibid., 58, 61.
46. Ibid., 116.
47. Ibid., 78, 79, 85.
48. *Map of New York & Erie Railroad and Its Connections: The Most Direct Route from New York to All Western Cities and Towns.* (New York: J. H. Colton & Co., 1855), wnyrailfan.net/erie_map_1855.htm.
49. *Map of the Erie Railway and Its Connections, 1866* (New York: G. W. Colton & C. B. Colton & Co., 1869), wnyrails.railfan.net/erie_map_1869.htm.

50. Switala, *Underground Railroad in Pennsylvania*, 115.

51. John T. Clarke, *Map of the State of New-York Showing Its Water and Rail Road Lines, Jan. 1855*, memory.loc.gov/cgi-bin/map_item.pl.

52. *Runaway Slave Advertisements.*

NEW YORK—THE EASTERN ROUTES

1. Siebert, *Underground Railroad*, 414–15.

2. *1850 County Level Census Data—New York*

3. Ibid.

4. Siebert, *Underground Railroad*, 124.

5. Ibid.

6. Maclean, *Underground Railroad in Hudson County.*

7. Federal Writers' Project, *New Jersey*, 275.

8. Karnoutsos, "Underground Railroad in Jersey City."

9. Siebert, *Underground Railroad*, 414.

10. Benjamin Quarles, *Black Abolitionists* (New York: Oxford University Press, 1969), 149.

11. Blockson, *Underground Railroad*, 223.

12. Siebert, *Underground Railroad*, 35.

13. "New Yorkers Active in the Underground Railroad," *New York History*, www.nyhistory.com/ugrr/people.htm.

14. One of the First to Fight Slavery, David Ruggles," *African American Registry*, www.aaregistry.com/african_american_history/1991/one_of_the_first_to_fight_slav...

15. Wilhelmina S. Robinson, *Historical Negro Biographies*, (New York: Publishers Company, Inc., 1967), 125.

16. *Henry Ward Beecher Abolitionism*, spider.georgetowncollege.edu/htallant/courses/his338/students/nhewitt/slavery.htm.

17. Robinson, *Historical Negro Biographies*, 148.

18. Still, *Underground Railroad*, 680, 682.

19. Kathleen G. Velsor, "The Long Island Freedom Trail," *Journal of Afro-American Historical and Genealogical Society* 22 (Fall 2003): 183.

20. Richard Shannon Moss, *Slavery on Long Island: A Study in Local Institutional and Early African-American Communal Life* (New York: Garland Publishing, 1993), 108.

21. Siebert, *Underground Railroad*, 113, 126.

22. Blockson, *Underground Railroad*, 60.

23. Siebert, *Underground Railroad*, 126.

24. *1850 County Level Census Data—New York—Population*

25. Velsor, "Long Island Freedom Trail," 179.

26. James Driscoll, "Samuel Parsons: A Long Island Quaker and the Anti-Slavery Struggle," *Journal of the Afro-American Historical and Genealogical Society* 22 (Fall 2003): 194.

27. Velsor, "Long Island Freedom Trail," 180.

28. Ibid., 178–79.

29. Ibid., 180–83.

30. Ibid., 183; Driscoll, "Samuel Parsons," 188.

31. Velsor, "Long Island Freedom Trail," 182–83.

32. Ibid., 180–81.

33. Ibid., 183–84.

34. Driscoll, "Samuel Parsons," 188–89, 194–95.

35. Siebert, *Underground Railroad*, 113; Alexander C. Flick, ed., *History of the State of New York*, vol. 7, *Modern Party Battles* (New York: Columbia University Press, 1935), 68.

36. Taylor, *Transportation Revolution*, 23, 33, 35, 58, 85.

37. Velsor, "Long Island Freedom Trail," 183.

38. Tom Calarco, *The Underground Railroad in the Adirondack Region* (Jefferson, NC: McFarland & Company, Publishers, 2004), 182–83.

39. "Peekskill Underground Railroad and Tunnel," *Forging the Freedom Trail*, www.freedomtrail.org/regions/peekskillug.htm.

40. Calarco, *Underground Railroad in the Adirondacks*, 184.

41. Ibid., 185–86.

42. Paul Stewart and Mary Liz Stewart, "People Who Supported the Work of the Underground Railroad," *Underground Workshop*, www.ugrworkshop.com/otherpeople.htm.

43. Ibid.

44. Ibid.

45. Calarco, *Underground Railroad in the Adirondacks*, 187.

46. Stewart and Stewart, "People Who Supported the Underground Railroad."

47. Ibid.

48. Siebert, *Underground Railroad*, 113.

49. Ibid., 414.

50. "New Yorkers Active in the Underground Railroad."

51. Paul Stewart and Mary Liz Stewart, "Underground Railroad Sites in the City of Albany—People, Places and Things," *Underground Workshop*, www.ugrworkshop.com/albanysites.htm.

52. "New Yorkers Active in the Underground Railroad."

53. Stewart and Stewart, "Underground Railroad Sites."

54. Calarco, *Underground Railroad in the Adirondacks*, 189.

55. Stewart and Stewart, "Underground Railroad Sites."

56. Calarco, *Underground Railroad in the Adirondacks*, 189.

57. Stewart and Stewart, "People Who Supported the Underground Railroad."

58. Calarco, *Underground Railroad in the Adirondacks*, 189–90.

59. Siebert, *Underground Railroad*, 113, 126.

60. Taylor, *Transportation Revolution*, 34, 78.

61. Siebert, *Underground Railroad*, 415.

62. "New Yorkers Active in the Underground Railroad."
63. Calarco, *Underground Railroad in the Adirondacks*, 96, 196.
64. "New Yorkers Active in the Underground Railroad.
65. Siebert, *Underground Railroad*, 113.
66. Ibid., 126.
67. Taylor, *Transportation Revolution*, 34–35.
68. Blockson, *Underground Railroad*, 224.
69. Calarco, *Underground Railroad in the Adirondacks*, 197.
70. Ibid., 202.
71. Stewart and Stewart, "People Who Supported the Underground Railroad."
72. Calarco, *Underground Railroad in the Adirondacks*, 204.
73. Ibid., 204–6.
74. Flick, *History of New York*, 68.
75. Calarco, *Underground Railroad in the Adirondacks*, 225.
76. Siebert, *Underground Railroad*, 127.
77. Ibid., 113.
78. C. Peter Ripley, ed., *The Black Abolitionist Papers*, vol. 3, *The United States, 1830–1846* (Chapel Hill: University of North Carolina Press, 1991), 42–45.
79. Flick, *History of the New York*, 68.
80. Stewart and Stewart, "People Who Supported the Underground Railroad."
81. Ibid.
82. Calarco, *Underground Railroad in the Adirondacks*, 216–17.
83. Ibid., 221.
84. Ibid., 227–28.
85. Taylor, *Transportation Revolution*, 34, 78, 85.
86. Stewart and Stewart, "People Who Supported the Underground Railroad.

NEW YORK—THE CENTRAL ROUTES
1. *County Level Census Data—New York*
2. Siebert, *Underground Railroad*, 414–15.
3. Taylor, *Transportation Revolution*, 33, 35, 78, 85, 87.
4. Ibid., 113.
5. Siebert, *Underground Railroad*, 126.
6. Kate Clifford Larson, *Bound for the Promised Land: Harriet Tubman, Portrait of an American Hero* (New York: Random House, 2004), xxii.
7. Calarco, *Underground Railroad in the Adirondacks*, 37, 132.
8. Payne, *African Methodist Episcopal Church*, 56–57.
9. Siebert, *Underground Railroad*, 415.
10. Rev. J. W. Loguen, *A Stop on the Underground Railroad* (Syracuse, NY: Hofman Press, n.d.; partial reprint of *The Rev. J. W. Loguen as a Slave and a Freeman* (Syracuse, NY: J. G. K. Truair, 1859), 7–14, 19, 25, 32.
11. Quarles, *Black Abolitionists*, 159.
12. Ibid., 34–51, 54–56, 58–65.

13. Siebert, *Underground Railroad*, 35, 113, 126, 414–15.
14. "New Yorkers Active in the Underground Railroad."
15. Still, *Underground Railroad*, 44, 108, 154.
16. Ibid., 158.
17. Ibid., 154.
18. Flick, *History of New York*, 68.
19. "New Yorkers Active in the Underground Railroad."
20. Ibid.
21. Payne, *African Methodist Episcopal Church*, 56.
22. Siebert, *Underground Railroad*, 113, 126, 415.
23. "New Yorkers Active in the Underground Railroad."
24. Still, *Underground Railroad*, 400.
25. Judith Wellman, *The Underground Railroad in Central New York: A Research Guide*, 5, www.oswego.edu/Acad_Dept/a_and_s/history/ugrr/guide.html.
26. *Asa and Caroline Mitchell Wing*, www.oswego.edu/Acad_Dept/a_and_s/history/ugrr/wing.html.
27. *George and Eliza Bragdon*, www.oswego.edu/Acad_Dept/a_and_s/history/ugrr/bragdon.html.
28. *D. Kilburne*, www.oswego.edu/Acad_Dept/a_and_s/history/ugrr/kilburne.html.
29. *Starr & Harriet Clark*, www.oswego.edu/Acad_Dept/a_and_s/history/ugrr/clark.html.
30. *Orson Ames*, www.oswego.edu/Acad_Dept/a_and_s/history/ugrr/ames.html.
31. *Charles and Flora Ann Smith*, www.oswego.edu/Acad_Dept/a_and_s/history/ugrr/ames.html.
32. *Tudor & Marie Grant*, www.oswego.edu/Acad_Dept/a_and_s/history/ugrr/grant.html.
33. *John B. and Lydia Edwards*, www.oswego.edu/Acad_Dept/a_and_s/history/ugrr/edwards.html.
34. *Asa Beebe and Mary Whipple Beebe*, www.oswego.edu/Acad_Dept/a_and_s/history/ugrr/beebe.html.
35. *James W. Seward*, www.oswego.edu/Acad_Dept/a_and_s/history/ugrr/seward.html.
36. Flick, *History of New York*, 68.
37. Siebert, *Underground Railroad*, 113.
38. Still, *Underground Railroad*, 45, 426.
39. Ibid., 426.
40. Ibid., 54, 104, 517.
41. Ibid., 221-23.
42. Flick, *History of New York*, 68.
43. Still, *Underground Railroad*, 158.
44. Calarco, *Underground Railroad in the Adirondacks*, 230–31.
45. Siebert, *Underground Railroad*, 113.

46. Binghamton, *New York: A Brief History*, www.cityofbinghamton.com/bing hamton_history.htm.
47. Paul A. Wallace, *Indian Paths of Pennsylvania* (Harrisburg: Pennsylvania Historical and Museum Commission, 1971), frontispiece.
48. Flick, *History of New York*, 68.
49. Siebert, *Underground Railroad*, 113, 414.
50. *Map of New York & Erie Railroad.*
51. Flick, *History of New York*, 65.
52. Ripley, *Black Abolitionist Papers*, 340–42.
53. Siebert, *Underground Railroad*, 113, 127, 415.
54. "In the Beginning . . . ," *Pages in the History of Elmira*, www.ci.elmira.ny.us/history/index.html.
55. "The Underground Railroad in Elmira," *Pages in the History of Elmira*, www.ci.elmira.ny.us/history/underground_railroad.html.
56. Switala, *Underground Railroad in Pennsylvania*, 102.
57. Wallace, *Indian Paths of Pennsylvania*, 46, 47, 75, 76.
58. Siebert, *Underground Railroad*, 35, 80, 113.
59. Larson, *Bound for the Promised Land*, xxii.
60. Siebert, *Underground Railroad*, 128, 415.
61. Carole Knowlton, "John W. Jones and Friends: The Origins of the Underground Railroad in Elmira, New York, *Journal of the Afro-American Historical and Genealogical Society* 22, (Fall 2003): 137–38.
62. Still, *Underground Railroad*, 530.
63. "Underground Railroad in Elmira."
64. Ibid.
65. *Map of the New York & Erie Railroad.*
66. Ibid.
67. Siebert, *Underground Railroad*, 415.
68. Flick, *History of New York*, 68.
69. Siebert, *Underground Railroad*, 113, 414.
70. "New Yorkers Active in the Underground Railroad."
71. Flick, *History of New York*, 68; "Underground Railroad in Elmira."
72. "Underground Railroad in Elmira."
73. Flick, *History of New York*, 68.
74. Ibid.
75. "Underground Railroad in Elmira."
76. Switala, *Underground Railroad in Pennsylvania*, 102, 118.

NEW YORK—THE WESTERN ROUTES
1. *1850 County Level Census Data—New York—Population.*
2. Siebert, *Underground Railroad*, 414–15.
3. Christopher Densmore, *Underground Railroad Agents in Western New York*, ublib.buffalo.edu/libraries/units/archives/urr/agents.html.

4. *American Anti-Slavery Society Branches in Western New York, 1837–38*, ublib.buffalo.edu/libraries/units/archives/urr/ASS-WNY.html.

5. Payne, *African Methodist Episcopal Church*, 56–57.

6. Taylor, *Transportation Revolution*, 23, 28, 35.

7. *Map of the New York & Erie Railroad.*

8. *Map of the Erie Railway and Its Connections, 1866* (New York: J. H. Colton & Co., 1855), wnyrailfan.net/erie_map_1855.htm.

9. Taylor, *Transportation Revolution*, 61.

10. Eber M. Pettit, *Sketches in the History of the Underground Railroad, Comprising Many Thrilling Incidents of the Escape of Fugitives from Slavery, and the Perils of Those Who Aided Them* (Fredonia, NY: W. McKinstry & Son, 1879; repr., Westfield, NY: Chautauqua Region Press, 1999), 42–43.

11. Siebert, *Underground Railroad*, 113; Flick, *History of New York*, 68.

12. *Map of the Erie Railway and Its Connections.*

13. Siebert, *Underground Railroad*, 415.

14. Densmore, *Underground Railroad Agents.*

15. David L. Dickinson, *African Americans in 19th Century Lockport*, www.lockport-ny.com/History/stories1.htm.

16. Pettit, *Sketches*, 86.

17. Ibid., 84, 85, 146.

18. Siebert, *Underground Railroad*, 415; Densmore, *Underground Railroad Agents.*

19. Still, *Underground Railroad*, 269, 333, 497.

20. Siebert, *Underground Railroad*, 113; Flick, *History of New York*, 68.

21. *The Covington Connection*, www.leroyny.com/news/2004/0830/Historical/005.htm.

22. *Map of the Erie Railway and Its Connections.*

23. Densmore, *Underground Railroad Agents.*

24. Pettit, *Sketches*, 13.

25. Switala, *Underground Railroad in Pennsylvania*, 102, 118.

26. Wallace, *Indian Paths of Pennsylvania*, 46–47.

27. Densmore, *Underground Railroad Agents.*

28. Siebert, *Underground Railroad*, 113.

29. Pettit, *Sketches*, 51.

30. Flick, *History of New York*, 68.

31. *Map of the Erie Railway and Its Connections.*

32. Densmore, *Underground Railroad Agents.*

33. Pettit, *Sketches*, 70.

34. Ibid.

35. Switala, *Underground Railroad in Pennsylvania*, 90, 98.

36. Densmore, *Underground Railroad Agents.*

37. Ibid.

38. C. R. Lockwood, *Catharine Harris and the Underground Railroad in Jamestown, New York*, ublib.buffalo.edu/libraries/units/archives/urr/jamestown.html.

39. Densmore, *Underground Railroad Agents.*

40. Siebert, *Underground Railroad*, 77.

41. Still, *Underground Railroad*, 590.

42. Pettit, *Sketches*, viii, 17, 46.

43. Christopher Densmore, *Quakers and Abolition in Western New York*, ublib.buf falo.edu/libraries/units/archives/urr/Quakers_and_Abolition.html.

44. Densmore, *Underground Railroad Agents.*

45. Pettit, *Sketches*, vii; Siebert, *Underground Railroad*, 113, 128.

46. Siebert, *Underground Railroad*, 113.

47. Densmore, *Underground Railroad Agents;* Switala, *Underground Railroad in Pennsylvania*, 90, 98.

48. Pettit, *Sketches*, 12.

49. Flick, *History of New York*, 68.

50. Pettit, *Sketches*, 42–43.

51. Drew, *North-Side View of Slavery*, 18.

52. Densmore, *Underground Railroad Agents.*

53. Siebert, *Underground Railroad*, 35, 236, 249.

54. *African American History of Western New York State, 1830 to 1865*, math.buf falo.edu/~sww/0history/1830-1865.html.

CANADA

1. "Follow the North Star—A Timeline of the Underground Railroad," *Ontario's Underground Railroad*, www.africanhertoour.org/story/timeline.html.

2. "Slavery in Early Canada," *The Underground Railroad*, collections.ic.gc.ca/free dom/page3.htm.

3. Ward, *Autobiography of a Fugitive Negro*, 292–93.

4. "Simcoe's Act, the War of 1812 and the Underground Railroad," *The Under-ground Railroad*, collections.ic.gc.ca/freedom/page6(14).htm.

5. Ibid.

6. Siebert, *Underground Railroad*, 27–28.

7. McDougall, *Fugitive Slaves 1619–1865*, 25.

8. "Follow the North Star—A Timeline of the Underground Railroad."

9. Ibid.

10. Siebert, *Underground Railroad*, 193, 195, 199–202.

11. Robin W. Winks, *The Blacks in Canada A History* (New Haven, CT: Yale University Press, 1971), 144.

12. *Historical Negro Biographies*, 89–90.

13. Siebert, *Underground Railroad*, 205–7.

14. Ibid., 202, 207, 210.

15. Ibid., 208.

16. "Conductors & Notable Figures," *Ontario's Underground Railroad*, www.afri canhertour.org/story/conductors.html.

17. Ibid.; "Follow the North Star."

18. "Conductors & Notable Figures."
19. "Salem Chapel, British Methodist Episcopal Church," *Ontario's Underground Railroad*, www.africanhertour.org/touring/site11.html.
20. "Follow the North Star."
21. "Conductors & Notable Figures."
22. Siebert, *Underground Railroad*, 113, 217–18.
23. "The Griffin House," *Ontario's Underground Railroad*, www.africanher tour.org/touring/site2.html.
24. "Mildred Mahoney Dolls' House/Bertie Hall," *Ontario's Underground Railroad*, www.africanhertour.org/touring/site7.html.
25. "Oakville Museum at Erchless Estate," *Ontario's Underground Railroad*, www.africanhertour.org/touring/site12.html.
26. "St. Catharines Museum at the Welland Canals Centre (Lock 3)," *Ontario's Underground Railroad*, www.africanhertour.org/touring/site13.html.
27. Still, *Underground Railroad*, 42, 57-59, 65, 76, 78, 80, 105, 119, 120, 137, 143, 144, 152, 160, 162–64, 192–200, 202, 213, 214, 224, 227, 234, 249, 261, 263, 264, 272, 289, 290, 292, 293, 300, 312, 317, 318, 324, 337, 378, 379, 385, 448, 461, 469, 490, 498, 545, 546.
28. Howe, *Freedmen's Report*, 15.
29. Gara, *Liberty Line*, 37.
30. Ward, *Autobiography*, 154.
31. Siebert, *Underground Railroad*, 220–23.
32. Ibid., 222, 223, 226.
33. Winks, *Blacks in Canada*, 145–46.
34. "Conductors & Notable Figures."
35. Still, *Underground Railroad*, 163.
36. Ibid., 78.
37. Ibid., 317.
38. Ibid., 229.
39. "The Turbulent 1850's," *The Underground Railroad*, collections.ic.gc.ca/free dom/page 21.htm.
40. Winks, *Blacks in Canada*, 148.
41. "Towards the End: The Civil War and Its Impact on Black Canada," *The Underground Railroad*, collections.ic.ga.ca/freedom/page23.htm.

BIBLIOGRAPHY

Abolition in New Jersey. www.njtimes.rutgers.edu.abolt.htm.

An Act for Regulating of Slaves. intranet.rutgers.edu/~clemens/slavelaw1714.html.

An Act for the Gradual Abolition of Slavery, and Other Purposes Respecting Slaves. intra net.rutgers.edu/~clemens/slavelaw1820.html.

An Act for the Gradual Abolition of Slavery (1804). intranet.rutgers.edu/%7Eclemens/slavelaw1804.html.

An Act Respecting Slaves. Acts of the General Assembly, chapter DCCXYVV.intranet.rutgers.edu/~clemens/slavelaw1798.html.

African American History of Western New York State, 1830 to 1865. math.buffalo.edu/~sww/0history/1830-1865.html.

Against Slavery and the Slave Trade in the District of Columbia and Florida. www.oswego.edu/Acad_Dept/a_and_s/history/ugrr/anti5.html.

Against the Annexation of Texas. www.oswego.edu/Acad_Dept/a_and_s/history/ugrr/anti3.html. and www.oswego.edu/Acad_Dept/a_and_s/history/ugrr/anti4.html.

American Anti-Slavery Society Branches in Western New York, 1837–38. ublib.buf falo.edu/libraries/uits/archives/urr/ASS-WNY.html.

Ames, Orson. www.oswego.edu/Acad_Dept/a_and_s/history/ugrr/ames.html.

Bailey, Thomas A. *The American Pageant: A History of the Republic.* Boston: D. C. Heath and Company, 1961.

Baney, Jack. "Hillsborough Backs Effort to Protect Ridge." *Packet Group*, June 22, 2000. www.pacpubservice.com/new/news/6-22-00/sourlands.html.

Beebe, Asu and Mary Whipple Beebe. www.oswego.edu/Acad_Dept/a_and_s/history/ugrr/beebe.html.

Binghamton, New York: A Brief History. www.cityofbinghamton.com/binghamton_history.htm.

Blockson, Charles L. *The Underground Railroad.* New York: Berkley Publishing Group, 1987.

———. *The Underground Railroad in Pennsylvania.* Jacksonville, NC: Flame International, 1981.

Bowen, Catherine Drinker. *Miracle at Philadelphia: The Story of the Constitutional Convention, May to September 1787.* New York: Book-of-the-Month Club, 1966.

Bragdon, George & Eliza. www.oswego.edu/Acad_Dept/a_and_s/history/ugrr/bragdon.html.

Brown, Ira V. *The Negro in Pennsylvania History.* University Park: Pennsylvania Historical Association, 1970.

————. *Pennsylvania Reformers: From Penn to 1848.* Philadelphia: Temple University Press, 1988.

Burlington, NJ. 08016.com/allison.html.; and, 08016/grubb_estate.html.

The Burned-Over District. history.acusd.edu/gen/civilwar/01/burned.html.

Calarco, Tom. *The Underground Railroad in the Adirondack Region.* Jefferson, NC: McFarland & Company, Publishers, 2004.

Certificate of Abandonment, Piscataway Township, New Jersey, 1806. www.scc.rutgers.edu/njwomenshistory/Period_2/abandonment.htm.

Christy, David. *Pulpit Politics; or, Ecclesiastical Legislation on Slavery in Its Disturbing Influences on the American Union.* New York: Farran & McLean Publishers, 1862. Reprint, New York: Negro Universities Press, 1969.

Clark, Starr & Harriet. www.oswego.edu/Acad_Dept/a_and_s/history/ugrr/clark.html.

Clarke, John T. *Map of the State of New-York Showing Its Water and Rail Road Lines, Jan. 1855.* memory.loc.gov/cgi-bin/map_item.pl.

Coffin, Levi. *Reminiscences.* Cincinnati: Robert Clarke Company, 1898. Reprint, New York: Arno Press and the *New York Times*, 1968.

Commager, Henry Steele, ed. *Documents of American History.* New York: Appleton-Century-Croft, 1986.

Cooper, David. "A Serious Address to the rulers of America on the Inconsistency of their conduct respecting slavery." Trenton, NJ: Isaac Collins, 1783.

"Conductors & Notable Figures." *Ontario's Underground Railroad.* www.africanhertour.org/story/conductors.html.

The Covington Connection. www.leroyny.com/news/2004/0830/Historical/005.htm.

Davis, David Brian, ed. *Ante-Bellum Reform.* New York: Harper & Row, Publishers, 1967.

Densmore, Christopher. *Quakers and Abolition In Western New York.* ublib.buffalo.edu/libraries/units/archives/urr/Quakers_and_Abolition.html.

————. "The Society of Friends in Western New York." *Quakers in Western New York.* ublib.buffalo.edu/libraries/units/archives/urr/Quakers_in_Western_New York.html.

————. *Underground Railroad Agents in Western New York.* ublib.buffalo.edu/libraries/units/archives/urr/agents.html.

Dickinson, David L. *African Americans in 19th Century Lockport.* www.lockport-ny.com/History/stories1.htm.

Dorwart, Jeffrey M. *Cape May County, New Jersey: The Making of an American Resort Community.* New Brunswick, NJ: Rutgers University Press, 1992.

Douglass, Frederick. *Narrative of the Life of Frederick Douglass, an American Slave, Written by Himself.* New York: Penguin Books USA, 1986.

"Downtown Jersey City Homes for Sale in Hudson County, New Jersey." *Downtown Jersey City.* www.downtown-jerseycity-homesforsale.com/cityprofile.htm.

Drew, Benjamin. *A North-Side View of Slavery: The Refugee; or, The Narratives of Fugitive Slaves in Canada.* Boston: John P. Jewett and Company, 1856.

Reprinted in *Four Fugitive Slave Narratives*, 22–25. Reading, MA: Addison-Wesley Publishing Company, 1968.

Driscoll, James. "Samuel Parsons: A Long Island Quaker and the Anti-Slavery Struggle," *Journal of the Afro-American Historical and Genealogical Society*, 22 (Fall 2003): 188–98.

Duberman, Martin, ed. *The Antislavery Vanguard: New Essays on the Abolitionists.* Princeton, NJ: Princeton University Press, 1965.

Dunaway, Wayland F. *A History of Pennsylvania.* Englewood Cliffs, NJ: Prentice-Hall, 1948.

Edwards, John B. and Lydia. www.oswego.edu/Acad_Dept/a_and_s/history/ugrr/edwards.html.

Elkins, Stanley M. *Slavery: A Problem in American Institutional and Intellectual Life.* New York: Grosset & Dunlap, 1963.

Ellis, Frank. *History of Monmouth County, New Jersey.* Philadelphia: R. T. Peck & Co., 1885.

Fabiano, John. "Historically Speaking: A Look at the Allentown–Upper Freehold of the Past." *Messenger-Press*, August 23, 2001. www.pacpub.com/site/news?cfm?newsid=2254354&BRD=1091&PAG=461&dept_i...

———. "Recrossing Crosswicks." Part 2 of 4. *Messenger-Press*, July 15, 2004. www.pacpub.com/site/news?cfm?newsid=12335558&BRD=1091&PAG=461&dept_i...

Fairbanks, Rev. Calvin. *During Slavery Times.* New York: Patriotic Publishing Co., 1890. Reprint, New York: Negro Universities Press, 1969.

Federal Writers' Project. *New Jersey: A Guide to Its Present and Past.* New York: Viking Press, 1939.

Filler, Louis. *The Crusade against Slavery, 1830–1860.* New York: Harper & Brothers, 1960.

First Federal Congress: Petitioning the Federal Government. www.gwu.edu/~ffcp/exhibit/p11/p11_4.html.

Fishman, George. *The African American Struggle for Freedom and Equality: The Development of a People's Identity, New Jersey, 1624–1850.* New York: Garland Publishing, 1997.

Fitzpatrick, John C., ed. *The Writings of George Washington from the Original Manuscript Sources, 1745–1799.* Vols. 28 and 29. Washington, D.C.: U.S. Government Printing Office, 1931.

Flick, Alexander C., ed. *History of the State of New York.* Vol. 7, *Modern Party Battles.* New York: Columbia University Press, 1935.

"Follow the North Star: A Timeline of the Underground Railroad." *Ontario's Underground Railroad.* www.africanhertour.org/story/timeline.html.

Foner, Philip S. *History of Black Americans: From Africa to the Emergence of the Cotton Kingdom.* Westport, CT: Greenwood Press, 1975.

Gara, Larry. *The Liberty Line: The Legend of the Underground Railroad.* Lexington: University of Kentucky Press, 1967.

Goodman, Paul. *Of One Blood: Abolitionism and the Origin of Racial Equality.* Berkeley: University of California Press, 1998.

"The Griffin House," *Ontario's Underground Railroad.* www.africanhertour.org/touring/site2.html.

"Grimes Homestead." *Aboard the Underground Railroad.* www.cr.nps.gov/nr/travel/underground/nj1.html.

Henry Ward Beecher Abolitionism. pider.georgetowncollege.edu/htallant/courses/his338/students/nhewitt/slavery.htm.

Higgins, Ross W., and Margaret Vetare. "Establishing Slavery in Colonial New York." *Historic Hudson Valley.* www.hudsonvalley.org/web/phil-slav.htm.

"History of Cranbury." *Early History—Cranbury, N.J.* www.cranbury.org/history/earlhist.html.

Hodges, Graham Russell. *Slavery and Freedom in the Rural North: African Americans in Monmouth County, New Jersey, 1665–1865.* Madison, WI: Madison House, 1997.

Howe, S. G. *Report to the Freedmen's Inquiry Commission, 1864: The Refugees from Slavery in Canada West.* Boston: Wright & Potter, Printers, 1864. Reprint, New York: Arno Press and the *New York Times,* 1969.

"In the Beginning . . ." *Pages in the History of Elmira.* www.ci.elmira.ny.us/history/index.html.

Interracial Committee of the New Jersey Conference of Social Work. *The Negro in New Jersey.* New York: Negro Universities Press, 1969.

Jackson, William J. *New Jerseyans in the Civil War for Union and Liberty.* New Brunswick, NJ: Rutgers University Press, 2000.

"Jacob's Chapel." *Mount Laurel Township.* www.mountlaurel.com/jacob.htm.

Kahn, Lea. "Canal's Past Revisited through Pictorial." *Lawrence Ledger,* January 17, 2002. www.pacpub.com/site/news?cfm?newsid=3012543&BRD=1091&PAG=461&dept_i...

Karnoutsos, Carmela. "The Underground Railroad in Jersey City," *Jersey City Past and Present.* www.njcu.edu/programs/jchistory/pages/U_Pages/Underground_Railroad.htm.

Kilburne, D. www.oswego.edu/Acad_Dept/a_and_s/history/ugrr/Kilburne.html.

Knowlton, Carole. "John W. Jones and Friends: The Origins of the Underground Railroad in Elmira, New York." *Journal of the Afro-American Historical and Genealogical Society* 22 (Fall 2003): 137–46.

Larson, Kate Clifford. *Bound for the Promised Land: Harriet Tubman, Portrait of an American Hero.* New York: Random House, 2004.

Learn, David. "Journey to Africa via Princeton." *Princeton Packet,* June 26, 1998. www.pacpubserver.com?new/news/6-27-98/slaves.html.

Life Pictorial Atlas of the World. New York: Time, 1961.

Lockwood, C. R. *Catharine Harris and the Underground Railroad in Jamestown, New York.* ublib.buffalo.edu/libraries/units/archives/urr/jamestown.html.

Loguen, Rev. J. W. *A Stop on the Underground Railroad.* Syracuse, NY: Hofman

Press, n.d. Partial reprint of *The Rev. J. W. Loguen as a Slave and a Freeman*. Syracuse, NY: J. G. K. Truair, 1859.

Maclean, Alexander. *The Underground Railroad in Hudson County*, part 11. 2002. www.cityofjerseycity.org/ur/undergroundrailroadinhudsoncounty eleven.shtml.

Magnotta, Christine. "Dream House Sours for Couple." *Pocono Record*, July 6, 1998. www.poconorecord.com/1998local.tjd70360.html.

A Manumission of Abigal, 1808. www.scc.rutgers.edu/njwomenshistory/Period_2/ manumission.html.

"Mildred Mahoney Dolls' House/Bertie Hall," *Ontario's Underground Railroad*. www.africanhertour.org/touring/site7.html.

Map of the Erie Railway and Its Connections, 1866. New York: G. W. Colton & C. B. Colton & Co., 1869. wnyrails.railfan.net/erie_map_1869.htm.

Map of New Jersey, 1826. mapmaker.rutgers.edu/NJ_1826jpg.

Map of New Jersey, 1856. mapmaker.rutgers.edu/NJ_1856jpg.

Map of New York & Erie Railroad and Its Connections: The Most Direct Route from New York to All Western Cities and Towns. New York: J. H. Colton & Co., 1855. wnyrailfan.net/erie_map_1855.htm.

Map of the Rail Roads of New Jersey and Parts of Adjoining States, 1869. mapmaker.rutgers.edu/HISTORICALMAPS/RAILROADS/rr_NJ_PA_NY.jpg.

Map of the State of NJ 1753. mapmaker.rutgers.edu/HISTORICALMAPS/NJ-1753 %20copy.jpg.

"Mass Meeting of Colored Citizens, October 3, 1850." *Buffalo Daily Republic*, October 4, 1850; and "Mass Meeting of Colored Citizens, October 17, 1850." [Rochester, NY] *North Star*, October 24, 1850. ublib.buffalo.edu/libraries/units/ archives/urr/Mass_Meeting_of_Colored_Citizens,1...1/13/2004.

McDougall, Marion Gleason. *Fugitive Slaves, 1619–1865*. Boston: Fay House Mono-Graphs, 1891. Reprint, New York: Bergman Publishers, 1967.

McKnight, W. J. *A Pioneer History of Jefferson County, Pennsylvania, and My First Recollections of Brookville, Pennsylvania, 1840–43, When My Feet Were Bare and My Cheeks Were Brown*. Philadelphia: J. B. Lippincott Company, 1898.

McMahon, William. *South Jersey Towns*. New Brunswick, NJ: Rutgers University Press, 1973.

"Meeting of Colored Citizens," *Oswego Palladium*, June 1, 1850. www.oswego.edu/ Acad_Dept/a_and_s/history/ugrr/palla3.html.

Morgan, Scott. "Shiloh Baptist Church Members Celebrate Black History Month at Their Bordentown City Church." *Register-News*, February 12, 2004. www.pac pub.com/site/news.cfm?newsid=3012543&BRD=1091&PAG=461&dept_i...

Morison, Samuel Eliot. *The Oxford History of the American People*. New York: Oxford University Press, 1965.

Moss, Richard Shannon. *Slavery on Long Island: A Study in Local Institutional and Early African-American Communal Life*. New York: Garland Publishing, 1993.

Munroe, John A. *Federalist Delaware, 1775–1815.* New Brunswick, NJ: Rutgers University Press, 1954.

National Park Service. *Aboard the Underground Railroad—Peter Mott House.* www.cr.nps.gov/nr/travel/underground/nj2.htm.

"New Jersey and Slavery." *New Jersey before the Civil War.* zorak.monmouth .edu/~njhist/NJTheCivilWar1.html.

New Jersey Slave Laws Summary and Record. www.slaveryinamerica.org/geography/ slave_laws_NJ.htm.

"New Yorkers Active in the Underground Railroad." *New York History.* www.nyhis tory.com/ugrr/people.htm.

New York Slave Law Summary and Record, www.slaveryinamerica.org/geography/ slave_laws_NY.htm.

"19th Century Mount Laurel," *Mount Laurel Township.* www.mountlaurel.com/ hist19c.htm.

"Oakville Museum at Erchless Estate," *Ontario's Underground Railroad.* www.african-hertour.org/touring/site12.html.

"One of the First to Fight Slavery, David Ruggles." *African American Registry.* www.aaregistry.com/african_american_history/1991/one_of_the_first_to_fight_ slav...

Payne, Daniel A. *History of the African Methodist Episcopal Church.* Nashville: Publishing House of the A.M.E. Sunday-School Union, 1891. Reprint, New York: Arno Press and the *New York Times,* 1969.

"Peekskill Underground Railroad and Tunnel." *Forging the Freedom Trail.* www.free-domtrail.org/regions/peekskillug.htm.

Pennsylvania Slave Laws Summary and Record. www.slaveryinamerica.org/geography/ slave_laws_PA.htm.

Pettit, Eber M. *Sketches in the History of the Underground Railroad, Comprising Many Thrilling Incidents of the Escape of Fugitives from Slavery, and the Perils of Those Who Aided Them.* Fredonia, NY: W. McKinstry & Son, 1879. Reprint, Westfield, NY: Chautauqua Region Press, 1999.

Price, Clement Alexander. *Freedom Not Far Distant: A Documentary History of Afro-Americans in New Jersey.* Newark: New Jersey Historical Association, 1980.

Quarles, Benjamin. *Black Abolitionists.* New York: Oxford University Press, 1969.

Ripley, C. Peter, ed. *The Black Abolitionist Papers.* Vol. 3. *The United States, 1830–1846.* Chapel Hill: University of North Carolina Press, 1991.

Robinson, Wilhelmina S. *Historical Negro Biographies.* New York: Publishers Company, 1967.

Runaway Slave Advertisements. www.runet.edu/~shepburn/web/Runaway%20Slave% 20Advertisements.htm.

"Salem Chapel, British Methodist Episcopal Church." *Ontario's Underground Railroad.* www.africanhertour.org/touring/site11.html.

"St. Catherines Museum at the Welland Canal Centre (Lock 3)," *Ontario's Underground Railroad.* www.africanhertour.org/touring/site13.html.

1790 to 1860 County Level Census Data—Sorted by State/County—New Jersey and New York. Fisher.lib.virginia.edu/cgi-local/censusbin/census/cen.pl.

Seward, James W. www.oswego.edu/Acad_Dept/a_and_s/history/ugrr/seward.html.

Siebert, Wilbur H. *The Underground Railroad: From Slavery to Freedom.* New York: Macmillan Company, 1898. Reprint, New York: Russell & Russell, 1967.

"Simcoe's Act, the War of 1812 and the Underground Railroad." *The Underground Railroad.* collections.ic.gc.ca/freedom/page 14.htm.

"Slavery in Early Canada." *The Underground Railroad.* collections.ic.gc.ca/freedom/page3.htm.

Smedley, Robert C. *History of the Underground Railroad in Chester and the Neighboring Counties in Pennsylvania.* Lancaster, PA: Office of the Journal, 1883. Reprint, New York: Arno Press and the *New York Times,* 1969.

Smith, Charles, and Flora Ann Smith. www.oswego.edu/Acad_Dept/a_and_s/history/ugrr/smith.html.

Smith, J. Calvin. *Map of the State of New York, Cities, Towns and Villages, 1844.* digital.nypl.org/images/w/434731w.jpg.

"South Brunswick Riding the 'Railroad' through Red Maple Farm." *Home News Tribune,* June 1, 2003. nl.newsbank.com/nl-search/we/Archives?s_site=thnt&f_sitename=Hom...

The State of New Jersey Compiled from the Most Authentic Information. mapmaker.rutgers.edu/HISTORICALMAPS/NJ_1753%20copy.jpg.

The Statistical History of the United States from Colonial times to the Present. Stamford, CT: Fairfield Publishers, 1965.

Stewart, Paul, and Mary Liz Stewart. "People Who Supported the Work of the Underground Railroad." *Underground Workshop.* www.ugrworkshop.com/otherpeople.htm.

———. "Underground Railroad Sites in the City of Albany—People, Places and Things." *Underground Workshop.* www.ugrworkshop.com/albanysites.htm.

Still, William. *The Underground Railroad: A Record of Facts, Authentic Narratives, Letters, &c.* Philadelphia: Porter & Coates, 1872. Reprint, New York: Arno Press and the *New York Times,* 1968.

Stoughton, Mary, and A. M. Locke. *Anti-Slavery in American from the Introduction of African Slaves to the Prohibition of Slave Trade, 1618–1808.* Boston: Ginn & Company, Publishers, 1907.

Sweet, William W. *The Story of Religion in America.* New York: Harper & Brothers, Publishers, 1930.

Switala, William J. *Underground Railroad in Pennsylvania.* Mechanicsburg, PA: Stackpole Books, 2001.

Taylor, George Rogers. *The Transportation Revolution, 1815–1860.* New York: Harper & Row, 1951.

Tiller, Louis. *The Crusade against Slavery, 1830–1860.* New York: Harper & Brothers Publishers, 1960.

"Towards the End: The Civil War and Its Impact on Black Canada." *The Underground Railroad.* collections.ic.gc.ca/freedom/page23.htm.

Trusty, Emma Marie. *The Underground Railroad: Ties That Bound Unveiled: A History of the Underground Railroad in Southern New Jersey from 1770 to 1861.* Philadelphia: Amed Literary, 1997.

"The Turbulent 1850's." *The Underground Railroad.* collections.ic.gc.ca/freedom/page21.htm.

"The Underground Railroad in Bucks, Burlington and Montgomery County," *Burlington County Times* (May 5, 2004). wysiwg://42/http://www.phillyburbs.com/undergroundrailroad/NJabolition.shtml.

"The Underground Railroad in Elmira," *Pages in the History of Elmira.* www.ci.elmira.ny.us/history/underground_railroad.html.

Velsor, Kathleen G. "The Long Island Freedom Trail." *Journal of Afro-American Historical and Genealogical Society* 22 (Fall 2003): 177–87.

Virginia Slave Laws Summary and Record. www.slaveryinamerica.org/geography/slave_laws_VA.htm.

Wallace, Paul A. *Indian Paths of Pennsylvania.* Harrisburg: Pennsylvania Historical and Museum Commission, 1971.

Ward, Samuel Ringgold. *Autobiography of a Fugitive Negro: His Anti-Slavery Labours in the United States, Canada & England.* London: John Snow, 1885. Reprint, New York: Arno Press and the *New York Times,* 1968.

Wellman, Judith. *The Underground Railroad in Central New York: A Research Guide.* www.oswego.edu/Acad_Dept/a_ and_s/history/ugrr/guide.html.

Winch, Julie. *Philadelphia Black Elite Activism, Accommodation, and the Struggle for Autonomy, 1787-1848.* Philadelphia: Temple University Press, 1988.

Wing, Asa, and Caroline Mitchell Wing. www.oswego.edu/Acad_Dept/a_and_s/history/ugrr/wing.html.

Winks, Robin W. *The Blacks in Canada: A History.* New Haven, CT: Yale University Press, 1971.

Woolman, John. "Some considerations on the keeping of Negroes." Philadelphia: James Chattin, 1754.

Wright, Giles R, and Edward Lama Wonkeryor. *"Steal Away, Steal Away . . .": A Guide to the Underground Railroad in New Jersey.* Trenton: New Jersey Historical Commission, n.d. www.state.nj.us/state/history/underground_rr. pdf.

Yetman, Norman R., ed. *Voices from Slavery: 100 Authentic Slave Narratives.* Mineola, NY: Dover Publications, 2003.

INDEX